PEOPLE, PATIENTS AND POLITICS

PEOPLE, PATIENTS AND POLITICS

The History of the North Carolina Mental Hospitals 1848-1960

Clark R. Cahow

ARNO PRESS

A New York Times Company
New York • 1980

Editorial Supervision: Brian Quinn

First Publication 1980 by Arno Press Inc.
Copyright © Clark R. Cahow, 1967 and 1978.
Reprinted by permission of Clark R. Cahow
HISTORICAL ISSUES IN MENTAL HEALTH
ISBN for complete set: 0-405-11900-3
See last pages of this volume for titles.

Publisher's Note: This dissertation was originally titled *The History of the North Carolina Mental Hospitals, 1848-1960.* This title has been changed at the request of the author.

Manufactured in the United States of America

Library of Congress Cataloging in Publication Data

Cahow, Clark R
    People, patients, and politics.

    (Historical issues in mental health)
    A revision of the author's thesis, Du-e University, 1967, issued under title: The history of the North Carolina mental hospitals, 1848-1960.
    Bibliography: p.
    1. Psychiatric hospitals--North Carolina--History. 2. Mentally ill--Care and treatment--North Carolina--History. I. Title. II. Series.
RC445.N78P46 1979   362.2'1'09756   78-22554
ISBN 0-405-11908-9

PEOPLE, PATIENTS AND POLITICS:
THE HISTORY OF THE NORTH CAROLINA
MENTAL HOSPITALS 1848-1960

Clark R. Cahow

Dedicated to Patricia Lee Cahow and to the people with whom she has worked and about whom this book is written.

Preface

This survey of North Carolina Mental Hospitals covers the period
from 1848 to 1960, the date of origin of the hospital system in North
Carolina to the year research funds were first allocated by the Legislature.
As the work of the Department of Mental Health in the years immediately
following this study and the more recent Department of Human Resources
rests directly on the early history and the more recent developments in
the state hospital system, the year 1960 seems to be a logical stopping
place in a seemingly never-ending narrative.

The provision of institutional care and treatment of the mentally
ill of the State of North Carolina from approximately 1848 to 1960 is a
history shaped in part by the medical, social, and administrative problems
inherent in the mental hospital program itself. Overriding these problems,
however, is the more powerful action of the political forces upon the system.
This action of forces is evident in every stage of the historical development
of the North Carolina mental hospital movement. This survey set out to
explore the changing response of the public, the elected officials, and the
professional administrators to the need for adequate care for the State's
mentally ill citizens. Certain questions have been raised. How effective
was the technique of expose in establishing social reform? What problems
developed within the institutions themselves and within the political structure
of the state that determined the programs of patient care and treatment?
What is the relationship between an effective and progressive mental hospital
system and the social, political, and administrative reaction to the problems
of mental illness? A comparison of events in 1960 with those that evolved

between 1848 and 1945 shows how far the state of North Carolina has progressed in little more than a hundred years.

The first hundred years of institutionalized care of the insane in North Carolina is best characterized as a period of public indifference and meager State appropriations which resulted in inadequate facilities, low salaries, insufficient and poorly trained staff, undermanned and overworked professional personnel, and a political structuring of the hospital system that fostered patronage and direct interference. This period was remarkable more for the persistence of a few dedicated doctors and laymen who fought a valiant holding action against the erosions of politics and a neglectful society than for its progressive achievements. The hospitals were partisan political institutions, though everyone including the politicians denied the fact. Not until the people of the State were aroused to the need for vigorous action and constant support first through the 1941 Jimison exposé and later by the constructive political leadership of John Umstead and the professional administrative staff he recruited did the movement become more than a mere custodial program for the mentally ill citizens of North Carolina.

Although a structure for reform emerged in 1943, it incorporated many of the practices of the past and failed to solve the problems of legislative indifference, political intrusion, and administrative inefficiency. In 1945 the threat of another investigation evoked the action of a politically astute, social-minded legislator.

Between 1945 and 1960, under John Umstead's leadership, the Board attempted to face the reality of its problems. The two-fold needs to expand and improve facilities and to develop staff and therapeutic programs were equally pressing. Experience gradually revealed that the necessary solution to these problems was a carefully structured partnership between the Executive and the

Legislature, the Hospitals Board of Control and the state's medical schools, and the hospital system and the people of the state. Only such a partnership could assure the support needed for a progressive, treatment-oriented hospital system.

Future progress in the care and treatment of the mentally ill in North Carolina will depend on the ability of professional and political leadership to keep history alive in order to avoid repetition of mistakes. If those concerned with mental health are to avoid the failures of the past, they must at the very least remain aware of the relationship of the parts to the whole; which is to say, they must comprehend the complex interplay in the roles of the Governor, the Commissioner, the Legislature, and the medical centers. And finally, if history is to have any meaning, future leaders must remain aware of the continual necessity to sell the concept of this relationship to the ever-changing political community. They must breed continuity of support and effective replacements on the political level and within the administrative structure of the hospital system itself. The North Carolina mental hospital system today as in the years 1848-1960 is political. The difference in 1960 as opposed to the early period is that this fact was recognized and used with candor to control attempts at interference and to promote a positive approach to the many problems existing in the hospitals and in the State.

I am indebted to Dr. Eugene Hargrove, former commissioner of Mental Health and to Dr. Charles Vernon for the funds made available by their department and to Duke University for granting me leave in order that I might pursue the research for this survey. To Professor I. B. Holley, I wish to express my special appreciation for his introducing me to the subject as well as for his guidance and criticisms during the research and writing of the manuscript.

Thanks are also due Dr. H. G. Jones, former State Archivist, North Carolina Department of Archives and History, and his staff for their assistance in helping me locate documents. Special thanks are due the late Mr. John Umstead and the many others who granted interviews to clarify the questions raised in my research that are not answered in the written records. While the insights afforded by these people were invaluable to me, the interpretations and con- clusions reached are mine, and I accept sole responsibility for them. I acknowledge with gratitude the assistance of Mrs. Olivia Truckner and Ms. Gail Bisplinghoff who devoted time to preparing and proofing the many drafts and the final copy of this work.

Finally, I owe a special debt to my wife, Patricia, and our daughter, Lee, in part for the near ascetic life they assumed during the period of research and writing, but more importantly for the critical insights Patricia brought to this effort from her experience with a Malaria Research Team, under the auspices of the United States Public Health Services, that brought her into direct contact with patients and personnel at State Hospitals in three states in the South.

Durham, North Carolina, 1978

CONTENTS

Chapter I

THE STRONG CLAIMS OF HUMANITY:

IMPETUS FOR REFORM

The strong claims of humanity prompt some men to champion causes that would otherwise go unnoticed or ignored by society. More than a century ago, the unbelievably bad treatment of the mentally ill in North Carolina brought forth the following exposé:

> In Lincoln County, near a public road, stands a decent dwelling; near by is a log cabin, strongly built and about ten feet square, and about seven or eight feet high; no windows to admit light; the square logs are compactly laid; no chimney indicates that a fire can be kindled within, and the small low door is securely locked and barred. Two apertures at right angles, ten inches long by four wide, are the sole avenues by which light and air are admitted within this dreary cabin, so closely secured, and so cautiously guarded. You need not ask to what uses it is appropriated, the shrill cries of an incarcerated maniac will arrest you on the way ... examine the interior of this prison, you will see a ferocious, filthy, unshorn, half-clad creature, wallowing in foul, noisome straw. The horrors of this place can hardly be imagined: the state of the maniac is revolting in the extreme .... For assuring public and private safety, his family have the only alternative of confining him on their own farm rather than seeing him thrown into the dungeon of the County jail.[1]

This quotation is part of a detailed description of the plight of the impecunious insane in North Carolina that Dorothea Dix presented to the Legislature in her successful crusade to gain a mental hospital for the state in 1848.

In the field of mental health, the actions of Miss Dix are not unique. Indeed, the exposé has been -- and continues to be -- one of the main weapons in the hands of those who would reform mental hospitals and the treatment of the mentally ill. Although Miss Dix denied coming to any legislative group solely "to quicken generous impulses ... by showing the existence of terrible abuses, revealing scenes of almost incredible suffering,"[2] she fully recognized the need for employing the muckraking technique to undergird her humanitarian appeal. The general reform movement of the mid-nineteenth century, in which Miss Dix played the leading role for hospital reform, radically altered the character of the mental hospital movement by opening the doors to the indigent insane. Between 1825 and 1865 the number of non-proprietary mental hospitals in the United States increased from nine to sixty-two.[3]

To be sure, the transfer of mental patients away from abuses in the local community to central state hospitals did not solve the problems confronting the insane patient, nor did centralization bring to an end the need for continuing reform. On the contrary, centralization often merely put the patient out-of-sight and, therefore, out-of-mind. Accusations of gross abuse and maltreatment seemed to gain greater attention when made within the context of a large state insane asylum.

Norman Dain, author of Concepts of Insanity in the United States, is correct in dismissing the problem of accusations in the form of public statements made against mental hospitals as "a curse" maligning the institutions attempting to help the insane.[4] An inherent fault of exposé literature, regardless of its factual content, is that it tends to be incomplete in its presentation, prejudicially one-sided, and overly simplistic in its suggested solutions for the problem at hand. The attempt to expose to the public the evils developed in an institutional structure is rarely coordinated with public effort to change the institution by pressure from the outside -- through legislative or legal action. It would be difficult to find a case where the technique of exposé was coordinated with administrative effort to reform an institution.

Exposé attacks in all directions result in a curse that maligns the institution, and tend to make the administrative staff -- from superintendent to

4

ward worker -- defensive and suspicious of change. Generally, public reaction is universally negative toward the obvious faults, and political reaction most often represents an effort to "smooth" over the situation by correcting the obvious. Exposé looks at the immediate symptoms of the problem and only rarely at root causes. Reaction to exposé sets in motion an effort to quiet public outcry. The end result, more often than not, is a glossing of the immediate problem, a failure to attack root causes and a deeper entrenchment of basic attitudes and practices within the institutional structure. Exposé, by its nature, may bring at least partial relief of a given condition, but the relief, usually temporary, frequently merely paves the way for further exposés of conditions that grow out of inadequate solutions to earlier problems.

Norman Dain fails, however, to acknowledge the existence of cruelty, maltreatment, and mismanagement in state hospitals, a condition that prompted many of the accusations and exposés of which he complains. His failure to treat this subject and its underlying causes weakens his discussion of the concepts of insanity. There were, it is true, unscrupulous and self-seeking individuals eager to make unfounded accusations against state hospitals in the nineteenth century, just as there are today. Such stories still find willing listeners as they did in the period before the Civil War about which Dain has written. Nevertheless, the validity of a great body of exposé literature which produced the shock of recognition of conditions and an awareness of the need for reform cannot be denied or ignored any more than the findings of Miss Dix from which the mental hospital movement gained its national character.

Dorothea Dix's use of muckraking techniques to correct the plight of the nation's insane set in motion a new system that was soon to suffer the same "evils" that she sought to eliminate.

One of the first major attacks against a state system came with the publication of The Prisoner's Hidden Life or Insane Asylums Unveiled by Mrs. E. P. W. Packard. Mrs. Packard was committed in 1860 to the Illinois State Hospital for the Insane at Jacksonville where she remained for three years. At the time of her commitment, the Illinois hospital, founded on an appeal by Miss Dix, was ten years old. Mrs. Packard's charges that she was confined on trumped-up charges and the description of treatment at the hospital caused a national sensation that prompted legislation that attempted to safeguard the mental patient. Unfortunately, the Illinois legislation requiring a jury trial left the fate of the insane and sane alike in the hands of laymen who were not competent to render such decisions.[5] The door was not closed to "railroading" in Illinois or in the other states, including North Carolina, that adopted a similar court hearing procedure.

One might suspect that accusations of railroading and mistreatment during the first few decades after Dorothea Dix were due, at least in part, to lack of proper legal controls and inexperience in the administration and medical treatment of patients in large state hospitals.[6] However, the description of the hospitals where Clifford Beers, founder of the Mental Hygiene Movement, was a patient at the turn of the century is different only in kind from that given by Mrs. Packard or many of the sensational exposés subsequently published from time to time in the nation's newspapers.

Indeed, railroading, not unlike that of the early period, still exists in spite of legal and institutional administrative attempts to prevent it. North Carolina rewrote its civil commitment procedures statutes in 1970 in an effort to protect a person's legal rights vis-a-vis admission to one of the state's mental hospitals. Yet, a review of admissions and commitment criteria in theory (statute) and practice conducted by six Duke University law students under the direction of Professor George C. Cochran revealed that the law is negated every day at every hospital.[7] The instances of abuse described in the Cochran study point out how easy it is for a person to be improperly committed to a hospital on an emergency status because a doctor is unwilling or unable to properly assess the patient's condition. The study also reveals how difficult it is for hospital authorities to refuse admission of an emergency patient -- even when commitment papers are improperly completed. The study's greatest merit is not in its attempt to describe the loopholes in the present commitment statutes, but rather is in the description of society's present-day attitude toward mental illness -- an attitude that is shared by physicians, lawyers, and the courts, as well as the general lay public. The historic public attitude toward mental illness and overt action and reaction against the mentally ill is described in a later chapter. The point to be made here is Cochran's study clearly points to the fact that while public discussion is openly frank about mental illness today, society's basic attitude toward the mentally ill, and the mentally defective as well, remains relatively unchanged. A series of exposé articles, using the Cochran studies as a base, did not attack public attitude, and the articles failed to produce any positive action for reform -- a basic fault of most exposé literature.

Commenting on the ineffectiveness of exposé as a method of reform, Albert Deutsch has written:

> However laudable the motives of individual narrators of asylum horrors might have been, however accurate their facts, few succeeded in bringing about even minor reforms. Their revelations might fill front pages as nine-day sensations, but comet like, they usually were lost to sight as suddenly as they had flared up.[8]

The validity of Deutsch's position is pointed up in the spate of exposé literature published during the 1940's in an effort to awaken the public conscience and spur reform. In spite of repeated sensational revelations, conditions in the mental hospitals of many states deteriorated markedly.

7

Muckraking productions ranged from fiction of the <u>Snake</u> <u>Pit</u> variety to factual biographical accounts and research reports replete with shocking facts that no longer shocked.[9] The description of life in "one of the better" state mental hospitals described in the <u>Snake</u> <u>Pit</u>[10] was popularized through the motion pictures and is probably one of the best remembered treatments of the horrors, personal indignities, and ludicrous regimentation suffered by patients in a mental hospital. This particular exposé helped significantly in publicizing the fact that most mental patients are sensitive people who know exactly what is happening to them.[11] Certainly the admixture of humor and pathos in the following episode from <u>Snake</u> <u>Pit</u> seems to confirm this contention.

> "We do not walk on our rug," the nurse said. "We have told you a dozen times. We do not walk on our carpet."
>
> "Why not?" asked Virginia.
>
> "Because we don't," said the nurse. "Understand? You can't come into this ward and do as you please. I don't know how you got along in your other wards but here we have rules and we stick to them. We do not walk on our rug. We are the only ward that has a rug."
>
> Virginia looked at the rug. It seemed very ordinary. Twenty-nine seventy-five you would guess. Maybe it covers a dangerous sink-hole. Maybe I barely escaped with my life. I was in a deep hole once and maybe that was the hole.
>
> "And we mean to keep it looking new," Miss Green was saying. "See that you don't go tramping all over it."
>
> "You might hang it on the wall," suggested Virginia.
>
> "Your wisecracks may have been appreciated in some wards," said the nurse, "but definitely in fourteen they do not go over. That rug is strictly safe where it is if you will keep your big feet off of it."
>
> Virginia studied Miss Green's feet. About size nine. What's she mean calling a five and a half big?[12]

As ludicrous as this episode may seem, the fate of the <u>Snake</u> <u>Pit</u> heroine was less shocking than the details related in Frank L. Wright's individual case studies of hospital facilities and patient care in eight states.[13] Furthermore,

the revised editions of Beers' autobiography and Deutsch's history in 1949 bear
a striking similarity. And earlier revelations made by Deutsch when he exposed
conditions in mental hospitals are shocking almost beyond belief.[14] While
North Carolina missed national notoriety from these widely publicized studies,
the state was not exempt from a similar, if local, thrust toward reform in the
early 1940's.

Slightly more than a month after the Japanese attack on Pearl Harbor,
the Charlotte News and the Greensboro Daily News announced a series of articles
of intense local interest to the people of North Carolina that would shock the
State almost as much as the Japanese attack had shocked the nation. Quarter-
page advertisements announced the beginning of a series of articles by Tom P.
Jimison entitled "Out of the Night of Morganton."[15] Calculated to gain the
attention of readers, the advertisement displayed a silhouette of the Morganton
Hospital. Above the picture was the caption, "Out of the Night of Morganton
... Comes a Pitiable Story." Below the picture, in boldface type the reader
was told:

> Here in the bastille of North Carolina - Here 2,700 mentally
> ill patients spend interminable days and years as a legion of
> "lost souls." Here through the parsimony of the State, a mere
> 17 cents is the daily allotment per person for food, clothing,
> medical, and custodial care. Here, within these dark, grey
> walls of misery, politics is a companion of despair.
>
> Tom P. Jimison, prominent lawyer and journalist, spent
> more than a year at the North Carolina State Hospital for the
> Insane at Morganton. During this period of incarceration he
> observed the deplorable conditions under which the hospital
> functions ... the inefficiency, the indifference that prevails.
> He associated intimately with the doctors, patients, staff
> members ... and he got a story that will shock North Carolina.
> In a series of sixteen articles, Mr. Jimison publishes the
> greatest commentary on a North Carolina institution ever
> written. The stark facts will appall you![16]

The editor's note which preceded each of the sixteen articles made it
clear that the papers did not "vouch for the statements contained in this series

of articles," but they were published for the people of the State to read because "the people have a right to know how the Morganton institution is being operated as related from the first hand knowledge of Mr. Jimison."[17]

Except for the statement in the advertisement and the editor's note, neither paper further identified Mr. Jimison or attested to his qualifications to write authoritatively about the Morganton hospital. Indeed, for many people of the State, Tom P. Jimison needed no further introduction, for he had long since established himself as zealous reformer. Some who did not recall his many previous feature articles and special news reports on social issues in the Charlotte News remembered him as a lawyer for the defense in the Gastonia labor trials of 1929-30 or as a labor organizer during the railway strike at Rocky Mount in 1932.[18] Still others knew Jimison as an ordained minister in the Western North Carolina Conference of the Methodist Church or as the fiery opponent of textile industrialist James Hanes in the race for Mayor of Winston-Salem in 1936. All who knew him remembered Jimison as a man possessed with a drive to serve a cause.[19] Proud of what he termed his "mulish mountaineer independence," and despite his unattractive physical appearance, Jimison was determined to make his presence felt wherever he went.

One of eight children born to Alexander and Mary Lou Jimison, Tom left his Smoky Mountain farm home in Haywood County, west of Asheville, to attend Emory and Henry College at Bristol, Virginia. Little is known of his early life from the time Tom graduated from college until he was received into the Methodist Church as a "preacher on trial" in 1917 at the age of thirty-one.[20] He was ordained an elder the following year but remained "on trial" until 1922 when he was received into full connection with the Conference. During his trial years, Jimison served a small rural charge in the western part of the state. His first major appointment was to the First Methodist Church at Spencer, North Carolina. Spencer was the headquarters for the Southern Railway

10

locomotive shops, and it was here that Jimison became interested in the labor problems that he later championed.

During his short pastorate, he was in constant demand as a revival preacher in the rural sections of the State. Sermons lasting an hour or an hour and a half were not unusual for him. His power to project himself into his audience led one of his ministerial colleagues to place his sermons in the Jonathan Edwards tradition. Ironically, Jimison succumbed to one of the very practices that the Methodist Church classes as a sin. No one is certain just when Jimison began to use alcohol, but by 1924 he was drinking so heavily that he was privately advised to leave the ministry voluntarily or face trial and certain expulsion. Accordingly, he asked for and received "permanent location without passage of character" as the language of the Conference put it.[21] In the same year, Jimison began the second of his many careers by entering the Law School at the University of North Carolina.

Jimison passed the State Bar Examinations after one year of formal training and was admitted to the North Carolina Bar in 1926. Except for one year in eleven years of practice when he was a partner in the law firm of Jimison, Edwards, and Gilreath, Jimison practiced in Charlotte, North Carolina, as an independent lawyer. His proclivity to serve the cause of the underdog was expressed by his social actions while a lawyer. The cause of the poor and the "outsider" was Jimison's campaign slogan in his only direct attempt to secure political office. His efforts to defeat textile industrialist James Hanes for the mayoralty of Winston-Salem came to an abrupt halt when he was arrested in the Twin City for possession of a container of "moonshine" liquor. Although his practice was never more than modest, Jimison remained an active member of the Mecklenburg Bar Association until 1937 when, again on the advice of friends, he withdrew from active practice rather than face the possibility of disbarment procedures because of excessive drinking.[22] By this time, Tom P. Jimison was an alcoholic. Without a law practice, Jimison turned to free lance writing for the _Charlotte News_ to earn his living. For two years he wrote special feature articles for the _News_ and is still remembered by the City Editor for his "stirring" Mother's Day and Fourth of July articles.[23]

Jimison's popularity as a preacher and a newspaper man resulted from a combination of fierce mountaineer independence and the ability to relate his opinions, whether on love, loyalty, patriotism, or the events of the day, in an appealing North Carolina dialect that "rang true" to the native listener and the reader. Brodie Griffith, then City Editor of the _Charlotte News_, tells of the time Jimison was assigned to cover the Barnum and Bailey Circus parade in Charlotte. The parade was to take place well before press time for the afternoon paper, but by ten minutes to press time there was no Jimison and no parade story. Convinced that Jimison had found his way to a bottle rather than to the parade, the editor was about to cancel space set aside for the special article when Jimison strode into the news room. Carefully placing his derby on the desk and hooking his cane over the back of his chair, the errant reporter inserted paper in the typewriter, pecked out two lines, retrieved hat and cane, and marched out of the office. While the rest of the _News_ staff watched, Editor Griffith removed the paper from the typewriter and read Jimison's account. "I seen the parade. Twern't much."

The newspaper people who knew Jimison were convinced that his career as a reporter could have been a successful one, but, without giving his reasons, Jimison suddenly decided to leave the _News_ and return to his law practice. He reopened his law office in Charlotte early in 1940, only to close it almost immediately when he voluntarily entered the State Hospital for the Insane at Morganton in April of that year. He remained there as a patient for fourteen months.

With his penchant for serving a cause, it is not surprising that Jimison could

see in Morganton the opportunity for a fundamental crusade on behalf of the

hospital's inmates. Indeed, he applied the knowledge and techniques of all

his previous careers in developing the series of articles that laid bare the

broad problems facing the mentally ill and the State Hospital.

Jimison recognized that society's attitude toward insanity was basic to

the myriad other problems he was to deal with in his articles. Chapter one in

the series is a description of his own admission to Morganton. Besides having

a "hankering" to see how the institution was run, as he put it, he sought ad-

mission on the grounds of alcoholism and a "social disease" his private physician

thought he had detected.[24] Jimison's first discovery was that it was "agin the

law to become demented." As a personal friend of the sheriff in the county where

he was committed, he was granted extra courtesies. Nonetheless, he could well

imagine the type of jails most patients were kept in while waiting for transfer

to the hospital. He was able to describe at first hand the feeling of terror

such patients must suffer while being taken to the hospital in handcuffs by

unsympathetic peace officers. Jimison depicted the attitude of society toward

the insane as one of downright hostility. The insane, like the criminal, he

wrote, deserved what he got because in the eyes of society, "drat 'em they should

not have gone crazy in the first place."[25]

In his mountaineer style, Jimison pointed up the basic public misunder-

standing of mental illness. "Society," he wrote, "does not believe that the

mind may slip its trolley pole as readily as the liver may lose its plumb."[26]

Coupled with misunderstanding, he found, was an admixture of guilt and embarrass-

ment that caused families to want to hide away their shame. These factors, he

declared, explain "why the physically ailing are tenderly nursed while the

mentally ill are hurried off to public asylums where they are incarcerated like

felons and practically forgotten by society."[27] It struck Jimison as ironic that

the more highly educated patient from the "better social brackets" received
fewer and more sporadic visits from his family than the poor, often illiterate,
patient whose needs were personally attended to by his loved ones. Rich or
poor, however, all patients received the same treatment from hospital staff.
Patients had to learn quickly to accept what was given to them and to be thank-
ful that their lot was not worse than it was.

Jimison's description of his first bath and the oversized hospital issue
of clothing that "swallowed" his "puny frame" was his way of telling the reader
how one was initiated into the society of those persons to be tolerated rather
than treated. In fact, the general attitude of hospital personnel was not much
different from that of the outside world. Each inmate was "jes another patient."
This callous attitude he portrayed graphically:

> One night Carl Phipps, a man in his late 30's, a quiet sort
> of chap, slipped through an unlocked door which led from D Ward
> to the attic. He climbed up there, got out on the roof, and either
> fell or jumped to the ground below, a distance of nearly 100 feet ....
> The Coroner looked at the body a moment, said it was suicide, and
> hurried home. But was it suicide? The door through which he had
> gone was supposed to be kept locked. Perhaps the poor man was home-
> sick for his wife and babies, and maybe his warped and tortured mind
> thought the open door led to them. But, the attendant said, "The ...
> wanted to break his damned neck, and that's what he done." He was
> jes another patient. [28]

Jimison recognized this intentionally-assumed attitude as being the result
of ignorance and gross indifference. He was able to bring the factors of ignorance
and indifference to light in a chapter dealing with his employment in the hospital
canteen where simple items were provided for the patients.

Only on rare occasions were patients allowed to visit the canteen in
person. Attendants usually purchased most of their requests - a service for
which they were "compensated." Holding back items purchased, over-charging the
patients, or directly assessing them for "services rendered" became so flagrant
during Jimison's hospitalization that the superintendent, Dr. James Watkins,

issued an order forbidding the practice of accepting "gifts and favors" from the patients. On one of these purchasing trips, an attendant asked Jimison for a nickel package of "Armadilla." Not knowing what was meant, Jimison asked if you "smoked it, ate it, or wore it." After threatening to "get" Jimison because of his "know-it-all, smart alecky" attitude, the attendant pointed to a small box of Arm and Hammer baking soda. The attendant could not read. Yet, this person was responsible for keeping a ward and for administering medication ordered by the doctors. Patients read labels on bottles and directions on charts for their illiterate keepers whose main responsibility was to maintain a clean and orderly ward.

The low educational level of the attendants precluded the possibility of any extensive psychiatric training that would develop in the attendant an interest and concern for his patients. The daily routine of maintaining a degree of cleanliness and order on an overcrowded psychiatric ward bred a stultifying attitude of indifference toward the patients. Getting the job done in a "passable manner" was the goal of most attendants.

Toward the goal of assuring a clean, well-ordered, quiet ward, the attendants developed a sort of lay psychiatry and treatment technique based on a system of rewards and punishment. While little personal concern was expressed for the patients, the attendants prided themselves in their ability to diagnose and prognosticate each patient's case. In fact, Jimison interpreted the pronouncement of the attendant in the Phipps case, as in all others relating to a patient's mental condition, not just an expression of indifference, but a diagnosis. He was quick to point out that the attendants were not entirely to blame for their attitude or the development of their lay practice.

The professional staff, Jimison observed, labored under a totally unrealistic work load.[29] The doctors, he concluded, were almost wholly dependent

15

upon the attendants for information as to the mental condition of the patients. This was so, he wrote, because they were required to make rounds twice daily, attend morning staff meetings, admit, treat the physical ills, and handle all the correspondence relating to the patients assigned to them. With over 450 patients in each doctor's care, it was little wonder that no professional psychiatry was practiced at Morganton, as Jimison charged. Rounds amounted to walking through the wards, listening to the attendant about problem cases, and casual remarks from the doctor to those patients closest to him. A more thorough routine was just not possible under the heavy burden placed on the attending physicians. Harried by the pressures of daily routine and administrative paper work and unable to meet even the basic medical demands of a "back-breaking" patient-load, the doctors themselves developed a protective air of detachment that Jimison contended was interpreted as indifference by attendant and patient alike. Under these circumstances, the actual control of the wards fell to the attendants who became masters of each patient's fate.

Patients soon found that it was imperative to "stand in" with the untrained, often illiterate attendants. Those who complained, those who created a disturbance on the ward, or were in any way deemed uncooperative, were reported as "disturbed." Such designation generally resulted in a transfer to one of the wards for degenerate inmates. These wards were the "hopeless wards" and patients feared being sent to them. To remain in good standing, patients volunteered to do the attendant's bidding regardless of the type of work involved.

While work therapy was considered a valid technique in helping a patient adjust to a social situation, Jimison charged that the practice of working patients was grossly abused by the "all powerful" hospital staff. Patients cleaned the wards, prepared food in the main kitchen, made and repaired hospital clothing, kept the grounds, and worked the farm. Even those with communicable diseases and otherwise too ill to work volunteered for job assignments. "It was a pitiful sight," he wrote, "to see patients marched off to work on cold rainy mornings when even prisoners from the nearby prison camps were allowed to remain indoors."[30] But no one complained; none dared to.

Work was more than an avenue to special favor. Work details afforded momentary escape from the wards and provided the only opportunity for physical exercise in an otherwise unplanned daily regime of sleeping, eating, and aimless waiting. Patients who worked could at least escape the hours of dreary wandering on the ward. Even more important, Jimison mused, there was a chance they might develop an appetite so as to stomach better the meals served in the central dining room.

The ex-inmate's description of the hospital diet served to drive home further revelations. The standard diet, which varied little from day to day, consisted of great quantities of "white horse" gravy, potatoes, turnips, fat back, dried beans, bread, black coffee, and an occasional serving of boiled beef and cabbage. Turkey was served at Thanksgiving and Christmas. All food was prepared in the central kitchen and then carried to the dining rooms, infirmary, and wards in open tubs or trays so that the food was always cold. The food was so bad by the time it reached the infirmary, Jimison wrote, patients got well out of self defense.[31] The diet, besides being monotonous and poorly cooked, was very often contaminated with roaches, spoiled food, and "jest plain dirt" from unwashed vegetables. Jimison claimed to have seen food, accidentally spilled on the floor, scooped up with a shovel and dumped into the serving tubs. Milk, eggs, and butter, produced on the farm, were used to supplement the diets of the critically ill and to enhance the fare in the staff dining room. Doctors rarely, if ever, visited the general dining room during meal hours. "The administration," he wrote, "was sensitive about food. And why not at 17¢ a day?"[32]

The reader's sense of revulsion and indignation at Jimison's vivid descriptions received a final thrust from his story of the meal served to a legislative appropriations committee invited to Morganton to discuss the general needs of the hospital and a $24,000 request for salary increases. In order to impress the visitors with the food service, cleanliness, and the overall efficiency of the staff, the group was given a tour of the hospital and served a dinner of barbecued hens, country ham and "all the fixings."

The stark contrast not only emphasized the plight of the patient, it provided Jimison with an opportunity to point up the futile deception employed by the staff in the operation of the hospital. The doctors, according to Jimison, formed a sort of "free masonry" to help each other.[33] No doctor spoke against another, and all were quick to defend a colleague when he was accused or an investigation was threatened. The attendants and nurses banded together to form a mutual protection society. News of staff decisions, private meetings, and "unannounced" rounds traveled via the hospital grapevine with the speed and efficiency of any modern communication system. All employees of the hospital bent every effort to "protect" the institution from outsiders. Every effort was made to present a solid front to the public in order to make the hospital look good. The special tour and dinner, which the cook dubbed "the feast of the gospel hens," was a prime example of the unified front in action.[34] The hospital was "spick and span" and the dinner was delicious. On return to Raleigh, the appropriations committee reported to the Legislature that conditions at Morganton were so good and the staff so well satisfied that it would not recommend any of the hospital's special requests. In terms of the salary issue alone, Jimison wrote, the "gospel hens" were served at a cost of $2,000 each. Such acts of deception, he argued, placed the hospital administration in the position of bowing to the dictates of politically motivated individuals and groups.

Compromised by the fear of scandal and a general unwillingness to reveal the true conditions of the hospital, the administration allowed the intrusion of politics into its operation. Jimison did not attempt to tell his reader how political considerations dictated many of the policies of the hospital administration. He contended that Superintendent Watkins often refused to make a decision on policy or general operation of the hospital without first consulting the chairman of the Democratic Party in Burke County. During the 1940 political campaign, Jimison charged, Dr. Watkins posted notices throughout the hospital requesting a ten per cent contribution of one month's salary to the Democratic Party chest. Although it was only a "request," Jimison likened it to the "Law of the Medes and the Persians."[35] This was the only specific charge of political pressure in Jimison's articles. Coupled with his repeated comments about insufficient funds allocated by the Legislature, however, it was enough to place the issue of politics on a par with the problems of gross understaffing, negligence and indifference, deceit and general mismanagement. After detailing his revelations in these areas, the crusading critic returned to the broader, yet no less significant, area of social concern for the insane.

In his final article Jimison prodded the conscience of both church and state. "The Church," he wrote, "has no message for the mentally infirm." The state assumes its problem is solved once the patient is admitted to a state hospital. Jimison believed funds to be the primary need and the answer to most of the hospital's internal problems. He called on the Legislature to provide the needed money and to name a new hospital board willing and able to inaugurate change. The series concluded with an emotional call to action by the citizens of the State.

The exposé which broke the scene in January 1941 is dealt with in greater detail in later chapters for three reasons. First, and probably least important in terms of long-range effect, the series of articles detailed the conditions that desperately needed correction at Morganton State Hospital. Second, the Jimison expose represents a bold attempt to go beyond obvious deplorable conditions at the Morganton hospital to lay bare political, social and institutional causes underlying those conditions and to assess responsibility for them. Third, the articles set in motion the political and institutional machinery of the state in a manner that is descriptive of predictable reaction to expose.

Concern for the mental hospital system is not unlike concern for mental illness itself. As long as men think the problem does not touch them directly they are prone only to be remotely concerned. National studies may shock momentarily. Local exposes, sensational muckraking attacks, and commission reports may temporarily arouse indignation or concern. However, an effective and progressive mental hospital system depends on an understanding of how problems develop within the institutions themselves and within the political structure of the state, why society reacts as it does to the problem of mental illness, how the mentally ill are affected, how programs are designed to treat patients, and how these programs relate to the social, political, and economic welfare of every individual in the state. Using North Carolina's Mental Hospital System as a model, the chapters that follow undertake to explore within a historic, political, social, and administrative context the problems of state institutions dealing with mental illness as those institutions attempt to champion a present day claim of humanity.

Chapter II

OUT OF SIGHT OUT OF MIND;

THE NORTH CAROLINA STATE MENTAL HOSPITAL EMERGES

The fundamental problems confronting state hospitals in the twentieth

century have their roots in the remote past and early beginnings of state programs

for mental health. The events in the early development of state hospital systems

varied in particular from state to state; nonetheless, the events surrounding the

North Carolina mental hospital movement are similar enough in kind to provide

a descriptive pattern of institutional form and structure that came to motivate

and direct the state mental hospital program throughout the nation. North Carolina

discovered the asylum as a method of care and treatment of the insane relatively

late in the reform movement of the nineteenth century. In the "Rip Van Winkle"[1]

state of North Carolina, during the first half of the nineteenth century, the major

problem was to secure social reform in a state that was "colossally ignorant"

and by far one of the least developed states in the union.[2] In the opinion of one

modern historian, no state was less developed or had more serious problems relating

to agriculture, transportation, commerce, finance, education, and emigration

than North Carolina.[3] In 1840 more than half the white population was illiterate.

Thousands of North Carolinians left the state to seek a better social, economic,

and political life, thus depleting its most valuable asset, human resources and

potential leaders.[4] To the factors of poverty, sparse population, and gross

ignorance was coupled a sectionalism that split the state politically.

On issues of internal improvements, constituional reform, extension of

slavery, and political reform, the cleavage in the legislature was between the relatively liberal, predominantly white, small farm holder in the West and the conservative, large farm-plantation owner and the slave-cotton economy of the East. The same cleavage prevailed on matters of federal internal improvements and state financial and banking policies.[5] The legislatures of this antebellum period were disinclined to accept any positive, constructive theory of government which would involve an outlay of funds. Thus, it is not surprising that North Carolina was dubbed the "Rip Van Winkle" state, especially as that title applied to her tardiness in joining the humanitarian movement that was sweeping the rest of the nation.

Although several attempts were made to launch social reforms prior to 1848, the pleas fell on deaf ears. "A Report on Penitentiary and Lunatic Asylums," published by a legislative committee in 1828, was the first official recommendation to the Legislature for an insane asylum. Similar requests followed from Governor Edward Dudley in 1840 and Governor John M. Morehead in 1842.[6] Morehead vainly urged action in the matter again in 1844 when he told the Legislature:

> For more than a century and a half the Legislatures of this
> state have been engaged in making laws for the benefit of that class
> of citizens which least needed aid, while the helpless and afflicted
> children of misfortune are almost wholly disregarded.[7]

The asylum measure finally became an official part of the Whig platform in 1844. The leading newspapers of both political parties, the Raleigh Register, Whig, and the North Carolina Standard, Democrat, published articles and editorials favoring the asylum.[8] Despite such bi-partisan support, however, the Whigs were unable to fulfill this part of their legislative program against the negative theory of the Democrats that the government which governed least and cost less governed best. As a result, even under the urging of Governor William A. Graham and a few progressive Democrats in 1846, the asylum issue rested between "ought and action."

22

When Dorothea Dix carried her crusade to North Carolina in 1848, the political situation in the state was unchanged. The Whigs and Democrats had equal strength in both the House and Senate in 1848, and neither party was willing to risk its political position in the state by voting additional appropriations.[9] It seemed certain that legislative action would be blocked again by the weight of the prevailing social attitude toward mental illness that had remained unchanged from the colonial period.

The sufferings of the insane were looked upon as the natural consequences of a stern, unbending Providence, meting out judgement to the wicked and the innately inferior.[10] The shame associated with such a concept bred an attitude of contempt for, and lack of interest in, the needs of the insane. The families that could afford special accommodations provided strong rooms to shut away the family shame, or sent the insane member to a neighboring state where institutional care could be purchased.

The dependent insane, who were not considered violent, were allowed to wander through the town, begging for food and becoming butts of ridicule of children or idlers.[11] Only those who were considered dangerous to the public welfare or who were a nuisance to the community received any public attention. Motivated by fear, communities used the local jail or almshouse as the common solution to the problem of public protection from the violent. There are no accurate records of the number of insane locked in the jails of the state at the time of Miss Dix' visit in 1848; but it was estimated that in 1854 there were over five hundred insane in jails, poor houses, and "such shelters as would seem alone fit for untamed beasts."[12] The combination of poverty, ignorance, prejudice, and political instability convinced the Whigs that any attempt to secure passage of the asylum bill in 1848 would fail.

Miss Dix was assured that there was no hope for her bill during the 1848-49 session. Writing to a friend in Philadelphia, she expressed the pre-

23

vailing opinion of those supporting the bill.

> They say nothing can be done here! ...It is declared that
> no word will be uttered in opposition to my claims, but that the
> Democrats, having banded as a party to vote for nothing that
> involves expense, will unite and silently vote down the bill.[13]

In the face of gloomy prospects, Miss Dix urged a leading Democrat, John W.
Ellis, to present the memorial to the Legislature. Ellis agreed, and a motion
to print passed the House without opposition.[14] A select committee, headed by
Ellis, reported the bill favorable, and it passed its first reading on December
8, 1948.

However, despite Miss Dix's memorial appealing to humanity, state pride,
and economic interests,[15] despite the early support of both party newspapers,
the Whig party, and a select group of Democrats, the House voted along party
lines. All arguments in favor of the asylum bill foundered in the face of a
requested appropriation of $100,000. Such an appropriation could hardly be
approved when the annual revenue of the state was less than $200,000 exclusive
of the literary fund.[16] The bill was defeated. Except for a motion to reconsider
and the impassioned plea of Democratic House Minority Leader James C. Dobbin,
the bill would have been forgotten.

Representative Dobbin was absent from the House floor during most of the
debate on the asylum bill to be at the bedside of his dying wife. The Dobbins
were staying in the Mansion House, and Miss Dix, also in residence there,
provided almost constant care for Mrs. Dobbin. In gratitude, Mrs. Dobbin
exacted a promise from her husband that he would "do what he could" for Miss
Dix's bill.[17] Immediately following his wife's funeral, Dobbin returned to
the House to ask for reconsideration:

> So ingenious (sic) and yet so clean were his arguments, and
> so earnest and yet so touching were the appeals which he made to
> the House, that all opposition to the project appeared to vanish
> into thin air.[18]

On a peak of emotion, the rules were suspended; and the bill passed both second and third readings on December 30, 1848, by a vote of 91 to 10.[19] The next day, a motion to reconsider was defeated by just two votes.[20] Ardor had cooled considerably in twenty-four hours. This now warm, now cool attitude expressed in the struggle over the first enabling act was a portent of the future for the hospital movement in North Carolina.

Seven years elapsed from the date of authorization before the hospital opened to patients. The long delay in construction was due, in part, to the method by which capital funds were provided. The legislature skirted an immediate appropriation by providing a special land and poll tax for a period of four years.[21] Funds for hospital construction could be spent only as they were received. The act further stipulated that paupers' expenses were to be borne by their respective counties, thus relieving the state of major operational costs once the hospital opened. The Legislature amended the original act in 1852 by renewing the asylum tax for three years. This act also reduced the superintendent's salary and required that "he be a skillful and competent medical man to reside continually at the institution"[22] on a two-year appointment or less if his services were not satisfactory to the Legislature. The superintendent was responsible for overseeing construction work and for keeping the hospital issue alive.

Construction of the hospital lagged to such a danger point by 1855 that Dr. Edward C. Fisher, the first superintendent, found it necessary to make an urgent appeal to the Legislature so that still neglected insane of the state might be cared for. As a result of this appeal, the Legislature incorporated the institution and established a rather formidable pre-admissions ritual and commitment procedure.[23] Testimony of a citizen, a physician, the decision of three or more justices, and confirmation by the board of directors were to precede commitment of a patient. The county support clause and poll tax were extended. An accompanying appropriation of $80,000 "to complete, furnish and enclose the asylum" made it possible to open the hospital on March 5, 1856.[24]

Although not yet completed, the new institution admitted forty patients in March and forty in April, 1856. Cost of construction was $184,938.58, almost twice the original appropriation. The water system and the gas lighting had yet to be installed, and the grounds were not enclosed. The Legislature approved a $35,000 bond issue for these purposes in 1857; but $13,000 of the issue remained unsold, and only a small portion of the fence was constructed.[25] Dr. Fisher's constant reminder that a fence should be constructed around the asylum was not prompted by any particular concern for the safety of the people of Raleigh. On the contrary, Dr. Fisher sought the fence in order to control the "citizens of Raleigh who come to the hospital, especially on Sundays, to watch and generally excite the patients."[26] In the same year the Legislature accepted, in part at least, Dr. Fisher's recommendation that the method and amount of financial support be changed.

The Superintendent argued that the $160 annual fee was insufficient to provide adequate care and treatment for patients. Also, the fact that "counties are held responsible to the state under such a complication and network of processes"[27] made payment from them both tedious and uncertain and most certainly "harmful to the patient in the hospital and to the insane still residing in the county."[28] The hospital could not operate without readily available funds. Furthermore, Dr. Fisher argued, counties that were unable or unwilling to pay the annual assessment for their indigent patients merely failed to complete admissions procedures. In these cases, the insane continued to languish under the deplorable conditions that the state hospital was supposed to eradicate.

The Legislature retained the county fee system, but it ordered such payments to be made to the state's general fund, made the state responsible for collecting the county assessment, and allowed the hospital to draw from the state

26

treasury for each indigent patient. As a further reform, the land and poll taxes were replaced by a direct appropriation.[29] Ten years had lapsed before the state began to recognize its responsibility for the operational support for the hospital it created.

A major task of every superintendent at Raleigh, and later at the other hospitals, was to keep reminding the Legislature of its continuing fiscal responsibility. As the superintendents succeeded in their task with the Legislature, they unwittingly developed one of several problems they were soon to regret. As the state became increasingly responsible, local government -- and, more important, local individuals -- began to assume that mental illness was not their responsibility. Unfortunately, those operating the hospitals were not attuned to the dangers of relegating complete responsibility for the mentally ill to a central state hospital. A relatively secure and simple hospital routine that was provided for a patient enabled him to avoid facing the more complex problem of life "on the outside," and a pathologic dependence on the institution was the result more often than not. Furthermore, local communities divorced themselves from any responsibility for their mentally ill citizens. Today, psychiatrists recognize the "malignant nature of pathologic dependence" and every effort is made to return the patient to his normal surroundings as rapidly as possible.[30] Recognition of this particular problem has prompted the movement toward community clinics and local mental health programs which are discussed in a later chapter.

Although the stinginess of the Legislature was a factor that created problems for the state hospitals, it cannot be charged entirely to a lack of understanding or appreciation for the hospital program. North Carolina was a poor state. The fiscal demands of the hospitals, however justified, were more than the Legislature felt it could meet in light of the total needs of the state. Besides, educational and highway projects, where the tangible results could be seen and weighed by the voter, had a greater appeal to the legislator. Nevertheless, the hospital superintendents continued to press demands for ever increasing capital and operating budgets in an attempt to satisfy a rapidly mounting hospital population growth rate while a significant number of patients remained in the local communities.

During no one year in the first ninety years of the hospital's history were there fewer than four hundred patients in the state who were barred from admission to a state hospital for lack of space. It was estimated in 1900 that among the white population the number reached nine hundred. Hospital superintendents contended that five hundred of this total were in "absolute need of hospitalization," and that five percent of the latter were lodged in jails.[31] No records were kept on the number of Negroes who were in need of hospital care. This situation remained relatively constant throughout the period 1900-1940.[32] Pressure for greater admissions came in the form of a constant demand on the local politician and the politically influential to secure admission to a state hospital for a relative or a friend. Such pressures could not be ignored by the vote-conscious politician or by hospital officials who looked to the politician for support in the Legislature. The three-fold result was a subtle intrusion of financial support from the Legislature, and further overcrowding. Even without this outside pressure, however, overcrowding could scarcely have been avoided.

In addition to providing hospital space for dire emergency cases that could no longer be cared for at home or in jails, superintendents willingly accepted every patient they could squeeze into the hospital if they considered the patient curable under the popular moral therapy of the day. Moral treatment consisted in removing the patient from his residence to an asylum where he could be cured by a therapy of kindness and consideration for his physical and emotional needs.[33]

Albert Deutsch, author of the first comprehensive history of the mental health movement in America, describes the prevailing approach to mental illness during the dominance of moral therapy as "a simple one: all the insane, or nearly all, could be cured in institutions, none, except a very few could be cured outside."[34] "The result," Deutsch contends, "was an emphasis on the mechanics of institutional arrangement. The important thing was to build hospitals."[35] Deutsch's position is borne out of the annual superintendent's reports describing the number of patients successfully treated and attributing failures to the extended duration of insanity before the patient was brought under treatment.[36] In reality, the percentage of cures in relation to total admissions declined so rapidly between 1850 and 1895 that the medical profession became disillusioned with moral therapy.[37]

Why did moral therapy, developed in France by Phillipe Pinel, and widely heralded in the United States as an effective and successful therapeutic method during the first half of the nineteenth century fall in disrepute by the end of the century? Part of the answer rests in the disillusionment from unrealistic, almost magical, hopefulness placed in moral therapy. The major reason for failure of the procedure can probably be attributed to the exuberance of superintendents who issued reports of high recovery rates to stimulate the founding of new mental institutions and to secure funds to enlarge existing ones. Dain, in his study of pre-Civil War institutions, points out that the resulting overcrowding and lack of adequate financial support of poorly equipped public hospitals made moral treatment impossible to practice.[38]

With no other medical approach available to replace the discredited practice of moral therapy, state hospitals became little more than custodial institutions.[39] Nevertheless, the outside pressures continued to exist. The end result of chronic overcrowding, with the concomitant pressures for larger facilities and expanded

appropriations, was a hardening of attitude in the Legislature toward demands made
by hospital officials. Deutsch attributes the action of the North Carolina
Legislature of 1873 in its refusal to appoint new members to the Board of Charities
as a reaction to such demands.[40] In point of fact, however, the basis for the
Legislature's action was both political and financial.

During the Reconstruction period, political interference in the operation
of the state hospitals became an established practice. North Carolina adopted
a new state constitution in 1868 which provided for a Board of Public Charities
with responsibility for overseeing the mental health facilities in the state.
During the period of reconstruction following the Civil War, the executive office
and the Legislature were controlled by Republicans and unionist sympathizers.[41]
It is not surprising, then, that the first members of the Board of Public Charities
were Republican and automatically considered suspect by their conservative opponents.
In its first annual report, the Board issued a detailed account of conditions at
the state's insane asylum and vigorously protested against the "abominable treatment of dependent insane in public institutions."[42] The report was a just and
soundly based account of prevailing conditions, but its major accomplishment was
to alienate further the conservative forces in the state who set out to destroy the
Board.

William W. Holden, Governor of North Carolina from 1868-1871, added insult
to injury when he refused to reappoint Dr. Fisher to another two-year term as
Superintendent of the hospital. Dr. Fisher, who had served as superintendent
throughout the Civil War, was popular with the conservative Democrats because he
had operated the hospital on a subsistence basis only because the State Militia
and ,later ,the Union Army had issued needed food and medical supplies.[43] Dr.
Eugene Grissom, a staunch, active Republican and a vowed unionist, Holden's
appointee, became Superintendent at the State Insane Asylum on July 1, 1868.

The Republican Governor's action was roundly denounced in the Legislature by State Representative Thomas J. Jarvis who accused him of introducing politics into the hospital.[44] In the meantime, the State Board of Public Charities continued to apply pressure on the Legislature for reform legislation. The conservative Democratic forces could only bide their time while they continued to rebuild their political strength.

When the Conservatives finally returned to power in 1871, they were able to muster enough strength to impeach Governor Holden. Dr. Grissom's second term was about to expire, and an attempt was launched to oust him and the Board of Directors. Thomas Jarvis, who had earlier denounced Governor Holden's action in appointing Dr. Grissom, now came to the Superintendent's support. As Speaker of the House in 1870-71, Jarvis left the Chair and told the Legislature that "When I denounced the appointment of Dr. Grissom, I meant to denounce the pernicious principle of carrying politics into this institution. I am as much opposed to doing so in 1871 as I was in 1868."[46] Dr. Grissom was reappointed by a vote of one hundred six to fourteen.[46] The fate of the Board of Directors for the asylum and the Board of Public Charities was not so favorable.

Acting on the principle that the right of appointment was reserved to the Governor and not the Legislature, Governor Tod R. Caldwell, Republican, 1871-1873, set out to remove the incumbents from office. When the hospital directors, previously appointed by the Legislature, refused to comply with Governor Caldwell's order to vacate office, he took the matter to the courts. The Supreme Court upheld Caldwell's action by ruling that the Governor alone has appointive power in all departments and agencies where appointment is not explicitly reserved to the Legislature by the Constitution.[47] The new hospital trustees assumed control in March, 1973. The Court's decision, however, opened the way for yet another maneuver by the Legislature. Since appointive authority over the State Board of Public Charities was explicitly reserved to the Legislature, that body, controlled

31

by the Conservatives, saw fit to exercise its authority in 1873 by refusing to appoint new members to the Board of Public Charities at the expiration of the terms of the incumbents. Thus, five years after its founding, the Board of Charities established by the Reconstruction legislature was dismantled by an act that further injected politics into the hospital movement.

Despite its short life and the antagonism it engendered, the efforts of the Board of Public Charities bore fruit. The first report of the Board, in 1868, emphasized the fact that a minimum estimate placed the number of insane in the jails and county homes of the state at seven hundred.[48] By 1873, the year the Board was abandoned, the situation was even worse. Dr. Grissom reported "776 insane and 976 idiots in the state," and of the 500 insane not in the asylum, over 250 needed treatment there. To accommodate the rising number of serious cases, the harmless incurables had been sent away and their places filled by acute or violent cases.[50] Besides emphasizing overcrowding and poor care provided the indigent, white psychotic, the Board criticized the total lack of state care for the Negro insane. So effective was the Board in keeping these facts before the Legislature that demands for an asylum in the western part of the state for white patients and one in the east for Negroes were successful.

The Legislature of 1874-75 appropriated $75,000 for the establishment of the North Carolina Western Insane Asylum, and Morganton was chosen over Asheville and Hickory Tavern for its location.[51] The first appropriation was used for the purchase of land and for the construction of the foundation for the main building. Each succeeding year for eight years, the hospital board had to request additional funds to complete the hospital. By the spring of 1883, the asylum was finally becoming organized. The south wing was completed and the first patient admitted in March of that year. When the hospital opened, the Legislature divided the state by a line north and south along the western

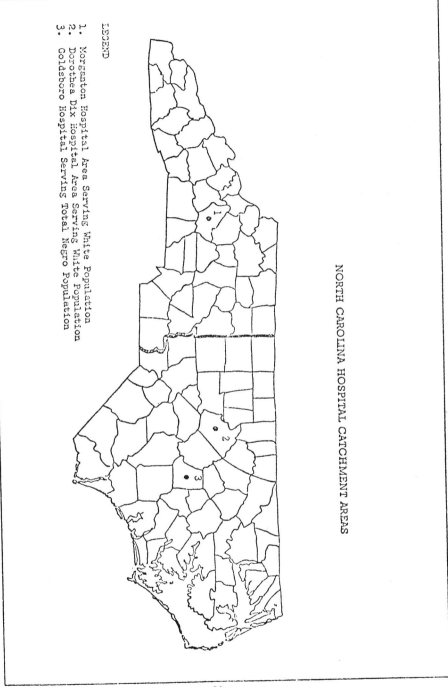

NORTH CAROLINA HOSPITAL CATCHMENT AREAS

LEGEND

1. Morganton Hospital Area Serving White Population
2. Dorothea Dix Hospital Area Serving White Population
3. Goldsboro Hospital Serving Total Negro Population

33

boundaries of Rockingham, Guilford, Randolph, and Richmond counties. White patients west of the line were sent to Morganton. Whites east of the line continued to enter Dix Hill (See map).

The Goldsboro hospital, established in the eastern part of the state where the Negro population was concentrated, was designed to serve the Negro population of the entire state. Although the Negro Asylum was not authorized until 1879, five years after Morganton, the hospital was completed and ready to accept patients in 1881, two years ahead of Morganton. The original appropriation of $40,000 was adequate to construct and furnish the one-hundred fifty-bed Negro asylum. North Carolina now had three asylums to testify, for the moment at least, to a change in the Legislature's earlier negative attitude toward state responsibility for the mentally ill.

Public attitude toward the cause of insanity had also changed somewhat in 1883. Insanity was no longer considered the punishment of a stern, unbending Providence, but rather the result of mental or physical defects that could possibly be cured. This change in attitude was evidenced by 1890 in the willingness of the Legislature to change the names of the three mental institutions from asylums to state hospitals "in order to disassociate the hospitals from the popular concept of craziness associated with the word asylum."[52] The shift in attitude did not, however, relieve a patient's family entirely from the social embarrassment of having a deviant in its midst. Nor did the change entirely alter the public attitude toward the mentally ill. All too often the mentally ill person continued to be regarded not as a sick person to be treated but as an undesirable charge to be tolerated. Once the public became convinced that hospitalization was an end in itself, the local community found it easy to forget the patients committed. Patients sent to a large, centralized, and somewhat isolated institution were now out of sight and soon out of mind.

While the individual patient was an embarrassment for his family to be set aside, collectively the insane were still a sight to see. The arrival of the special asylum train at Morganton in 1883 created an air of excitement akin to that of a circus coming to town. The event was so momentous that fifty-five years later a Morganton resident could:

> remember very distinctly as a lad of eleven the morning that they brought about a hundred patients on a special train from Raleigh to Morganton. The train arrived here just about daybreak and of course at that time seeing a "crazy person" was something of a curiosity and I was there at the station with everyone else to see them unloaded. They walked them over to the hospital in pairs.[53]

Reaction to the arrival of the asylum train was an expression of the ill-defined public attitude on the status of mental illness and the function of the mental hospital. If the public at large held such views, it was scarcely to be expected that the attitudes of the members of the state legislature would be far different. Nonetheless, whether the public and the representatives were hostile, callous or indifferent, those in charge of the state hospitals had somehow to win their support.

Dr. Patrick Murphy, first superintendent at Morganton, recognized the importance of establishing and maintaining a good rapport with the Legislature and the local community; and he bent every effort to keep the lines of communication open to these two sources of support for the hospital. Dr. Murphy took advantage of the fact that besides being the seat of Burke County and the center of Republican strength in the state, Morganton was on the main east-west railroad line of the state. Virtually every legislator traveling west had to pass through Morganton. Since the asylum was the only major state institution west of Raleigh, it was relatively easy for the adept Dr. Murphy to develop an area-wide sense of pride in the hospital. Both state and local politicians visted the hospital whenever they had the opportunity. Dr. Murphy encouraged such visits and took pains

to make every legislator's visit a special event. Friday night dances, a part of
Dr. Murphy's moral therapy, were held on the second floor of the main building.
These dances became the weekly social event of the area. Once having visited
the asylum, legislator and local citizen alike went away as lasting and personal
friends of the institution and its superintendent.[54] The happy visits to Morganton
were recalled with great political effect by Dr. Murphy when the hospital's biennial budget was presented to the Legislature. Dr. Murphy further sought advice
and counsel from the leading citizens of Morganton on matters relating to the
hospital. This close relationship with the town was to benefit Dr. Murphy when
political winds shifted in the state. Later, however, under a different superintendent, this close political relationship was to prove a source of embarrassment
to the hospital.

Since there was no efficiently organized central administration for the
hospitals, each superintendent was left to his own devices not only for maintaining
a good rapport with the local community, but also for developing techniques of
treatment, managing the physical operation of the institution, establishing
personnel procedures, and successfully presenting to the Legislature the needs
of his particular hospital. The total operation of the hospital centered in the
superintendent, and the success or failure of the hospital's program rested on
his ability to carry out his policies. Although there was a delegation of responsibility to the assistant physicians, chief matron, engineer, farm manager, and
others for functional operations, the authority to determine how these operations
were to be accomplished rested solely with the superintendent. As a result,
important organizational functions grew up by local tradition and administrative
rule of thumb rather than by law or regulation. The authority delegated to supervisory personnel varied with the willingness of the superintendent to grant it.

The therapeutic techniques employed in each hospital differed from the others
to the degree that a superintendent favored a particular method.

Dr. Murphy, for example, was an enthusiastic advocate of colony treatment.[55] Under this system, less disturbed patients were placed in small groups
where they worked and lived together as a unit under the supervision of an attendant.
The basic purpose of the colony was to provide employment as a means of treating
and caring for the insane in a way that could not be accomplished in the large
central hospital plant. Besides providing work as an approved method of treatment,
a colony unit could be built and maintained at a lower per capita cost than the same
patient space would require in the central hospital - a key factor in Dr. Murphy's
ability to secure legislative support for this program.

Dr. Grissom of Dix Hill, on the other hand, was an advocate of moral
theraphy modified by a "sound and necessary application of restraint." Dr.
Grissom's paper on the use of mechanical restraint, read before the Association
of American Institutions for the Insane, was the source of a national debate
for several years. [56] The position he took was used against him when an effort
was launched to have him removed from office in 1889. In any case, superintendents
were the final authority in all phases of hospital operation; and rarely if ever,
did the board of trustees directly determine policy, although by indirect pressures
they influenced the application of policy. The demands thus placed on the superintendents tended, therefore, to make rigid and authoritarian internal organization
of the hospitals a necessity. Probably the greatest of all demands was for a rigid
economy in the use of funds appropriated by the Legislature.

The Legislature, already firm in its opposition toward increases in general
appropriations, was now faced with three separate demands to support one state
operation. The highly individualized and totally uncoordinated methods employed

by the three hospitals in approaching the Legislature for general support and specific appropriations increased the demand for economy at every point. A reading of annual reports from the three hospitals, especially after the turn of the century, leaves the impression that what began as an honest effort to economize, soon became an open effort to gain legislative favor for the hospital that could cut its per capita costs the closest. One superintendent at Raleigh took offical note of the fact that he was able to return $42,000 to the general fund as an unused portion of his hospital's appropriation.[57] This was at a time when the hospital was understaffed and the salary scale for qualified personnel was not competitive even within the community.[58] In the same report, the superintendent noted the urgent need for repairs to a men's ward, the lack of an operating room and nurses' quarters, the need for a dentist on the staff, and the general rundown condition of the chapel and the main women's ward.

The superintendents continual efforts to reduce the per capita cost, although proved to be a false economy, was the result of an honest, if misdi-rected, effort to accommodate the increasing demands for hospital admissions. While the uncoordinated rule of thumb operation at the local level was becoming the established pattern for developing the hospital system in North Carolina, the superintendents were repeatedly forced with one hand to woo the Legislature and with the other ward off attempts at direct political intervention into the opera-tion of the hospitals.

Two of these attempts constituted power plays of major proportions. The first came in 1889 when the Democratic legislature lodged charges of cruelty and immoral conduct against the Republican appointee, Dr. Grissom. The charge of immorality against Dr. Grissom was based on circumstantial evidence and could not be substantiated. The charge of cruelty was made on the basis of Dr. Grissom's

use of mechanical restraints, but evidence from a number of the nation's psychiatrists supported Dr. Grissom, and the charge was dropped.

Nonetheless, because of the sensationalism surrounding the trial, Dr.
Grissom felt his effectiveness as a superintendent was beyond repair. Following
the trial, therefore, he published "A Statement to the Friends of the North
Carolina Insane Asylum, 1889" issuing his resignation and charging that the entire
proceeding was nothing more than the culmination of a determined effort by his
political enemies to have him removed.[59] Grissom's statement accused Governor
Daniel Fowle of inducing a hospital steward to institute the false charges against
him in order to remove a Republican from a high and respected state office.
Grissom also described how the controversial nature of his appointment and the
long running debate on his advocacy of mechanical restraint were used as tools
against him. Although Dr. Grissom was vindicated, the political effort to force
him to resign was successful. This success in the face of the evidence only
served as a precedent for further political intervention of an even more threatening
character.

The next attempt to make the state mental hospital system into a political
plaything came in 1895 when the Fusionists, a coalition of Republicans and
Populists, elected Republican Daniel L. Russell governor and attempted to remove
all incumbent board members and superintendents of the three hospitals in favor
of a new crop of political appointees. One of the first acts of the Legislature
was to change the title of Board of Directors for the hospitals to Board of Trustees.
Under this thinly disguised "reorganization" Governor Russell assumed authority
to name a new slate of trustees for the three institutions.

At this juncture, the long standing friendship developed between Dr. Murphy
and the leading citizens of Morganton proved its worth.[60] When the new slate of
trustees was received at Morganton, Dr. Murphy's friends offered financial and

moral support to fight the Governor's action. The case was carried to the Supreme

Court. In the case of <u>Wood</u> <u>vs</u> <u>Bellamy</u>, the Supreme Court ruled against the

Legislature and the Governor.[61] Justice Montgomery castigated the Legislature

for obvious political intent in instituting the name change.[62] The unanimous

opinion of the court brought to an end overt attempts to incorporate the hospital's

administrations into the political spoils system of the state. Unfortunately, the

subtle practice of pressure by individual politicians continued to influence ad-

missions practices and continued to be a factor in the personnel policies of the

hospitals. Thus, within the first fifty years of operation, there developed in the

North Carolina mental hospital system all of the problems that would continue

to prevent effective therapeutic treatment of the mentally ill for the next fifty

years.

With the death of Dr. Murphy in 1908, the pretense toward the application

of moral theraphy as a positive therapeutic tool passed from the scene. Changes

in treatment of patients and organization of institutions came from practical

experience rather than as the result of research or experimentation. The hope

for an early return home had died. By 1900 the state's hospitals were not much

more than custodial institutions serving the primary function of keeping the

mentally ill out of sight.

Chapter III

A SAD BUSINESS:

THE ERA OF CUSTODIAL SUPERVISION

As managers of custodial institutions, the state hospital superintendents continued to perpetuate earlier assumptions and practices that served to aggravate further a deteriorating situation. The practice of attempting to cut per capita costs despite continual hospital population increase was maintained in order to persuade the Legislature to appropriate funds for physical expansion. To get the patient into the hospital was still regarded as the most important objective. The economy of operation plus the plight of the insane still lodged in jails and poor-houses was the basis for an appeal to the state in 1900 by the North Carolina Board of Public Charities for a physical expansion of all three hospitals.[1] Nonetheless, the development of the Morganton and Goldsboro hospitals and the periodic expansion of all three units failed to keep pace with the needs of the mentally ill in the state. The uncoordinated efforts of the three hospitals, lack of efficient management, political pressure for increased admissions, the demand for rigid economy, and the development of the rule of thumb system prompted one observer to note, "improvements that were made, were adopted in a spirit of alleviating a necessary evil and in a manner that would entail the least expenditure of time and money."[2]

Progress in the care and treatment of patients after 1900 continued to be marginal. Improvements were introduced, to be sure, but these were largely confined to the construction of facilities for concentrating patients in functional units for specialized care. For example, special facilities were established at Raleigh for epileptic patients in 1910, all white inebriates in 1922, and for the criminally insane in 1925. The Goldsboro hospital for non-whites opened special buildings in 1909 for the epileptic and tubercular patients and a building for the criminally insane in 1926. A school of nursing was established at Raleigh, and a training program instituted at Morganton helped relieve the personnel problem of the hospitals.

The School of Nursing at Raleigh had originally begun in 1868 as a simple training program under the direction of Dr. Grissom. Training was in psychiatric nursing only, and the school's graduates were not registered; but the school did help to fill the hospital's need for qualified staff members. The Raleigh school was reorganized in 1913 under Superintendent Albert Anderson and incorporated by the Legislature in 1916. In his annual report of that year, Dr. Anderson justified the reorganization and explained the training program, saying that "in this way we can give our patients skilled nursing attention with no added expense and at the same time qualify our graduates for state registration."[3] In effect, the training program served as yet another device for keeping costs down while providing a source of labor. A similar training program at Morganton, established in 1906, had to be discontinued in 1930 for lack of funds.

The major innovation, beyond construction and reorganization of existing facilities, involved the expansion of the state mental health program to provide institutional care for mental defectives.[4] The first facility for mental defectives was established in 1911 when the Legislature authorized the Caswell Training School. The purpose of the school was to:

> segregate, care for, train, and educate mental defectives; to
> disseminate knowledge concerning the extent, nature, and
> menace of mental deficiency; to initiate methods of control,
> reduction, and ultimate eradication from our people; to main-

42

tain a bureau for instructing the public with reference to the
care of mental defectives who remain in their homes; to maintain a psychological clinic for study and observation of mental
defectives charged with crime.[5]

The key word which gives away the underlying motivation for establishing this

institution, not unlike the mental hospitals, is "segregate" - again, out of sight,

out of mind. The duties and responsibilities of the school were already so broad

in scope that not even the first goal of admitting eligible children, let along all

the various categories of adults, could be achieved in the first twenty-five years

after the school began. By 1935, Caswell School had 621 inmates, but studies

showed that there were over 1,600 feebleminded in the state who need to be in-

stitutionalized. The actual waiting list stood at 800 in 1935.[6] Under these

conditions; and with no let-up in the demand for strict economy, the school op-

erated under the same pressures and decentralized administration that developed

over the years in the state's mental hospitals. As a result, conditions at Cas-

well were described in 1937 as "very poor." There were not enough toilets,

baths, or locker spaces. Many of the buildings were described as fire traps.

Physical education was inadequate, and in the lower grades the children were

too often neglected and simply allowed to vegetate.[7] Ironically, the prevailing

political psychology that encouraged operating on a continually reduced per

capita cost basis in order to secure expanded facilities and larger patient en-

rollments made it exceedingly difficult to obtain an honest judgement on the

part of the Legislature as to the real needs of the institutions.[8]

Although politics intruded upon the operation of the state hospital system,

it is difficult to criticize the members of the Legislature for their failure to

understand the broad problems of the mental hospitals since there was no specific

person or agency to advise them. To remedy this defect, the Legislature attempted

43

to provide a central agency for the three state hospitals by placing them under a single board in 1917. In 1919, a supplementary act included the Caswell Training School as well. Because each institution was represented by three members who had special interest in their own institution and very little in the others, the hoped-for centralization of control and coordination failed to materialize.[9] The old order was restored in 1921, and separate, independent boards re-established for each of the units in the state system.[10]

After the abortive attempt at centralization begun in 1917, no further consideration was given to unification until 1936. Each superintendent continued to fight his own battles, promote his own hospital, and institute his own internal programs as he saw fit. There was, to be sure, at least one agency that might have afforded some degree of coordination. The North Carolina Board of Charities and Public Welfare seemed to have been the logical body to develop and direct a statewide hospital program. Unfortunately, state law limited the activities of the Board of Charities to an annual inspection of the hospitals and to the function of advising the separate hospital boards. This practice followed the general pattern in North Carolina which favored decentralization of state authority and the fostering of local systems of government for state agencies. The lack of a unified approach to the over-riding problems of the state hospital program almost inevitably led, as one observer put it, to the development of an extemporizing policy according to which the needs and inadequacies of the mental hospitals were treated as if they were merely temporary disturbances in an otherwise ordered system.[11] Two such "disturbances," selected from many others arising after the turn of the century, lent credence to this contention.

The chronic problems of overcrowding and insufficient appropriations focused public attention, at least briefly, on the hospitals. The first exposé came in 1905 when the <u>Charlotte Observer</u> charged that patients were unlawfully

admitted on the basis of favoritism which resulted in a neglect of the poor.
The paper stated that if these well-to-do patients were discharged, there would
be room for the indigent insane.[12] An investigation by Governor Robert B. Glenn
proved the Observer's charges to be unsubstantiated.[13] At the time of the
Observer's allegations, there were only two non-indigent patients at Raleigh
and two at Morganton. All four had been admitted prior to a Supreme Court ruling
on the definition of "indigent" in 1898.[14] The Governor and the Chairman of the
Board of Directors both praised the administration of the hospitals and defended
the integrity of the superintendents. The Observer supported the findings, and the
matter was closed.

The second exposé involved the trial, in 1924, of Dr. Albert Anderson on
charges of misappropriating hospital materials and of cruelty to patients by working
them for his own personal gain. The practice of using patients to perform menial
tasks was one of long standing. The general theory of moral therapy and the
colony plan originally employed by Dr. Murphy at Morganton relied on a super-
vised work program as a therapeutic tool. The argument for such employment was
that patients kept busy had less time to brood and an opportunity to develope and
work in a more normal social context than mere ward confinement provided. Of
course, the lack of funds for hiring adequate maintenance and farm personnel
afforded a no less compelling justification for this practice. Charges leading
to Dr. Anderson's trial were filed by a member of the hospital staff who sought
to discredit the Superintendent because of a difference of opinion over the fiscal
operation of the hospital.[15] The lower court conviction was overturned by the
Supreme Court for lack of sufficient evidence.[16]

Both exposés provided an opportunity for a thorough investigation of underlying causes. Once the specific cases were settled, however, the hospitals were
allowed to return to their routine operations while needs and inadequacies mounted.

The weak administrative structure of the hospitals is attested by failure of the Board of Trustees at Dix Hill to act when charges were leveled against Dr. Anderson. The court admonished the trustees for not assuming their proper responsibility for investigating the matter and for not settling an issue that "should never have found its way into the courts."[17] The investigation of charges made against Dr. C. B. McNairy, Superintendent of the Caswell Training School, brought about his dismissal in 1925; but there is no evidence that conditions were markedly improved following the report of the committee appointed to investigate the school.[18] When Dr. F. M. Register assumed the superintendency at Caswell in 1933, he initiated a number of administrative changes and introduced several training programs at the school. Dr. Register's ability to accomplish these ends was more a tribute to his recognized talent and personal devotion to the institution than to change in attitude by the general public or any significant increase in appropriations by the Legislature.[19]

Increasingly, it became evident that there was no one to accept responsibility for the hospitals. Those who blamed the Legislature resorted to a form of "scapegoating" by placing responsibility for medical and political leadership on so many individuals that it was virtually impossible to assign responsibility. On the other hand, those who placed final responsiblity with the executive branch and the hospital administrators were faced with even more basic questions. Who was to advise the executive brance of state government? Who was to support the hospital administration?

While it would seem logical for the three hospital superintendents to fulfill the advisory function, the historical development of North Carolina's three mental hospitals seemed to preclude this possibility. From their inception each hospital had been treated as a separate entity, a relatively self-contained and isolated community. The state's hospitals fit well S. Kirkson Weinberg's description of the historical social structure of the state mental hospital as "a community where change comes slowly, innovations are suspect and disruptions in the patterned routine are often opposed."[20] There is no existing evidence that the superintendents communicated with each other on matters of patient care and treatment techniques, nor were details of administrative routine shared or discussed among the competitors for the legislative dollar.

Governor J. C. B. Ehringhaus sought to improve the state hospital system by establishing a commission in 1936 to study the care and treatment of the insane in North Carolina. The commission was charged with recommending programs to upgrade the administrative structure, therapeutic programs, and physical facilities of the hospitals.[21] When the question of a unified board was raised again by the Commission, open opposition was expressed by the superintendents.

At a meeting of the Governor's Commission and the state hospital superintendents, Dr. Federick M. Hanes of the Duke Medical School, the Commission Chairman, expressed the opinion that not only could a centralized program focus on the Legislature one man and one department for the sake of emphasis, but also the centralized approach "would avoid the political trick of playing one institution against the other," dividing the strength of those who supported the hospitals.[22] Dr. J. W. Ashby, the superintendent at Raleigh, opposed a unified board on the dual grounds that the three superintendents could get the necessary job done by meeting together informally and that an overriding commissioner would probably not understand the needs of the separate institutions while at the same time he and his staff would require funds desperately needed by the hospitals.[23]

Ashby's real objective, of course, was a defence of the existing character of the hospitals against an outside agency that might diminish the authority of the superintendents. He was only reiterating an attitude that had played a significant role in defeating the earlier attempt at unification and that also served to block any effective efforts to improve the lot of the hospital program in North Carolina.

In addition to a normal or "built in" resistance to change, political factors such as those present in North Carolina's hospital system created a climate of insecurity that tended to make superintendents hypersensitive to and fearful of political aggressions. In 1937, practically every admission to a North Carolina State Hospital came after a somewhat complicated Superior Court procedure. The Governor's Commission noted that "exceptions are these commitments made on patient's own application." All admissions," the Commission further noted, "are governed by available bed space. Almost every county has a waiting list."[24] In fact, however, the obvious problems created by overcrowded hospital conditions and the red tape involved in court procedures were further complicated by a tangled pattern of political influence that tended to justify the superintendent's fears. For example, to the friend of a seventy-year-old woman who could no longer care for her feebleminded son, one governor wrote, "I appreciate the difficult situation in which you find yourself. However, the only thing I can recommend is that you follow the regular procedure for having a patient committed to the State Hospital. If the son is violent, the court can have him locked up until there is room to admit him at one of our hospitals."[25] On the other hand, in response to a request from "an old friend," the Governor told Superintendent Ashby he would "appreciate his assistance in gaining admission for a patient."[26] When the Governor was urged to speed up acceptance of an "emergency case" from his home county, he wired confirmation of immediate admission to the Morganton hospital "when legal papers are completed."[27] A similar request from another county fared less well; in this instance, the Governor suggested that the routine admissions procedure be followed.[28]

Political interference was by no means confined to the Governor's office. For example, the Chairman of the Board of Trustees for Dix Hospital was not unaccustomed to assuming the role of admissions officer. Not infrequently he would send these letters to the Superintendent saying. "I am sending (patient) by the county sheriff for admission to Dix." On at least one occasion he was a little more expansive: "I am sending Sheriff _____ to pick up (patient). He is needed at home during the tobacco harvest. He will be returned to the hospital when the crops are in. The parole should do him good."[29] Whether these patients should or should not have been admitted or paroled, or were equal candidates for admission, the fact remains that such decisions were often made by the political officials and not by qualified hospital staff members. In an effort to insulate themselves against such actions, the superintendents were led to prefer seclusion for themselves, their staff, and their patients. Institutional loyalties and routines became the center of administrative policy. Resistance to change, the traditional authority-minded pattern of the hospitals, and a climate of political insecurity - in-short, a defense of the status quo - prevented the superintendents from serving the executive branch in any concerted advisory capacity. These same factors along with the legislative demand for operational efficiency combined to create a pressure that led the superintendents beyond a merely defensive posture to the practice of deception.

Throughout the state, medical men regarded it an honor to be selected as a member of the Board of Visiting Physicians. In a characteristic reaction, one prominent physician of Asheville thanked the Governor for his appointment and expressed "a feeling of great pride in being allowed to serve the state's hospitals because of the excellent care they provided the insane."[30] Yet, almost at the same time, the Governor received a letter from an Episcopal Rector:

> About 5:45 o'clock, November 7 ... an undertaker of Roanoke Rapids, phoned me to come to his funeral home. I went in about twenty minutes and saw a sight capable of arousing the indignation of any respectable citizen of North Carolina, as it did mine. I write to register as strong a protest as I can.

On the work table of the embalming room ... I saw the body
(of a woman) which had just a few minutes before arrived in the
hearse from Raleigh for burial. One could have expected to see
a body in such condition in a primitive land or less respectable
state but not in our state where people boast of civilization,
culture, and deep interest and sympathy for the unfortunate and
ill. I am told (this woman) died of "paralysis of the insane" as
stated on the death certificate. The body was poor and unclean
and evidenced neglect. The hair of the dead was alive with lice
from an eighth of an inch in length ... to as small as the eye
could see. Back of the ear and for two inches down the neck
these vermin clung so thick they looked like scales or scabs,
the undertaker took a small knife and raked the vermin off into
a bottle in large numbers.31

Fearful lest his informant fulfill the threat to take his revelations to the

newspapers if action was not taken, the Governor ordered an immediate investigation

of the Dix Hill Hospital where the patient had been confined. In the report

requested by the Governor, Superintendent J. W. Ashby flatly declared that he had

inspected his institution and that there were no vermin there. Patients were

properly examined and treated by competent help. What is more, with unconscious

humor, he supported his contentions by affidavits from three funeral homes attesting

to the good condition of bodies received from the State Hospital. The staff

physician, Dr. J. F. Owen, stated that he saw the patient daily and saw no evidence

of pediculi. Similarly, Dr. G. G. Foster said he had examined the patient on

admission and saw her twice daily from the time she came to Dobbin Infirmary on

September 21, 1937, until her death there on November 7. Two registered nurses

supported the doctor's statements. A senior nursing student attested to bathing the

patient daily, and twenty-two affidavits from other nurses and attendants testifeid

to proper care for the patient and to "no signs whatever of pediculi."32 This

overwhelming attestation of proper care and medical attention must have bordered

on the ridiculous in the light of the notation by the Governor's Commission that

the ratio of patients to nurses and attendants was sixteen to one. The committee

observed that:

With over 400 resident patients and about 140 admissions a year for each physician, routine duties consume practically the full time of the physician, leaving little chance for thorough psychotherapy or other individual medical attention.[33]

While denying the charges of uncleanliness in his hospital, Dr. Ashby appealed for an understanding of the problems he faced at Dix Hill by stressing the overcrowded condition of the hospital and the heavy burden carried by his under-staffed institution. In the particular case recounted here, neither the family nor the minister was satisfied with the explanation; but they let the matter drop. For the Governor, however, quieting this particular complaint did not mark the end of his difficulties.

He had no sooner dismissed the episode at Dix Hill, when another accusation from a different unit in the state hospital system threatened his administration with unfavorable publicity. The Governor sent the letter of complaint to Harry T. Riddle, Secretary of the Board of Morganton hospital. "I am enclosing a letter from the family of a former patient at Morganton," he wrote:

> I would appreciate your looking into the matter. I send these complaints to you as Secretary of the Board rather than to the hospital because I know you can make an impartial investigation as an outsider who knows the inside. Of course I send this in confidence.[34]

This letter concerned a patient admitted to the Morganton Hospital on May 7, 1938, and paroled twenty days later to the custody and complete responsibility of his family. The patient died two days after returning home. The family complained to the Governor through an attorney that his body was covered with large, deep bruises indicating severe mistreatment while the patient was said to have been locked in an isolation room on a "disturbed" ward during his hospitalization. The investigation consisted of an interrogation of the doctor, two male attendants, and one patient on the ward. All agreed that the patient was uncooperative and refused to stay in bed but that he had received proper care and was probably bruised by rubbing himself along the concrete floor of his cell. Accusations of cruelty or mistreatment were implicitly denied.[35] The three-page report was duly accepted by the Governor after Riddle indicated that the family was "satisfied" and would not pursue the matter further.[36] While hospital authorities stressed the pressures of outside factors, outsiders stressed the internal structure of the state hospital as the primary source of difficulty.

According to one student of mental institutions in the nation at large, the social structure of the state hospital relegates the person most directly concerned with the patients' welfare to the lowest level of the social hierarchy. Significantly enough:

> the immediate authority in the life of the patients rests with the ward attendants, the lowest paid, least respected group in the hospital .... Supervision of attendants is very formalized especially in larger hospitals. Beyond holding them responsible for general equanimity of their wards and visible accidents to patients, the administrative staff leaves them to handle the patients according to the dictates of a coercive behavior system which has evolved over the centuries.[37]

This view conforms almost exactly with the formalized description of staff duties found in the by-laws of each hospital in North Carolina.[38] That a coercive system existed in the North Carolina mental hospitals is borne out in the letters of patients and families of patients addressed to the Governor's Office over the years. Again and again, these pathetic appeals seeking relief or requesting investigation of irregularities testified to the pattern of coercion found in the state hospitals. Jimison's description of patients being marched to work in weather too bad to bring prisoners out[39] parallels the graphic stories of Frank Wright's volume Out of Sight Out of Mind.

Ironically, the very concept of a reward-punishment system, which opened the door to brutal abuses and exploitation of patients, was initiated by Dr. Phillip Pinel, the father of moral therapy.[40] It need not be assumed that a reward-punishment system is _ipso_ _facto_ wrong; the point is simply that the system, as

it existed in the first half of the twentieth century in North Carolina, was mis-

used or existed in a primitive, non-clinical form. A modified reward-punishment

system is still considered a basically valid reinforcement method of learning and

treatment.[41] To protect their position of authority on the ward, the attendants

established a kind of collective defense which would offset the inspection of

their methods of supervising patients. Frank Wright's description of the prepara-

tions made for the state inspectors typifies the defense system of ward personnel

in the early forties:

> Ward 20 was in an uproar when Bruce came on duty after his
> morning off. Never had he seen such activity. A crew of worker
> patients was waxing the floor using two big cans of paste wax-
> the kind Bruce had been ordering regularly for two months without
> results. The smell of pine disinfectant came from the shower
> room ... the exterminators were busy in the dormitory ... beds
> which had been without sheets for months were being made up
> with two sheets, a pillow case, a blanket, and a bedspread.
> And to cap the climax Miss Vollmer came sailing around the
> corner at the head of a cavalcade of potted plants and framed
> pictures. She looked a little harried but triumphant as she
> looked at Bruce. "Get on a fresh white coat," she ordered,
> "and keep these patients in line until after the visit. The
> state inspectors will be here at two o'clock sharp, and we want
> everything to be ready ... at four o'clock you can help them
> store these things away again.
>
> So this was the cause of all the fuss, Bruce thought. Wax
> he could have made last for weeks, sheets enough for two weeks
> at the normal rate - all expended in one great rush. And why?
> So that the very people who alone could improve conditions
> wouldn't see things as they really were.[42]

The masking of actual conditions on the wards was not a defensive practice

peculiar to attendants. In an effort to maintain the favorable facade of the

hospital before the Legislature and the general public, the chief administrators

made certain that the hospital was bright and shining and in proper order when

state officials made their investigations. As a result, the Commissioner of

Public Charities and Welfare and visiting legislators often came away from a hospital visit with the false notion that all was well. Jimison's episode of the "gospel hens" pointed out the futility of such ill-conceived deception by hospital officials.[43] Not only were legislative investigators often deceived by this fascinating contradictory attitude that the hospital administrators developed, the practice of hiding patients from public view and masking the real conditions within the hospitals effectively blocked what little attempt was made to change public attitude toward mental illness. In fact, the traditional notions and fears concerning mental illness were reinforced through lack of information and public contact with the hospitals' administrators and patients. When Dr. Murphy, Superintendent at Morganton, died in 1908, the practice of keeping alive a public awareness and support for the hospitals that he so carefully developed was no longer actively pursued.[44]

As a result of the National Mental Hygiene Movement founded by Clifford Beers, an opportunity to present the case of the hospitals to the public was afforded in 1914. In the wake of this movement, Dr. Albert Anderson of the Dix Hill Hospital and others founded the North Carolina Mental Hygiene Society. Dr. John McCampbell, Superintendent at Morganton, and Dr. W. W. Faison, Superintendent at Goldsboro, were members of the executive committee of the Society.[45] Little, however, was actually accomplished by the Society, and it made no organized effort to secure funds or introduce programs for the hospitals. The major activity of the N.C.M.H.S. was providing lecturers to interested groups in the state on the prevention of mental illness and work being done at the hospitals. Interest was sporadic and scattered at best. In only two towns, Charlotte and Winston-Salem, were active chapters founded. The society died a natural death of inaction in 1921 and was not reorganized until 1936 in conjunction with the work of Dr. Lloyd Thompson and the Governor's Commission on Mental Health in North Carolina.[46] While the members of the Mental Hygiene Society ostensibly supported the work of the hospitals, their efforts were not coordinated with those of the separate institutions. The closed system of separately run, defensively oriented units largely discouraged outside voluntary movements and prevented them from being of real service. The hospital staff itself, as it evolved in the first half of the twentieth century, helped to keep the patient out of sight and out of mind. Significantly, the Legislature and the general public were not alone in being misled by the system at the cost of the patient and the hospitals.

Complaints lodged against the institutions and pleas for admission were directed to the Governor of the state. Without a central administrative agency to act as a clearing house for such matters, every Governor relied on the hospital's superintendents or the boards of trustees to investigate charges or to weigh the merit of an admissions appeal.[47] Some complaints of mistreatment written by paranoid patients may well have been exaggerated or groundless. Nevertheless, the end results of an investigation conducted by the accused is all too obvious, especially in cases where factual evidence seemed to support the charges. Such a weak and indefensible administrative procedure worked against the patient by allowing superficial investigations and the well-nigh inevitable "white washing" of charges whenever possible.

While the procedure may have served to protect the hospital administrations from the scrutiny of outside investigators, it made the same administrations vulnerable to political pressures in admissions policies and operations procedures. The superintendents faced the reality of having to accept patients whose requests for admission to one of the mental hospitals were endorsed by the Governor or other key political figures in the state. "I would appreciate your looking into this matter at your earliest convenience," and "Admission as soon as possible seems warranted," were sentences synonymous with "admitted."[48] Referral to the regular admissions procedures or reference to extremely overcrowded conditions

and waiting lists were the official reasons for denying a patient immediate admission to one of the state mental hospitals. The same references, when used
by the Governor, were accepted by the hospital administration as an indication
that such cases constituted no political pressure. Regardless of the good intent
of the superintendents who sought only to care for their patients and to protect
their hospitals, the defensive system that developed in the hospitals served to
foster deceptive and coercive practices that worked against these same men.
Superintendents were caught in a vicious cycle of seeking to better their lot
while perpetuating the very practices that prevented betterment.

The sociological characteristics of North Carolina's mental hospitals
were undoubtedly important factors in the development of deceptive and coercive
practices. Yet, it is all but impossible to determine whether the social structure created the situation or whether the factors of misunderstanding concerning
the role of the state hospital, the threat of political interference, the honest
attempt to maintain the integrity of the hospitals, and the legislative demands
for rigid economy under conditions of extreme overcrowding were not the molding
forces that set the social structure of the hospitals and forced the superintendents
into compromising situations. Not all the problems uncovered by the Commission
were purely political. Most certainly the low intellectual and technical level of
attendants and the physical condition of the hospitals added to the superintendents' administrative problems. The Commission report pointed out that:

> No formal instruction except some courses in Ethics and
> Practical Nursing is given to attendants, but they undoubtedly
> learn from the student nurses.[49]

A counterpoint to the Commission's notation on training is found in the quarterly
report of Superintendent McCampbell at the Morganton State Hospital. "On
August 31, 1937," McCampbell informed the trustees, "J. M. A., a patient on

Ward X, hanged himself. In this instance, the accident was due, we thought to negligence on the part of the attendant in charge, and he was relieved from duty on that account."[50]

The facts disclosed by the study commission concerning the physical plant at the various state hospitals were no less depressing than its observations on the shortcomings in staff and procedure. Throughout the commission report, there were references made to porous floors in the wards, poor ventilation, and bad odors even where ventilation was good. Page after page of testimony described the poor physical condition of the facilities, dark halls, crowded dormitory-type wards, untidy patients, and understaffing at all hospitals. Per capita costs, the investigators learned, were invariably used as a gauge of the economic efficiency of the hospitals. As a consequence, superintendents were under continual pressure to keep costs down. The Commission noted prophetically that the pecuniary attitude of the hospital officials was unfortunate. Savings were obtained through decreasing staff, lowering salaries, and postponing repairs, all of which could only bring discredit rather than honor to the hospitals.[51] The daily per capita cost at Morganton hospital was less than $1.10; only seventeen cents of this amount was allotted for food. The Commission found better than sixty percent of the wards in need of repair and fifteen percent totally unsuited for patient care or custody. One third of the wards at Morganton, for example, were unscreened, allowing flies to swarm freely. Dr. Ashby's plea to Governor Hoey in 1938 for an understanding of the problems he faced as a result of overcrowding and understaffing was a typical defense borne of the frustration of the superintendents who were attempting to perform a vital service under adverse conditions. Given the situation of a rigid internal hierarchy, an unrealistic budget, and a poorly qualified, ill-trained overworked staff, it is not surprising that coercion, to the point of occasional brutality, prevailed in North Carolina's mental hospitals.

Just how serious the personnel problem was may be seen from a comparison of staff levels in North Carolina's three mental hospitals with national averages and the American Psychiatric Association's recommendations. From the opening of the hospitals through 1936, no hospital staff reached the full strength actually authorized by the Legislature. Turnover in medical staff, nurses, and attendants was extremely high. Of the twelve physicians employed at Morganton between 1916 and 1936, seven stayed for periods less than four years.[52] In a twenty-year period, the patient-doctor ratio at Raleigh State Hospital jumped from a low of 259 to 1 in 1916 to a high of 639 to 1 in 1936.[53] By American Psychiatric Association standards, there should not be more than 150 patients per physician, excluding the superintendent; and there should not be over 40 annual admissions per doctor.[54] In North Carolina, the Commission noted that the ratio was 528 to 1 in 1935 while the national average was 252 to 1. In the same year the number of admissions per physician averaged 138.[55]

Patient-nurse-attendant ratios were even worse. Minimum standards of the A.P.A. set the patient-nurse-attendant ratio to 8 to 1. In North Carolina the average ratio was 17 to 1 in 1936.[56] The national average was 11 to 1. The Morganton Hospital had one registered nurse and eight graduates of the training school in 1936. The one hundred twenty-six other "nurses" and attendants had no formal training. Nurses and attendants were on duty twelve hours a day. They had one afternoon off duty each week and forty-eight consecutive hours off once a month. A breakdown of salary scales is not readily available; but with a daily per capita cost of seven cents for professional care, salaries could not have been more than marginal.[57] Ratio studies can sometimes be misleading, but at these levels, as Governor Ehringhaus' Commission noted, "It is humanly impossible for the patients to obtain the proper care and attention they should have."[58]

Many allied services, standard in other states, were not available in the North Carolina mental hospitals. There were no psychiatric social workers, and no therapists were available to operate the physio- or hydro-therapy equipment at the hospitals. No hospital had pathology or research laboratories, and funds for remunerating consulting physicians from outside the staff were nil.[59] At Goldsboro, all clinical laboratory work was done by the physicians themselves who also had to type their case histories and other records.[60]

Governor Ehringhaus' Commission noted further that while the Legislature had recommended an increase in the attendant staff at all hospitals in 1935, no funds were made available for such an increase.[61] With the onset of the Depression, the state decreased the annual per capita allowance and completely cut off all capital funds for improvements and expansion. Between 1930 and 1936, there had been a marked deterioration in the physical plant of the state's mental hospitals.[62] With the federal funds under the Public Works Administration in 1936, the state launched the first in a series of jointly sponsored major renovation and expansion projects in an effort to restore the hospital buildings to standard serviceability.[63] This program was a prime example of an extemporizing policy established to alleviate two necessary evils, unemployment and deteriorating public facilities, without adequate thought being given to the long-range needs of the hospitals.

That North Carolina was not overly concerned with its mental hospital program beyond meeting the bare minimum of requirements is evidenced by the reaction of the state to the overall report of the Ehringhaus Commission and the specific recommendations it proposed. The Commission offered two alternative courses of action for dealing with "those whom unfortunate necessity has caused through mental disorder to become wards of the State."[64] One alternative was the existing policy of parsimony and inaction which meant "limiting the activities

59

of institutions to those necessary for purely custodial care until time or death relieves the State of the burden."[65] The other alternative would be a forward-looking policy designed to meet squarely "by preventive activities and adequate early treatment: the challenge of restoring to an active and productive life the largest possible number of persons suffering from mental illness.[66] The latter approach demanded a re-evaluation of the mental hospital program in North Carolina and a vastly increased expenditure of state funds. The report of the Governor's Commission provided the foundation for such a re-evaluation and called upon the Legislature to provide the necessary funds.

The Commission based its entire argument for re-evaluation on economic factors. In the biennium 1935-37, the Commission reported,

> the yearly State appropriation for maintenance of the state hospitals and Caswell Training School ... is in large part a dead loss to the taxpayers ... The part of the expenditure which is not a loss but an excellent investment is that which goes to restore patients to a community. In every restored case not only is the state relieved of maintenance costs but the patient may be returned to the ranks of productive workers and become an economic asset.[67]

The same basic argument was used in urging the state to expand a Division of Hospitals and Medical Service to coordinate the mental health program in North Carolina. Here was a forthright challenge to the whole state, a call for a bold and imaginative break with the past.

Unfortunately, the leaders of the state were apparently not yet ready to respond to such a call. The newly reorganized North Carolina Mental Hygiene Society urged acceptance of all the recommendations made by the Commission when Dr. Hanes submitted the report to Governor Ehringhaus on December 8, 1936.[68] The Commission's report was a model of thoroughness and accuracy. Yet, despite Dr. Hanes' warning that "it is too often the fate of official reports to find themselves quietly interred in the oblivion of dusty pigeon holes,"[69] this was precisely what happened. Unfortunately, the report was not ready to be submitted to Governor Ehringhaus until the last month of his term as governor. Lack of vital concern is suggested by the fact that the original copy of the Study was not transmitted to Governor-elect Hoey but ended up in the files of The Ehringhaus Administration in the Department of Archives and History.[70] When Dr. Hanes, the chairman of the investigating committee, died in 1946, the retired editor of the Winston-Salem Journal recalled that it was only through his efforts that a copy of the Study was found at Duke University and made available to Governor Hoey late in 1937.[71]

In spite of the valiant efforts of the Governor's Commission, the people of North Carolina were not able to shake off the "out of sight out of mind" attitude toward the mentally ill. Official reaction to the Commission's report confirmed the state's traditional practice of custodial supervision for mental patients under an extemporizing policy of least cost, least effort. Instead of awakening an "alarm minded and action oriented"[72] public, the highly analytical and dispassionate report became a substitute for remedial action. Against continual deficits of staff and material, against occasional instances of indifference, neglect, or outright abuse, against public apathy and a self-perpetuating administrative system, the progressive programs and attempts at reform in the North Carolina hospital system were frustrated.

A literally explosive social and political atmosphere had been allowed to develop. Logical argument based on economic factors failed to win the Legislature to the initial hospital movement in 1848; the same was true of the movement for reform in 1936. Emotion had carried the day in 1848, and once again in January, 1942, when an ex-inmate of the Morganton hospital, Tom P. Jimison, touched off one of the most sensational exposés ever launched against a North Carolina institution.

Chapter IV

A NEW DAY DAWNS:

AN EFFORT TO REFORM

The Jimison articles, discussed earlier, and the newspaper publicity
attendant to them were calculated to gain the attention and reaction of the
public at large. In this respect, they were a complete success. Indeed, official
reaction set in before the first article was published. Mr. J. Ed. Dowd, editor
of the Charlotte News and sponsor of the Jimison articles, sent Dr. Watkins, the
superintendent at Morganton, an advanced notice of the series the day before
publication. Recognizing its explosive nature, Watkins attempted to protect
himself and the hospital and at the same time discredit the series in a letter to
Governor J. Melville Broughton.[1] Watkins hoped to bring the Governor to the
side of the hospital in any ensuing debate by implying that the press was meddling
in matters that should properly be taken up by the Governor and Legislature. Re-
lying on the same defensive approach that had served in the past, Watkins insisted
that it was painful to have someone needlessly claim inefficiency and carelessness,
especially when the hospital had nothing to hide. Governor Broughton obviously
recognized Watkins' letter as a rather naive and desperate attempt to secure his
immediate support against Jimison's accusations.

Editor Dowd sent Governor Broughton word in advance, also.[2] Broughton,
not to be trapped by either side, set in motion a series of actions designed to
insure his control of a politically dangerous situation. The Governor made it
perfectly clear in his response to Dr. Watkins that if the problems at Morganton
were solely due to insufficient funds, then he had no cause for alarm. Since

the institution could act only within funds appropriated, and if these funds were inadequate, this was a matter for the Advisory Budget Commission and the General Assembly. Broughton then shifted the problem back to Watkins by insisting that other factual matters that might be contained in the articles relating to negligence, carelessness, or improver treatment were subjects not related to the size of appropriations. The Governor failed to recognize the relationship between inadequate appropriations and the resulting salary scale that forced the hospital to operate with an inadequate staff at all levels. On the competitive job market the hospital had to satisfy itself with hiring untrained, incapable and often unsympathetic semi-illiterates to perform attendants' duties that required semi-professional skills. In an obvious attempt to get Watkins to accept the responsibility of answering the attack on the hospital, Broughton suggested that Watkins initiate an immediate and full investigation by the hospital's board of trustees.[3] Anticipating Dr. Watkins' response, Broughton wrote immediately to Mrs. W. T. Bost, Commissioner of the Board of Charities and Public Welfare, suggesting that her Board initiate an investigation at Morganton as provided by the Constitution.[4] In spite of the Governor's recommendations and rising public protest, neither Dr. Watkins nor Mrs. Bost took any positive action.

In fact, Governor Broughton was forced to cope with negative reactions from both officials. The Commissioner of Public Welfare, Mrs. Bost, wrote the Governor defending the hospital and requesting the opportunity to discuss the matter with Broughton and her staff member Dr. James Watson, Director of the Division of Mental Hygiene, at a later date after the series of articles had run its course. She did not even mention the investigation Broughton had strongly urged her to make. The failure of Dr. Watkins to act prompted the Governor to write to Dr. Guy S. Kirby, Chairman of the Board of Directors of the Morganton Hospital, concerning the adverse sentiment created by the Jimison articles and

63

editorial comments in the press. He urged the Chairman to go very thoroughly into all the accusations and prodded him further by stating that the Governor's office would doubtless feel it necessary to have a thorough and independent investigation made of the entire institution at a later date.[5] Broughton made every effort to get the hospital officials to clean their own house voluntarily as was evidenced by his reminding Mrs. Bost, for the third time in ten days, that in view of the press coverage and the general public attitude an investigation would be necessary.[6] At the same time the Governor was urging his officials to act, he was attempting to keep in check the adverse public sentiment fostered by the exposé.

Reaction from the general public began to pour into the Governor's office. In the two weeks after Jimison's articles appeared, Broughton received seventy-five letters from mill-hands, business leaders, club women, ex-patients, and relatives of patients. Without exception, the letters from patients and their relatives supported the charges made in the articles. Ever sensitive to the political implications of the political outcry, Broughton answered each of these protests personally. To a textile worker at Concord who had written on a post-card, " ... Things don't look so good at Morganton, hey. Prisoner (sic) are treated more humanly (sic) ... Now ain't that a _____ of a way to treat patients!," the Governor graciously replied that he was grateful for the communication and assured the writer that a prompt and complete investigation would be made. In this and all other letters the Governor wrote relating to the Jimison articles, he tacitly defended the hospital. "While no management is perfect, and mis-management is subject to investigation," be observed, "the Morganton hospital is a great institution that had done a great work."[7]

By the third week of the Jimison series the Governor realized that drastic action would be necessary. Determined to maintain control of the rapidly worsen-

64

ing situation and to be prepared for any eventuality, Broughton decided to order a full-dress, independent investigation.[8] At the same time he requested a ruling from the Attorney General as to the procedure that might appropriately be followed.[9] The Attorney General informed him that the Constitution provided the Governor with authority to request an investigation of any state agency through the Attorney's Office or by any board designated by him. Broughton now had a clear path for independent action. Despite growing public concern and continuing newspaper pressure, the Governor delayed taking any direct action in order to allow the hospital officials maximum opportunity to act first. Probably the greatest of all the pressures placed on Broughton came from the press.

Only three papers in the state actually carried the series, but articles summarizing the series, as well as editorial comment, were statewide, with editor Dowd taking the lead. Dowd's attack on the hospital administrators and not the Legislature was characteristic of the crusading editor's penchant for finding fault with individuals and not institutional structures. In the light of evidence to the contrary, he remained convinced that Dr. Watkins should have been summarily dismissed because the Superintendent did not care for people, did not build an adequate medical staff, and did not go to the Legislature for funds.[10]

From the beginning, Dowd backed the credibility of the Jimison articles. In a series of editorials, the Charlotte editor attacked the hospital administration for being "inexcusably remiss and derelict" in its responsiblities.[11] His most devastating editorial was an indictment of "individuals and not institutions."[12] The editor readily agreed that part of the trouble at Morganton - wholly inadequate medical staff, accommodations, quality and turnover of nurses and attendants - could be traced to insufficient appropriations:

> But the state is not primarily to blame. It is those in charge at Morganton. Lack of money cannot explain lack of feeling or mistreatment ... One should not be condemned without a trial, but

we have read Jimison's story, and enough else to drive home that
it is the hospital administration and not the state that should go
on trial.

As each article in the Jimison series appeared in the <u>Charlotte News</u>, Editor Dowd sent the Governor a copy along with the editorials he had written to highlight Jimison's allegations. Apparently pleased with the impact already made, he told Broughton he was launching a new series of articles by still another former patient at Morganton who promised to tell "the woman's side of the story."13 Upon learning that an investigation by the local hospital staff was in the offing, Dowd urged the Governor to make it as searching as possible. He offered the names of several former patients who were willing to testify even though, as he put it, "some of them are fearful of doing so. They are afraid they'll wind up there again some day."14

J. Ed Dowd, for all his reforming zeal and penchant for seeing justice done, was as blind to the realities of institutional form and structure as was Governor Broughton. The mental hospital movement was founded on what is known today as programmed problem solving. Patients sent to a centrally operated insane asylum could and would be treated and cured--or at least properly cared for within the institution. Neither the founders of the movement nor those who later attacked its inadequacies understood the implications of institutionalized programming. Movements that become formalized in a bureaucratic structure take on a momentum and, in many cases, a direction of their own not necessarily intended by their founders or those persons within the system responsible for its management.

Clearly, the mental hospital movement represents a prime example of how external and internal forces impinge upon a system to give direction to the institutionalized form and structure. As the majority of his contemporaries, Dowd could see evil only in people and not in the institutions they construct. When

66

Jimison exposed the conditions at Morganton, the mode of patient care, administrative routine and political direction had long since become entrenched routine.
No superintendent or local politician could have broken the mold. Indeed, their
actions, though weak in some instances--indefensible in others, was only what
should have been expected given the structure within which they were forced to
work.

Editorial reaction to the Jimison articles throughout the state was some-
what mixed. The Gastonia Gazette argued that reform might well be needed at
Morganton but doubted seriously that Jimison's articles were the proper approach.[15]
The Fayetteville Observer, the Raleigh News and Observer, and the Asheville
Citizen all agreed that there might be a need for an investigation, but questioned
Jimison's reliability.[16] The Greensboro Daily News defended the articles after
checking into the credibility of Jimison as a person and his reason for entering
the hospital. Significantly, the editorialist did not state how he had "checked
the credibility of Jimison" or his reason for entering the hospital. "Someone
had to plead the cause of the patients" and what better person than an honest,
forth-right ex-patient?[17] The Greensboro paper differed with the Charlotte News
by stating that what was really needed at Morganton was more funds. The hospital
administration had explained its needs. "Yet, nothing was done. The blame lies
with the Legislature."[18]

The character of the widspread editorial comment following the Jimison
series caused Governor Broughton no little concern. For the moment, he could
do little more than wait until the Board of Trustees at Morganton responded to
his request of January 31 calling for a thorough investigation. Alarmed by the
rising furor, and by now thoroughly on the defensive, the Trustees established
an investigating committee composed of five members who were not on the Board
at the time Jimison was at the hospital.[19] Dr. Watkins sent the Governor a copy

of the resolution adopted by the Trustees appointing the investigating committee and enclosed a covering letter inviting the State Board of Charities and Public Welfare to make an investigation and promising his full cooperation.[20]

Eight days after the Trustees' investigating committee was appointed, its members reported to Broughton that they were " ... unable to find grounds for any substantial complaint in connection with the administration of the State Hospital at Morganton other than the fact that the employees and especially the attendants and nurses work long hours for compensation which is not very substantial."[21] Shrewdly, Governor Broughton gave no publicity to this report. Now the Governor found himself trapped by the closed defensive oriented system. The factual data in the Trustess' report could not be used to support the hospital administration or to aid the Governor in his effort to counter the attack made against a state institution for which he was ultimately responsible. Whatever it merits, after the publicity given to Jimison's charges, the findings would appear to be nothing less than a whitewash. When all eight copies of the Trustees' report were quietly dropped into the files, Governor Broughton was free to act.

Within a week after receiving the trustees' report, Broughton announced to the press that he had assembled a five-member board of inquiry of his own choosing to investigate conditions at Morganton and "to make reports and recommendations concerning the operation, maintenance, equipment and other phases of the institution."[22] Members of the Board were former Superior Court Judge Marshall R. Spears, Durham, Chairman; Dr. Wingate M. Johnson, Past President of the North Carolina Medical Society, Editor of the North Carolina Medical Journal and a member of the faculty of the Bowman-Gray School of Medicine, Winston-Salem; L. C. Gifford, Editor of the Hickory Record; Mr. Word Wood, Charlotte banker; and Mrs. E. L. McKee, former State Senator from Jackson County. At the suggestion of the Attorney General, Charles A. Hines, a partner in the largest law firm in Greensboro, was appointed legal counsel for the board.

In addition to naming the members of the board and praising their public spirited consciousness, Broughton reiterated the reason for assembling the group:

> The recent series of newspaper articles and press communications ... have been such as to warrant a full inquiry and investigation ... This is a public institution, built and operated out of money of the taxpayers of the state, and the people of the state are entitled to the fullest disclosure of its affairs. It should be stated to the credit of the Board of Trustees and of the Superintendent and staff of the institution that they have not only not objected to such an inquiry, but have urged that it be made.

Prior to issuing the news release, Broughton held a meeting with the Board of Charities and Public Welfare and secured agreement from the members that it would be better to have a separate board of inquiry. This agreement came after the Governor had already selected the members of the board. When the press and the public spoke, the Governor had listened. He would continue to listen, and then, he would act.

The newly appointed board lost no time getting started. While Charles Hines, legal counsel for the board, began to secure witnesses willing to testify before the inquiry, Judge Spears asked Governor Broughton to outline the general scope of the inquiry so it could be made a part of the record and serve as a guide to the board.[23] The Governor replied promptly, suggesting that the board investigate the following:

> (1) The adequacy of the physical equipment. (2) The quality of the food and method of serving same. (3) The adequacy and competency of the medical staff. (4) Adequacy and competency of trained or professional nurses and attendants with special attention being given to charges of negligence and cruelty. (5) Attitude, demeanor, and general conduct of the Superintendent. (6) Make such recommendations as to adequacy of appropriations, sufficiency of medical staff, changes in policy, and such changes to the law as may be deemed essential.[24]

On the question of whether or not the hearings should be held in public or private sessions, the Governor showed great political sensitivity. While "leaving it wholly to the discretion of the board," he reminded Spears of the editorials appearing in some of the leading newspapers of the State which were "strongly on the side of public hearings." He urged the board to "give this matter considerable attention," suggesting that "in the event public hearings are decided on, there can be an understanding with reporters ... that in the case of any witness who makes the request, the name and testimony of such witness shall not be published."

Although the Governor professed to be willing to leave the issue of open or closed hearings to the board members, he did not let the matter drop. When Spears did not answer his letter immediately, the Governor wrote to inquire as to the progress of the board toward beginning hearings. Spears replied on March 9 that a full meeting of the board would be held March 12 at Statesville.[25] Broughton wrote on March 11, sending Hines editorial clippings concerning the question of public hearings and suggesting only that they were "worthy of consideration." Governor Broughton's indirect approach appears to have been highly effective. At any rate, following the Statesville meeting, Hines informed him that "the committee decided to make hearings public except where witnesses desire executive session."[26]

The initial sessions of the board were given entirely to hearing testimony from patients, ex-patients including Jimison, relatives of patients, and expert witnesses from outside the state.[27] Non-professional testimony overwhelmingly supported the accusations made in the Jimison articles. The expert witnesses testified as to the advisability and purpose of solitary confinement. The experts agreed that it should be used only for the protection of violent patients and never as a mode of punishment. On March 27 the board recessed to give the stenographer

70

an opportunity to transcribe the testimony. Chairman Spears asked him to have the record available within ten days.

When some fifty-six days lapsed without any further action by the board, Broughton wrote to Spears and Hines asking for a progress report and some indication as to when the investigation would be completed.[29] Hines replied the next day that the delay was no fault of his; he, himself, had written Spears on three different occasions to ask this very question, he declared, but to date had received no reply.[29] Finally, at the end of May, Spears wrote to Broughton to say that the board would resume hearings at Morganton on June 2. The "apparent delay," Spears explained, had been caused by delays in receiving transcripts of the evidence already taken and by his own enforced absence at the trial of a number of cases in the Superior Court and the Supreme Court.[30] The three-day Morganton session was similar to that of the earlier hearings after which a twelve day recess was provided to bring the transcript of testimony up to date so the hospital administrative staff could read it prior to offering testimony on the last day of the hearings.

Verbal fireworks erupted at the final session when Harry Riddle, Secretary of the Morganton Board of Trustees, was questioned concerning accusations that he used political pressure and influence to run the hospital. Testimony showed that Riddle had once ordered the business manager of the hospital to buy building supplies and clothing for inmates from local merchants who were his personal friends without first placing the orders for competitive bids and without receiving clearance from the State Board of Purchasing and Contracts. The Charlotte News carried a banner headline: "Riddle Plays Politics with Hospital Affairs."[31]

Subsequent testimony put a rather different face on the charges. Prices paid for the building material were in line with current state contract prices.

71

The women's coats purchased from Harry Wilson, owner of the Lazarus Department
Store, were originally valued at seventy-five dollars, but because they were two
years old and a discontinued style, the hospital was able to buy them at twelve
dollars a coat. Nonetheless, the fact that Wilson was currently a member of the
State Civil Service Board added fire to the charges of political intrigue and gross
interference in the operation of the Morganton hospital made by the Charlotte News.

Why not purchase coats from friend Harry Wilson--they were needed and
could be had at sub-bargain rates. The fact that Harry Wilson was a personal
friend and political ally or that he held a responsible state position, or that the
Department of Purchase and Contract was circumvented may never have entered
Harry Riddle's mind. At worst he most likely dismissed those issues as unim-
portant as they related to securing needed material for the hospital. Dealings
of this nature were routine at all the hospitals. Exposure of such actions in the
press brought to light a political relationship that had become an integral part
of the hospitals' operation. Active support of a hospital, for every good reason,
too easily became a trap for the politician at the local level. To be sure, the
politician's influence in patient commitment procedures and general administrative affairs was formidable. His effort to secure desperately needed funds for
his "own" hospital placed him in a position of unique authority vis-a-vis the
hospital administration. At the same time he found himself in a political de-
pendency relationship in the state. Not unlike the hospital superintendent and
the general administrative staff, the political spokesman soon assumed a
defensive, secretive and sometimes deceptive role in the effort to make his
hospital look good to the outsider--the public and the legislature-- which was
his source of funding. As he secured favors he also incurred political debt.
Regardless of his motives or good intentions, the actions taken by Riddle and
his counterparts at other hospitals did constitute inferference in the operation
of the hospitals. Conflict of interest could hardly be avoided for a person who

was both a member of the hospital's board and a key figure in area politics with direct ties to the Legislature. But this was the system the local politician was forced to work within if he was to aid the hospitals at all.

The inflammable character of the accusations against Riddle made a public resolution of the question more than ever imperative. Nonetheless, after the June 16 hearing, there ensued another lengthy delay. Word Wood, a member of Spears' investigating board, began to grow restive. In no little distress, he wrote a "confidential" letter to Governor Broughton expressing his embarrassment over the "two and a half months lost in the hearings." There was talk in Charlotte, he reported, that the delays were designed to "whitewash" the whole situation. Wood concluded his letter by reminding Broughton that it was politically important to him as Governor, as well as to the committee, that no further delay be permitted.

Actually, Wood's statement concerning "talk of a whitewash" may have reflected something less than widespread public discontent. Wood's appointment to the Board of Inquiry was his first appearance at the state level of public service, and he may have been somewhat inexperienced in his appraisal of the situation. At any rate, it is not without interest that Pete McKnight, Morganton reporter for the Observer, believed that Wood was in a hurry to "get the job done" and wanted to present a strongly worded report. When a lag in the investigation occurred, the newspaper coverage suffered a corresponding decline. Dowd was intent on keeping the issue alive and before the public. Moreover, he was fearful that undue delay might tend to soft-pedal the committee's action and report. Playing on Wood's apparent political innocence and his eagerness to finish the investigation, McKnight deliberately planted the hint of a whitewash, and Wood followed through.[33]

Broughton, heeding Wood's admonition and attempting to ward off apparent dissention in the board, again prodded Spears to action.[34] Although Broughton's statement that his letter was not meant as "a criticism as to delay" appears on the surface as a subtle hint that criticism was voiced, later events served to indicate that the Governor was sincere in his statement. He was not as distaught or embarrassed over the delays as were some of the board members, and he had complete confidence in Spears' handling of the investigation.[35] Broughton's letter produced prompt action from Judge Spears and did much to quiet the exasperation of the other board members. Hines wrote the Governor a "personal and confidential" letter expressing concern over the delay in the investigation although he stated that Spears had promised that meetings would begin July 31 and continue without interruption until the work of the committee was completed.[36] True to his word, Judge Spears submitted the board's final report on August 7; and the Governor immediately announced to the press the full results of the inquiry.

The "Report of the Board of Inquiry" was an eighteen-page document that summarized the board's conclusions after interviewing 89 witnesses, considering 108 documentary exhibits, and evaluating 1718 pages of evidence.[37] Although the board concerned itself with problems of physical plant as well as personnel, findings on the latter held the center of the stage.

Perhaps the most dramatic revelation of the board concerned the medical staff, comparing the patient load per doctor at Morganton, 425 to 1, with the average for the nation, 248 to 1, and the recommended average of the American Phychiatric Association, 150 to 1.[38] The salary scale was no better. The highest paid doctor received $300 per month, the lowest, $250. Although these ill-paid physicians made rounds twice a day, the high patient load and the total absence of professional nurses made it virtually impossible to keep adequate records. At least one-third of the doctor's time was required in talking to relatives and answering correspondence since there were no counselors or secretaries at the hospital for these purposes.

The constantly changing population of the hospital created an especially vexing administrative problem. In one year alone, 692 patients were admitted, 376 discharged, 590 paroled, and 178 died at the hospital. All of these changes required time and thought, and perhaps examination, on the part of the staff physicians.[39]

The board's findings of the nurses and attendants were scarcely less distressing.[40] The report stated flatly that "there was no conflict in the testimony as to the question of the utter inadequacy of the number of nurses and attendants." At the time of the investigation, there were sixty-five nurses and eighty-five attendants working in shifts in order to have someone on duty twenty-four hours a day. If all the nurses and attendants had been able to go on duty at the same time, with 2,650 patients at the hospital the ratio of patients to nurses and attendants would have been seventeen to one. This ratio "made it humanly impossible for the patients to obtain the proper care and attention." The Board stated that this condition was "readily admitted and deplored by the officials of the institution."[41] Dr. Watkins testified that there were times when one nurse had the responsibility of two wards, each ward holding more than fifty patients. The national ratio of patients to nurses and attendants at the time of the investigation was nine to one. The A.P.A. recommended ratio was eight to one at all times.

Because salaries for female attendants ranged from $20 to $30 per month and for male attendants from $35 to $45 per month, turnover in staff constituted a major problem. The board discovered that turnover in nurses and attendants ran as high as 400 percent per year or a change every three months in half the employees. In desperation, the hospital had to take what it could get; no previous experience in nursing was required or expected. Statements made by Dr. Watkins to the Advisory Budget Commission for the 1941-43 biennium were incorporated into the report to show that the hospital administration was well aware of the desperate need for more, better paid, better qualified nurses and attendants to provide individual care of the mentally sick patients at Morganton.

Accusations as to mistreatment of patients by nurses and attendants were corroborated by the board. Instances of such mistreatment were laid to untrained personnel. The board concurred that such mistreatment was the exception rather than the rule but hastened to point out that when inflicted in the presence of other patients it engendered in them a fear which not only postponed their recovery but rendered subsequent service by the nurse or attendant in question of doubtful value.

Patient care was thoroughly discussed in the board's report.42 Sufficient quantities of food were found to be served, but the board agreed there was "evidence of too great monotony in diet and preparation, an over abundance of carbohydrates, and far too little in the way of green vegetables, fruits, and dairy products." A typical sample of the utterly colorless daily diet is revealed by the steward's menu: Breakfast - bread, bacon, oatmeal, molasses, coffee, milk; Dinner - cornbread, white beans, cabbage, buttermilk; Supper - bread, molasses, brown gravy, grits, coffee. It was pointed out that the only equipment available for food preparation was stem kettles for boiling food. There were no frying or baking facilities in the main kitchen. The management agreed that the food was unsatisfactory and that employees, not patients, should prepare and serve food.

With the equipment and funds that were available to the hospital for food service, the only way to cook food was to boil it. The only way to prepare and serve it was to use hospital patient help. The average annual appropriation per patient for all needs in 1942 was $169.26, a drop of $70.00 from 1926-27. The national average was $291.27. North Carolina ranked forty-fifth in the nation. Superintendent Watkins pointed out that under current appropriations "only $71.90

is allowed annually for food per patient, and this includes an estimated $20.81 for farm produced items." Thus, the daily food cost for each patient at Morganton was only a fraction more than nineteen cents.

The Board of inquiry discovered that the same lack of equipment and funds prevented the hospital administration from instituting many therapeutic and administrative programs that were desperately needed at Morganton. Occupational therapy was negligible, and there was no recreational therapy provided for the patients. While the members of tne board concurred with the testimony of Dr. C. Fred Williams, Superintendent of the Hospital for the Mentally Sick in South Carolina, that solitary confinement should be kept at a minimum, that records should be thorough and up-to-date, and that patients should be more carefully screened and classified according to the various types of mental diseases, they did recognize the difficulty involved in effècting such improvements with the hospital's grossly insufficient staff.

Finally, a review of the procedure for commitment of patients brought unanimous agreement from the Board of Inquiry that the present system was "arcnaic" and resulted in the "railroading" of men and women into the institution at Morganton for reasons other than treatment of mental disorders. It was a relatively easy matter to get one's self admitted to a state hopital as Jimison's experience showed. For the admission of a family member without showing just psychiatric cause for commitment, tne procedure was a trifle more complicated; but someone with political influence or knowledge of court procedure could obtain tne necessary professional testimony and court approval. The prevailing practice of admitting patients to state hospitals on the order of board chairman was certainly open to the suspicion of "railroading."

In the light of all the evidence received, the Board of Inquiry sustained the accusations of Tom Jimison and leveled a two-pronged attack on the needs and inequities of the hospital system - specifically those at Morganton.[43] The board first made a series of recommendations aimed at relieving the immediate problems disclosed by the inquiry. The upgrading of the physical plant was to include repair or abandonment of certain buildings at the hospital, the installation of baking equipment for the kitchen, the purchase of additional farm land, the enlargement of the dairy herd, the erection of benches on the porches, courts, and grounds for the use of the patients, and the screening of all windows.

To relieve the problem of understaffing and to provide better patient care, the board recommended the establishment of a patient-nurse ratio of ten to one with adequate and systematic training of all members of the nursing force and the additional employment of twenty-five professional nurses above this figure for supervisory purposes. Salary increases were recommended in order to bring the hospital in line with the national average and to reduce the high rate of turnover. To protect patients from brutal treatment and the fear of coercion, the board recommended that patients be more carefully classified. Solitary confinement was to cease as a means of punishment and to be used only when absolutely necessary and then under strict regulations. As a solution to the most obvious problem at Morganton, the board urged the employment of a full-time registered dietician who could provide a better balanced diet for patients and who would oversee the preparation and serving of all food by regular hospital employees.

Conscious of the grossly inadequate professional care at Morganton, the board called for the number of physicians to be doubled in order to establish a patient-doctor ratio of 248 to 1. At least one occupational therapist was recommended, as were out-patient clinics that would provide care for paroled and discharged patients. Finally, to mollify those who were calling for Dr. Watkins' resignation, the board recommended that "the management of the physical plant and the supervision of the staff and treatment of patients be separated." Dr. Watkins who had no formal training in psychiatry, was to be made superintendent of the physical plant and farm program. No mention was made of the attacks against Watkins during the investigations. To direct the medical program, the board urged the employment of a young and aggressive physician, properly trained in psychiatry and with experience in the treatment of mental illness, as Chief of the Medical Staff and Clinical Director in complete control of the treatment of patients at the hospital. After attending to the immediate and obvious problems, the board attacked at least two of the underlying causes of the disturbances at Morganton as the causes were spelled out in the Jimison articles.

The Board of Inquiry recognized that little could be done beyond temporarily solving the immediate problems at any of the state hospitals until the entire system had a proper budget and professional staff freed from local political interference. To this end, they proposed a unified board of control comprising fifteen members appointed by the Governor and representing the Western, Piedmont, and Eastern sections of the state with responsibility for consolidation and coordination of the control of all State Mental Hospitals in North Carolina. To supervise the work of institutions, the Board recommended the employment of a General Superintendent of Mental Hygiene. This person was to be one who had demonstrated executive ability and a doctor of medicine with special education and substantial experience in psychiatry and the treatment of mental diseases. The final recommendation of the board dealt with revising the law governing patient commitment procedures.

Nowhere in the Commission report is there a single reference to the "out of sight-out of mind" attitude of the general public that allowed the conditions at Morganton to develop. Discovering what it did at Morganton, the Governor's Commission was not prompted to raise questions about affairs at the State's other hospitals and training schools. No one in the state, including J. Ed Dowd, raised

the issue at all with the Commission or effectively with the Govenor. The scope
and direction of the investigation--structured by the Governor--and the report of
the Commission underscore Jimison's comments that it was "agin the law to become
demented...drat em they should not have gone crazy in the first place...society
does not believe that the mind may skip its trolley pole as readily as the liver
may lose its plumb...so the physically ailing are tenderly nursed while the
mentally ill are hurried off to public asylums where they are incarcerated like
felons and practically forgotten by society." Perhaps the pressure of time and
the outcry of the public and the press prevented any thorough investigation of
the self perpetuating social, political and administrative structure that served
to promulgate an ever increasingly bad set of conditions at the state's hospitals.
The Commission's failure to contend with the most important facet of its investigation left the door open to near collapse of its reform efforts. Ironically, the
same failure created an atmosphere among key legislators that prompted a state-
wide review that resulted in a complete overhaul of the hospital superstructure
within two years.

At a press conference the day following receipt of the Inquiry report,
Governor Broughton expressed his complete agreement with the work of the board.[44]
"The recommendations of the board as to the plant and physical facilities were
most timely," he said, "and would be carried out as early as may be possible ...
under present war conditions." All other matters that required additional appropriations and therefore legislative action were to be put before the General
Assembly with the Governor's firm approval. This included the Board's recommendations concerning a unified board and changes in the law concerning commitment
as well as the assignment of Dr. Watkins as superintendent of the physical plant.
Broughton was willing to relieve Dr. Watkins from direct contact with patients in
order to satisfy those, notably editor Dowd, who had clamored for his dismissal.

In a politically charged reform atmosphere change is not necessarily made for the sake of reform nor is reform necessarily effected. Broughton's concern was to restore order at Morganton without being unduly harsh on Dr. Watkins.

In addition to the factual aspects of the news release, Broughton began laying the foundation for favorable support for his future actions by praising the press of the state "for its leadership in bringing these conditions forcibly to the attention of the people and in helping to create a public sentiment that will support needed improvements."[45]

The Governor's prompt and positive response to the Inquiry report received favorable newspaper comment. Dowd editorialized that the Governor had placed the investigation in sound hands and was wise in accepting the recommendations of the Board of Inquiry. To keep the issue open, however, he warned that it would remain to be seen what steps would follow to implement the report.[46] Citizens throughout the state congratulated the Governor on his support of the board's report, and he was urged to follow through on all recommendations.[47] Broughton submitted a copy of the report to each member of the Morganton board of trustees and to the Advisory Budget Commission. He made no mention of forwarding a report to the Commissioner of Public Welfare, and his later actions made it obvious that he did not intend to entrust implementation of the report to the Commissioner or the Board of Public Welfare. The Governor had been unable to prod the hospital officials or the Commissioner to action earlier, and now he would personally guide implementation of the report.

In the days that followed, Governor Broughton's superb political skill was of great advantage. To make certain that problems at Morganton were properly dispatched, the Governor announced that he would attend the regular September meeting of the Board of Trustees of the Morganton Hospital.[48] This announcement prompted editor Dowd to write to Broughton asking that he be allowed to cover the meeting.[49] At the same time, Dowd published an editorial including ten recommendations for the Governor to consider prior to the Morganton meeting. When Broughton sent Dowd notice that the Morganton meeting would be held September 15, he suggested that it might be better if no reporters were present since he wanted a frank and open discussion with the trustees and other hospital personnel.[50] Dowd agreed with this position but argued that his reporter would be discreet and not print what was considered to be confidential information.[51] If, however, the Governor still felt the meeting should be "closed," Dowd agreed to bow to the Governor's preference and not even allow his reporter, Pete McKnight, to eavesdrop. Dowd concluded by asking for an advance copy of the recommendations which the Governor proposed to make. If Dowd thought he had the Governor in a position where he could press him into compliance, he misjudged the political adroitness of his man.

Broughton replied, praising the Charlotte News as the best afternoon paper in the territory. The Morganton meeting would be over by 1:00, he hinted, and the "News with its alert afternoon instinct would probably not object to the timing."[52] But the Governor made no mention of an advance copy of his recommendations. Apparently this ploy worked, for Dowd sent another letter to the Governor thanking him for his praise of the paper and his efforts on behalf of Morganton.[53]

The day before Broughton's visit to Morganton, the hospital trustees approved the report of the Board of Inquiry and sent the Governor a formal memorandum to that effect. Uncertain as to Broughton's plans and clearly anxious to make their position known on at least one issue before meeting the Governor, the trustees went on record as being "unanimously loyal and faithful to Dr. Watkins," who they felt had been maligned without cause.[54] At the same time, Broughton sent Dowd a summary of the remarks and recommendations he was to make at

Morganton. This letter was sent "confidential - Special Delivery" with the statement, "This is of course for release any time after 10:00 a.m., September 15."[55]

At the Morganton meeting, Governor Broughton told the trustees he would give the report and recommendations of the Board of Inquiry his full support. He listed seven points that he would urge the Legislature to act upon favorably. These included increased appropriations for patient care and increased staff, laws providing an adequate parole system and more effective commitment procedures, and, most important, a special law providing for the unification of all mental hospital administration under a central board of control. Recommendations of the report that could be acted upon without legislative approval were to be carried out with dispatch.

Aware of the tension between the forces seeking Dr. Watkins' dismissal and the politically important trustees supporting him, Broughton displayed great political sagacity by satisfying both groups. The Governor concurred in "the finding of the board of inquiry relative to the excellent work done by Dr. Watkins ... and in the recommendation that he should be relieved of some of his work." He stated, however, that:

> In view of the fact that I shall urge the Legislature to enact provisions for a central, unified board for all mental institutions in the state, with a general superintendent of mental hygiene in charge of all such institutions under the direction of such unified board; and in view of the fact that such legislation, if enacted will probably result in some reorganization of the management of the various institutions of the state, which action, if taken by the Legislature, will occur within the next few months. I do not recommend any present change in the superintendency of the institution. Any change made now might be subject to further change when reorganization is effected.

Dr. Watkins was to remain as superintendent. The Governor's adroit action in not relieving Dr. Watkins for the reasons stated prevented hard feeings from erupting among the trustees of the hospital, and it quieted editor Dowd's demands, momentarily at least, for the discharge of Dr. Watkins. The same tactic was to be used at a later date when Dowd again called for Watkins' dismissal.

Dowd was so impressed with his advance notice of the Morganton meeting that he ran an editorial in the News on September 15, which he entitled "A New Day Dawns."[56] The editor praised the Governor's action and commented on the fact that his recommendations paralleled those of the News with one or two minor exceptions. In a letter of the same date, Dowd thanked the Governor for enabling the News "to carry the Morganton story fully and in detail in our first edition which goes over the territory."[57] The Charlotte Observer noted that the Governor had given the News a "scoop" over all other state papers since the general news release was issued from Morganton at the time of the meeting, too late to make most afternoon editions.[58] The Observer ran an accompanying editorial praising the Governor for "moving with dispatch and commendable promptness."[59] The editorial lauded Broughton:

> for making no adverse recommendation as to the future of the Superintend-ent Watkins who had been more sinned against than sinning ... The board of trustees of the institution are loyal and faithful to Dr. Watkins. They know the difficulties he has confronted and the limi-tations to which he was subject.

The Governor's action received general statewide approval from the press and the public. Dr. Wingate Johnson, a member of the Board of Inquiry, thanked the Governor for recommending Watkins's retention as superintendent and suggested that the new board of control have a member from each of the state's medical schools.[60] The Governor tactfully replied to Johnson's letter using the same reason for retaining Watkins that he gave at the Morganton meeting. Then, going a step further to assure effective support for his legislative program, he urged

Johnson to see Senator Irving Carlyle and the members of the House from Forsyth County about supporting legislation for the mental hospitals. To give Dr. Johnson some incentive, he promised to put one representative from each of the medical schools in the state on the board should be bill pass.[61]

If the Governor's actions to this point did not make it clear that he was assuming complete responsibility for the implementation of his recommendations and for developing solid support for his program, his actions of September 21 did. Broughton directed Robert G. Deyton, Assistant Director of the Budget, to carry out every one of the investigating board's recommendations that did not need legislative action.[62] He listed in detail the recommendations he had made to the Morganton trustees on September 15 which could be completed immediately. Then he sent a copy of this directive to editor Dowd under cover of a "personal and confidential" letter suggesting that the information was not for publication since he wanted nothing said about this phase of the matter "until we are in a position to announce the accomplishment of those things specified in my communication. The next report I give to the people will be of things done." Broughton again praised the News:

> In view of the leadership which you and your papers have taken in this matter, I shall continue to try as best I can to make news announcements about these matters available first to the afternoon papers ... I do this simply in recognition of the outstanding public service which your paper, an afternoon paper, has rendered in this important matter.[63]

The Governor's praise of Dowd and his willingness to reward the News in "recognition of public service" paid dividends in less than a month. Broughton had hoped to have all his recommendations completed by October 15, and he told Dowed as much. But by mid-October, no news had come from the Governor's office relative to a "report of things done." Pete McKnight, Morganton reporter for the

<u>Charlotte News</u>, addressed a letter to Deyton at the Budget Office reminding him of the Governor's promise that "action would be forthcoming immediately." Since no further announcements had been made on the progress of the reform program, McKnight asked Deyton to outline "at your earliest opportunity ... the detailed steps which have been taken on each of these proposals with the understanding that such information will be for publication."[64] Dowd intercepted McKnight's letter and forwarded it to Broughton for his consideration.

At the same time, Dowd sent Broughton a copy of one of his recent editorials demanding a complete change in the administration at Morganton.[65] In an effort to gain support for his position, Dowd wrote "confidential" letters to Word Wood and Dr. Johnson asking for comments on the editorial; but both men refused to take Dowd's bait. Instead, they sent Dowd's letters to Broughton along with their personal veiws on the matter.[66] Unable to gain support for his position, Dowd let the matter drop. The Governor commended Johnson and Wood for refraining from making any comment and again repeated his previous reasons for not making any change in the superintendency. Both men were informed that progress was being made.[67]

Deyton kept the Governor informed as to the steps being taken by him and the new business manager at Morganton, Mr. R. M. Rothgeb, toward accomplishing the Governor's recommendations. Almost every piece of equipment and every item of material needed by the hospital was on a government priority list. When the orders were finally placed, additional delay was encountered because of the backlog of orders. Between September 21 and December 10, when most of the projects were completed, Deyton and Rothgeb submitted six progress reports directly to Broughton.

As the non-legislative portion of Broughton's program neared completion, the Governor wrote two letters of interest. One was to Judge Spears asking that he draft a bill to be presented to the Legislature that "would effectuate the recommendation relative to a unified board."[69] The other was to editor Dowd enclosing a press release for December 10 announcing improvements at the State Hospital at Morganton.[70] The press release stated that "all steps that can be taken prior to legislative action have now been completed." It then listed each accomplishment.[71] The announcement of "things done" just three weeks prior to the convening of the Legislature focused attention on the hospital issue and opened the way for Broughton's legislative program. The fact that the Chairman of the Board of Inquiry was drafting the bill for the Hospital Board of Control added further prestige and political strength to the Governor's recommendation to the Legislature.

Broughton urged passage of legislation providing for a unified board of control for the state's mental hospitals and an increase in appropriations to these hospitals. For reasons that the available records do not make clear, he made no recommendation in his address relative to a revision in the state commitment laws.[72] He may, of course, have decided that it was wiser not to muddy the water with too many requests at one time. Within a month from the time of his legislative message, Broughton was ready to send Judge Spears' draft of a hospital bill to the Legislature.

To assure effective management of this major piece of legislation, Broughton secured the support and services of two influential veteran legislators. William T. Clark, a member of the Senate and Chairman of the Dix Hill trustees for more than twenty years, and Representative C. W. Spruill, also a Dix Hill trustee, submitted similar bills in the two houses of the Legislature on February 5, 1943. The bills were referred to the respective committees on mental institutions. The Senate took first action, issuing a favorable report from the committee on February 11. The bill passed the second and third readings the next day and was sent to the House without engrossment. The House Committee reported its bill out with favor on February 15, but in light of the earlier Senate passage of the same bill, Spruill moved that the House bill be postponed indefinitely. The Senate bill was placed on the House Calendar February 15 and passed second reading that day. The third reading was approved the next day.[73] The bill was ordered engrossed and sent to the office of the Secretary of State thirteen days from the date it was introduced.

The measure so promptly enacted by the Legislature established a unified board of control to govern the operation of the state mental hospitals at Morganton, Raleigh, Goldsboro, and the Caswell Training School at Kinston. The law provided for a fifteen member board to be appointed by the Governor for terms of one, two, three, four, and five years, respectively. To provide state-wide representation, board members were to be selected from the Eastern Piedmont, and Western sections of the state. The board was charged with overall supervision of the hospitals. This included hiring a General Superintendent of Mental Hygiene who would assume direct supervision of all aspects of the hospitals but with particular responsibility for the medical care of patients. A general business manager would supervise the functions and activities of the separate hospital business managers in cooperation with the General Superintendent. Under this dual control system, both men reported directly to the Board of Control.

By-laws to govern the several institutions were to be drawn up by the board, and it was given the responsibility for fixing all salaries and making a single request for appropriations to the Advisory Budget Commission for all hospitals. In addition to the dual control feature, the significant aspect of the law was the separation of the board from the Department of Public Welfare as a separate entity reporting directly to the Governor. The Legislature approved Broughton's reform program without question.

Success in the Legislature, however, did not solve all of Broughton's problems, and his political ability was again put to the test through an unexpected turn of events. Dr. Watkins, who had been in failing health during the investigation, died March 8, 1943. On receiving this news, the Governor sent a telegram to G. S. Kirby, chairman of the Morganton Hospital board of trustees, suggesting that there be no selection of a permanent Superintendent but that Dr. Saunders be made Acting Superintendent "in view of the new legislation adopted at this session with reference to a unified board of trustees."[74]

Editorial comment on Broughton's action was immediate. The Hickory Record, edited by a member of the Board of Inquiry, accepted the appointment of Saunders as a temporary expedient. At the same time it urged that a permanent Superintendent be employed as quickly as possible since it doubted the ability of Dr. Saunders to serve effectively in the light of the adverse criticism launched against him.[75]

The Governor acted promptly to ward off any possible charge of politics in the selection of a superintendent by sending a "personal and confidential" letter to Board Secretary, Harry Riddle, against whom the press had lodged charges of political interference. With the letter, he enclosed a copy of the Hickory Record editorial. Broughton warned Riddle that the Record's reaction was typical of other editorial expression in different papers of the state and repeated the recommendation he made to Chairman Kirby. Broughton stated with no uncertainty where he stood on the matter of Dr. Saunders' appointment:

> I am beginning to receive some communication that there may be a campaign started on behalf of Dr. Saunders. I do not know what the general board will do in respect to choosing a general superintendent at this institution, but it would not be helpful to Dr. Saunders or to the institution for anyone to attempt to bring pressure in his behalf. This whole thing will be decided on its merits, and not on the basis of friendship, politics, or anything else.

I send this to you in confidence because I feel that you are entitled
to know the reaction that has occurred.76

Obviously heeding the Governor's telegram to Kirby and the letter to Riddle, the

Morganton trustees delayed action on naming a replacement for Dr. Watkins until

March 23 when they named Saunders Acting Superintendent until July 1, 1943.

Broughton had not only received full compliance with his wishes, he had also

kept the way clear for any action the unified board might want to take.

By action of the Legislature, the Hospitals Board of Control was to come

into being on or after July 1, 1943. Broughton began recruiting members for the

new board in May, and by July 8 he had secured the stipulated number of fifteen.77

Dr. Wingate Johnson of the Board of Inquiry was appointed to a three-year term.

Three members of the Morganton board were appointed to the new board: Dr. R. H.

Crawford received a five-year appointment; Dr. C. C. Poindexter and Harry Riddle

were each appointed to one-year terms. Three members of the State Legislature

were appointed to the board: Representative C. W. Spruill, Senator N. E.

Edgerton, and Senator William Clark. Clark and Spruill were also trustees of

the Dix Hill Hospital. The other members were doctors, lawyers, and business

leaders from throughout the state. The Governor asked Judge Spears to accept the

chairmanship of the new board, but Spears declined because of other responsibilities

The appointment of Riddle, Spruill, and Clark satisfied Broughton's political debt

to these men - Riddle for his control of the Democratic Party in sometimes

Republican Burke County; Spruill and Clark for their support in the Legislature

and their years of service to the Dix Hill Hospital. The only negative reaction

to the new board came in opposition to Harry Riddle.

Burke Davis, who became editor of the Charlotte News when Ed Dowd entered

military service, protested Riddle's appointment.79 The News editors were not

willing to accept appointment of a man they described as being the source of

90

political interference at Morganton. Broughton replied that evidence did not support statements that Riddle derived personal gain from his association with the hospital. Granting that Riddle might have been "somewhat indiscreet" in some of his actions, the Governor felt that he was honest and sincere and had always cooperated in any venture that was to the benefit of the hospital.[80] Broughton sent a copy of the Davis letter to Riddle, stating that he realized that there would be criticism of his action, but in view of Riddle's twenty years of service to the hospital he felt the appointment was justified. The Governor insisted that no one seek personal or political gain from his connection with the hospital. Again he warned Riddle not to conduct a compaign for Dr. Saunders and asked him to leave politics and personal feelings out of selection of the Superintendent.[81]

Broughton further justified his appointment of Riddle on the day the newly appointed board was sworn in by releasing a letter from Dr. James N. Vernon of Morganton, President of the North Carolina Medical Society.[82] Dr. Vernon supported Broughton's selection of board members and praised the work of Harry Riddle. Vernon wrote that Riddle "does not deserve the criticism some have directed toward him, but should be praised for long faithful service." After the board members received the oath of office, Broughton cited the organization of the board as "the beginning of a new era in the administration of the State's hospitals."[87]

In a final attempt to divorce politics from the operation of the hospital system, the Governor reminded each member that:

> No political consideration whatsoever has entered into the selection of this consolidated board; and politics should have no part in any of the board's functions. I urge that it be made the fixed policy of the board that the employmentment of staff and personnel, the admission or discharge of patients, and every other administrative phase of these several institutions be kept entirely free from political manipulation, pressure or control.

91

I also urge as a fixed policy of this board and these several
institutions under its management, that the employees and
staff members be strictly enjoined against any political activity
other than the free and individual exercise of voting privilege.
If any member of this board should undertake to use his position and influence politically in connection with employment of
personnel or admission or discharge of patients, or the use of
the staff for political purpose, I shall consider it my duty to
request such member to resign.[84]

Broughton then reiterated his remarks by raising the question of the superin-

tendency at Morganton. The institution at Morganton, he reminded the board, had

been operating under an acting superintendent since the death of Dr. Watkins.

To give the board an opportunity to effect a smooth transition of authority and

mindful of the press reaction to Dr. Saunders, Broughton suggested that the board

study the whole Morganton situation before electing a superintendent.[85]

The pitiable revelations that poured forth in "Out of the Night at

Morganton" had seriously shaken public confidence in the state hospitals. Governor

Broughton was faced with the task of restoring that confidence. The Governor showed

great political sagacity in keeping personal control of an explosive situation.

His deft maneuvering of the press and state officials enabled him to establish an

independent Board of Inquiry charged with making a much needed and thorough

investigation of the Morganton Hospital. Since the Board was responsible for re-

porting directly to him, the Governor was able to keep abreast of each development

during the course of the deliberations.

Probably Broughton's greatest achievement during the hospital crisis was

his ability to gain almost immediate and complete confidence from the public and

press that he would see justice done at Morganton. Not once during the eighteen

months between the exposé and the swearing in of the newly established Hospitals

Board of Control did Broughton do or say anything to shake public confidence in

the program. He gave his full support to the investigation committee, reserved

udgement on the hospital administrators, and acted to calm the tirades of J. Ed
owd, the leading press critic. When the Board of Inquiry filed its report,
overnor Broughton gave prompt public support to all its findings and recommenda-
ions - an action that gained wide acclaim.

The members of the Board of Inquiry made a sound, fair, and thorough
eview of the charges leveled against the state hospital. Their conclusions and
ecommendations showed that they were concerned with more than an expedient
olution to surface problems, and they presented the Governor a rare opportunity
o effect wide reaching reform of the entire hospital system.

Governor Broughton accepted the challenge to reform without hesitation.
he renovation of the Morganton hospital was no easy accomplishment under war-
ime restrictions. Within six months, the chief executive had completed all
lanned improvements in the hospital plant and had lined up the necessary forces
o assure smooth passage of the legislative portion of his program. The swearing-
n ceremony in Raleigh was the climax of a series of skillful maneuvers by
overnor Broughton that had enabled him to lay the groundwork for an efficient
oordinating mechanism.

Chapter V

RESISTANCE TO CHANGE

NEW FORMS, OLD ROUTINES

The greatest achievement for Governor Broughton appeared to be his

successful establishment of the Hospitals Board of Control. Unlike the abortive

attempt at unification in 1919, the new board had the expressed support of the

separate hospitals, the state medical society, the State Mental Hygiene Society,

and the press. Broughton charged the Board to expel the intrusion of politics

from the operation of the hospitals. The centralized program, according to

Broughton's plan, was to focus the responsibility for one man, the General

Superintendent, and one program on the Legislature thus preventing the division

of strength of those who supported the hospitals. For the first time, the new

board provided an opportunity to attack the underlying causes that plagued the

North Carolina hospital system and produced the Morganton debacle. But could

the newly-created central board rise to the opportunity so skillfully shaped

by the Governor?

When it convened at Dix Hill following the Governor's swearing-in ceremony,

the Hospitals Board of Control in its first actions provided a portent of the

future for the state hospital program. In the first order of business, Dr. Roscoe

McMillan of Red Springs, North Carolina, moved the election of Dr. Saunders to

Superintendent of the State Hospital at Morganton. Representative Wayland Spruill

seconded the motion, and it carried.[1] The action of the Board was in direct oppo-

sition to the expressed wishes of the Governor and the position the press assumed

in regard to Dr. Saunders. The Board's action was ostensibly the result of support

94

for Saunders from two influential sources.

Throughout the Morganton investigation, members of the medical profession defended the integrity and the loyal dedication of the physicians at Morganton. Dr. Saunders was specifically singled out for his ability and devotion to duty under extremely difficult conditions. Dr. James N. Vernon, president of the North Carolina Medical Society, and Dr. Wingate Johnson of the Bowman Gray School of Medicine both supported Saunders during the investigation in letters to Governor Broughton.[2] A copy of Dr. Vernon's letter was sent to Dr. McMillan in his capacity as Secretary of the North Carolina Medical Society. Equally strong support came from members of the Board who had served as hospital trustees under the old system. Dr. Vernon was a personal friend of Dr. Saunders and a colleague. Regardless of the merits of the case, Dr. Vernon's letter to Dr. McMillan, who was now a member of the new board, might be construed as representing a conflict of interest. More importantly, the action of support by all of the trustees who served under the old system was to prove indicative of the new board's resistance to change.

Press reaction to the appointment was immediate. Burke Davis, editor of the Charlotte News, protested Saunders' appointment and warned of the consequences of allowing a key figure of the Morganton exposé to remain in charge of the hospital. Davis asked editorially if the action of the Board were an indication of a return to the earlier system that condoned inefficiency, brutality and indifference.[3] The press reaction might have been cause for alarm, but Governor Broughton effectively silenced the critics by supporting the Board's decision as a sound one in "the light of the current shortage of qualified doctors" and the support Dr. Saunders had received from the medical profession.[4] More significant than the Saunders' appointment, which was not entirely without merit, was the second action taken by the Board at its organizational meeting.

To assure the maintenance of operational control over the hospitals and to conform with the requirements of the law, the unified board established separate executive committees responsible for overseeing each of the units in the state system. The Morganton committee was chaired by Dr. J. H. Beall with Mrs. Andrews Blair, Dr. R. H. Crawford, Dr. Wingate Johnson, and Mr. Harry L. Riddle as members. Senator W. G. Clark was named chairman of the Dix committee. Representative C. W. Spruill, Dr. Lois Stanford, and Mr. N. E. Edgerton completed the Dix group. The Goldsboro unit was chaired by Mr. W. A. Dees with Mr. Dwight Barbour, Dr. H. M. Baker, and Dr. Carl V. Reynolds as members of the executive committee. Mr. L. L. Oettinger, Mrs. Rivers D. Johnson, and Dr. C. C. Poindexter comprised the executive committee for Caswell Training School.[5] Oettinger chaired this committee. Beall, Riddle, Clark, Spruill, Dees, and Oettinger had all been board members of the respective hospitals before unification.

The executive committees functioned in much the same manner as the separate boards did under the old system. Rather than place authority for granting discharges in the hands of the hospital staff, the executive committees continued to require the authorization of three of its members before a patient could be discharged.[6] Matters relating to the day-to-day operation of the hospitals were discussed and resolved at the monthly meetings of the executive committees. Letters of complaint received by the Governor continued to be forwarded to the hospital superintendents or to members of the executive committees for action - with the same results as before. Hiring of personnel above the attendant level required the approval of the Governor. Board Chairman N. E. Edgerton recommended the appointment of three psychiatric social workers, but Governor Broughton had to approve final action.[7] In fact, throughout the remainder of his administration, Governor Broughton kept a close check on the activities at the four hospitals by asking for regular progress reports from Assistant Director of the Budget Robert Deyton[8] - not from the new

96

board. The net effect of the Hospitals Board's action in establishing the executive committee structure for governing the hospitals was the insured retention of the old, established administrative routines. Although a sub-committee of the Board was appointed to secure a General Superintendent, there is no indication in the minutes of the Board from July, 1943 to December, 1944, that any concerted effort was made in this respect. Was the Hospitals Board of Control purposely dragging its feet?

The first annual report of the Board noted its inability to secure a General Superintendent and attributed the lack of success in this effort to the war-time shortage of qualified psychiatrists.[9] The report makes no mention of other factors that contributed to the failure to secure a man for the position. Throughout the history of the state hospitals, there had been little in the way of professional stimulation to attract physicians to the system. Dr. Maurice H. Greenhill of the Department of Neuropsychiatry, Duke University School of Medicine, noted in 1945 that only the more fully equipped and modern facilities for psychiatric practice are able to obtain doctors to do their work.[10] Not only were the facilities not modern, the State Hospitals of North Carolina had shown no significant improvement from the national position noted by Dr. Lloyd Thompson in his 1936 Study.[11] The state of affairs in the hospitals presented an unattractive picture to prospective physicians. Problems inherent in the structure of the Hospitals Board of Control and the legislation by which it was governed made the position of General Superintendent even less attractive.

The composition of the Board itself presented the first major problem. Of the sixteen members appointed by Governor Broughton, there were five physicians, one dentist, and ten interested lay individuals. There was not one psychiatrist appointed to the Board, nor was there a social service administrator or anyone representing psychiatric nursing. No member of the Board had experience as a

hospital administrator. As a matter of fact, through 1960, there was not a pro-
fessionally trained hospital business administrator on the Board, at any of the
hospitals, or in the Department of Mental Health, nor did the Board have the
advice of the psychiatric profession. While a considerable body of opinion favors
wholly non-professional boards, if such are adopted, then careful provision must
be made for ready access to outside professional talent for specialized judgments.
The Board had no such access. Since the presumption that the superintendents of
the hospitals would provide excellent counsel to the Board proved faulty in 1917,
and was the source of failure to secure support for unification in 1936, there was
no reason to assume that such counsel would be forthcoming in 1943. Because of
their positions and responsibility to their separate units, it is doubtful that
the Superintendents could fulfill such a role at any time. Despite efforts to
bridge the gap between the separate units and the central administration, there
is not yet a viable system of communication and counsel between the superintendents
and the commissioners' office. Superintendents meet together to discuss their
mutual problems and to initiate conferences with political leaders to gain support
for programs. Superintendents still individually urge legislative action on matters
relating to the hospitals--in some cases their specific units--with some degree of
success. Furthermore, in the 1943 legislation establishing a unified hospital
structure, no provision was made for a professional staff for the General Superintendent. The statute not only failed to provide a professional advisory staff for
the superintendent but, through the stipulations governing tenure, it further re-
stricted the possibility of securing a qualified psychiatrist for the office. Under
the law, the Superintendent's appointment was for two years "to be renewed at the
discretion of the board."[12] The political implications of such a tenuous appointment were obvious. New therapeutic programs or administrative reorganization that
threatened the status quo would hardly be worth attempting on the basis of a

two-year tenure. Coupled with the restriction as to tenure was the division of administrative responsibility and authority between the General Superintendent and General Business Manager. The man responsible for the care and treatment of patients was to have no authority over the allocation of funds or the general management of hospital facilities. The concept of dual control was a major point of concern for the first General Superintendent, and it has continued to be a bone of contention ever since.

Still another factor contributing to the board's failure to secure a General Superintendent was the constitutional mandate which vested the North Carolina State Board of Charities and Public Welfare, headed by Commissioner Bost, with the responsibility for all mental institutions in the state. When the Hospitals Board of Control was established, there was considerable confusion over the respective functions of the two bodies. Dr. James Watson, Mrs. Bost's subordinate, was the first to recognize the inter-agency problems created by the legislative action of 1943. In an effort to avoid confusion, he listed the ten duties of the Division of Mental Hygiene, which he headed, and their possible overlapping with some of the responsibilities of the Hospitals Board of Control.[13]

Dr. Watson contended that the responsibility for providing psychiatric examination service to institutions both public and private was now a responsibility of the Hospitals Board of Control. In Watson's opinion, the psychiatrist in the State Board of Welfare was now"... free to give all his time to consultation service to county welfare departments." In like manner, the interstate transfer of mental patients was to be a function of the new board. All county and state data cards concerning mental patients, Watson recommended, should be transferred to the Hospitals Board"... since it should now serve in the capacity of state clearing house for all mental patients." The development of research and preventive measures "along mental hygiene lines" fell, he believed, under the direct control of the Hospitals Board of Control. "The old theory of life-long custodial care," Watson argued, "with ever-increasing need for new buildings and increasing personnel, with ever-increasing expenditure should be abandoned as a relic of the middle ages ... and this can be done only through effective research in the State Hospitals and medical schools." A logical outgrowth of such research and, therefore, the responsibility of the Hospitals Board was the assembly and interpretation of statistics on mental health, the inspection of State Hospitals, the licensing of all private mental hospitals, and the development of child guidance and mental hygiene clinics. Only three of the original ten duties, in Watson's estimation, were still logically the partial responsibility of the Division of Mental Hygiene. On a basis of shared responsibility and joint cooperation, both agencies were to support educational services, provide consultant services for all state agencies, and work to integrate local welfare departments with state hospitals services for supplying case histories and financial investigations.

Dr. Watson's forward-looking approach to eliminating duplication of effort and confusion concerning authority and responsibility between two state agencies seemed to offer a sound basis for the immediate development of a state-wide mental health program. Unfortunately, while his memorandum to Mrs. Bost did bring about a meeting of representatives of the two agencies together with Governor Broughton and the Attorney General in February, 1944, it fell far short of Watson's expectations. At this meeting, it was decided that the Hospitals Board of Control was an operating organization for the four state institutions and the State Board of Charities and Public Welfare would have supervision over it.[14] Supervision was construed to mean the continuation of the annual inspection of state institutions for the mentally ill. This decision left unanswered the considerations raised in Dr. Watson's memorandum so that in January, 1945, Dr. Greenhill, of the Duke Medical School, could still report that the relationship between the two boards "has not been completely clarified ... and the issue is confused."[15] The lack of qualified personnel on the unified board, the unrealistic term of office authorized for the superintendent, the dual control administrative system with no specific guidelines for operation, and the confusion growing out of overlapping with other agencies with no clear-cut areas of responsibility together presented political and administrative roadblocks to the recruitment of a general superintendent.

Why were none of these issues raised by the agency responsible for bringing to light problems of such magnitude? Perhaps the new board was unable or unwilling to recognize the significance of the issues. Dr. Greenhill attributed the failure to secure a superintendent to the lack of qualified professional representation on the Board.[16] Board reaction to the proposal for reorganization in 1945 indicates that the influential members of the Hospitals Board of Control were satisfied with the organizational structure and the laws undergirding the Board. The significant number of Board members carried over from the old separate boards and the executive committee structure for each hospital under the new plan suggests the possibility that the Board members were unwilling to pursue the selection of an executive officer or call attention to weak points in the administrative structure of the new system for fear that such actions might further diminish the autonomy of the local hospitals.

A second look at the composition of the Hospitals Board and the part some of its members played in securing passage of the Hospitals Bill in 1943 will serve to substantiate this claim. Of the ten laymen appointed to the Hospitals Board of Control, six were carry-overs from the old system and all were either directly or indirectly engaged in political activity on the state or district level. Senator Clark and Representative Spruill, who introduced the bill to reorganize in 1943, were members of a legislative block that was not always strong enough to push its programs through the Legislature but had enough strength to kill any bill it did not wish to see passed.[17]

Clark and Spruill not only introduced the Hospitals Bill in their respective chambers of the General Assembly, they managed its successful passage. If the two-year appointment clause or the provision for administrative executive committees for each hospital was objectionable to these men, it is doubtful that they would have supported the bill. Reviewing Senator Clark's and Representative Spruill's support of the bill in the light of later events, it becomes clear that, as objectionable as certain features of the bill proved to be, it was supported by these two and the carry-over members of the Board because it assured their continued control of the hospitals. To point out the administrative and political weaknesses of the Hospitals Board of Control when the issue was before the Legislature might have opened the door to changes and the possible loss of control that the carry-over Board members continued to enjoy under the new system. Operating on the assumption that the trouble at Morganton was a temporary disturbance in an otherwise well ordered system, it appears more likely that no one saw the flaws in the bill that experience uncovered.

While the Board members' failure to grapple with the problems that stood in the way of effective action seems, in retrospect, to be indefensible, their position is not to be taken as a basis for impugning their motives. The years of service rendered to the state hospitals by this group testifies to their personal and public concern for the care of the mentally ill. The position of the carry-over members of the Hospitals Board was no different from that of Dr. Ashby in 1936 when he expressed fear of the loss of control of Dix Hospital - his hospital - through the creation of a unified board. Already there was a certain degree of loss of local autonomy under the new Hospitals Board of Control, and old Board members were not prone to "rock the boat" any further by giving up complete control of the units to which they had devoted so much time and effort. Commitments of the past prevent future action, and the majority of the members on the new unified board were still committed to the old way of doing things.

For eighteen months after the creation of the Board of Control, the hospitals continued to operate under the same rule of thumb and uncoordinated procedures of the past. The people of the state seemed to have assumed that the establishment of the Hospitals Board of Control as a separate state agency would in itself eliminate the evils uncovered by the investigation at Morganton. At any rate, for all practical purposes the issue was considered closed; and the Hospitals Board of Control was left with the task of re-establishing order in the system.

In the attempt to return to normal and to solve some of the more obvious problems facing the hospitals, the Board probably performed as well as could be expected under the circumstances. It established standing committees to select a Superintendent and to meet with the State Board of Charities and Public Welfare, as well as committees on by-laws, building and equipment, personnel and the equalization of salaries and wages, division of territory and the admission of patients, publicity, agriculture (livestock and provision), dentistry, care of patients, psychiatric standards and policies, as well as a committee on legislation. The Board set as its goal " ... a program to do all in its power to see that the treatment and care of the mentally ill in North Carolina be improved to equal that of the best institutions of like kind, and surpassed by none.[18] The recommendations of the standing committees, included in the annual report, dealt with suggestions for improvements and additions to existing physical structures, for construction of new buildings, for providing necessary equipment, and for more adequate personnel with higher salaries, including an increase in the number of graduate nurses, recreational directors, occupational therapists, teachers, laboratory technicians, psychiatric case workers, and at least one physician for each 200 patients.

The work of the Board and the "First Annual Report" came between legislative sessions so it is difficult to assess the effect it might have had on the Appropriations Committee or the General Assembly. However, the approach of cataloging needs, no matter how thoroughly justified, was an old one that had stirred few souls and moved no one to action in the past. For practical purposes, the problems that were the most pressing were dealt with first. Morganton still held the primary attention of the Board and Governor Broughton because of the investigation. Improvements were carried forward at Morganton while similar needs went unattended at Dix, Goldsboro, and Caswell. The operational philosophy by which these other hospitals operated was still that of custodial care. This point was made abundantly clear in the report of the General Business Manager, R. M. Rothgeb, who interpreted his responsibility as that of "doing what we must to contribute to their (the patients) general comfort and welfare."[19]

Actual conditions in the hospitals were brought to light again by the first significant annual inspection made by the Board of Charities and Public Welfare in 1944. For the first time, the Welfare Board secured the services of a qualified psychiatrist to conduct the inspection. In December, 1944, eighteen months after reorganization, Dr. Maurice Greenhill filed a forty-four page report detailing the results of his inspection.[20] Dr. Greenhill's visit to each hospital included:

> ... conversations with the Superintendents and all members of the Physicians Staff, the Superintendent of nurses, Chief Attendants and the Record Librarian; and an inspection tour of the entire hospital during which particular attention was paid to the state of the physical facilities and the quality of patient care, sanitation, medical equipment, dietary facilities, organization of the hospital in general, and the state of patient care.[21]

Dr. Greenhill found Morganton far above the other state hospitals in its physical equipment and care of patients "probably because of the criticism and investigation two years ago."[22] Yet, there was still no occupational therapy or

104

hydrotherapy at the hospital. Per capita cost for the 2,707 patients at Morganton was still a low twenty-three cents. With a staff of five doctors having an average patient load of 541 per doctor, medical care, at best, was inadequate. There was no follow-up on patients after release or parole and no re-examination of paroled patients at the time of discharge.[23] Dr. Greenhill found no liaison between the Hospital and the County Welfare Department. Parole and discharge rates were considered low, and duration of hospitalization was termed "prolonged" by Greenhill.[24] There were four registered nurses, 58 female attendants, and 81 male attendants employed at the time of the inspection. All attendants worked twelve-hour shifts, and there were no training classes for this group. The end result of the overall staff problem, Greenhill reported, was that chronic patients were almost never examined. "It is possible," Greenhill pointed out, "for a patient to go for years without re-examination or re-evaluation of his condition."[25] The hospital was found to operate on a custodial care basis with no specific therapy for any of the patients.[26] The conditions reported at Morganton indicated that the state had not dealt with any of the underlying causes that produced the Jimison expose three years earlier.

Conditions at Raleigh were worse. Greenhill found the Central Building to be a "disgrace ... reminiscent of the 17th Century."[27] Beds almost touched each other in some wards. In Wards S and R, there were only two toilets for 475 patients. The attendant-patient ratio at Dix was 1 to 75 during the day and 1 to 250 at night. The report classed the female infirmary as a potential fire trap and noted that "several plumbing leaks dripped from the floor above into the dining room."[28] Per capita cost for the 2,465 patients at Dix was 22 cents. With seven physicians, fourteen nurses, and twenty-two cadet nurses, the respective patient ratios of 1 to 353 and 1 to 176 were considerably better than at Morganton but still far above the recommended levels set by the American Psychiatric

Association.[29] There were no facilities for hydrotherapy or occupational therapy at Dix. Of necessity, the hospital was operated on a custodial basis. Despite the conditions discovered at the Raleigh hospital, Dr. Greenhill praised the medical staff for "making the best of a difficult situation for which they are in no sense to be blamed."[30] Greenhill laid all the difficulties at Dix to the Legislature's failure to provide adequate funds for the administration of the hospital.[31]

The fact that the State Hospital for Negro patients at Goldsboro was rarely mentioned or given public attention commensurate with that of the hospitals at Raleigh and Morganton did not warrant the conclusion that conditions there were better. Conditions were worse. The doctor-patient ratio was 1 to 641 and the nurse-patient ratio was 1 to 1,282. There were only 103 attendants to serve the 2,564 patients.[32] The per capita cost of 29 cents, the highest of the three state hospitals, was attributed to the market value of the large supply of farm products grown by the Negro patients at Goldsboro. While there was no waiting list at the hospital, there was gross overcrowding on the wards. Small iron cages were still used at Goldsboro to restrain violent patients. Most of the buildings were described as being in "poor condition." Dr. Greenhill praised the medical staff for its devotion to duty under adverse conditions, and he offered a special commendation for certain innovations that the staff had accomplished on its own. One such innovation was the "strange yet apparently fruitful"[33] practice of placing excited patients in locked rooms where the floor was covered with three or four feet of corn cobs. Instead of risking the destruction of all too scarce hospital equipment and supplies by keeping the patients in a general ward, they were allowed to work off their excess energy by alternately burying and uncovering themselves in the cob-filled room.[34]

At the Caswell Training School, Dr. Greenhill reported a student population of 825. There was one physician, the Superintendent, on the staff along with one nurse, one consulting physician, five practical nurses, seven school teachers, and one principal out of a total of 88 employees. Per capita cost of 39½ cents a day was the highest in the state. There was no psychiatrist nor psychiatric social worker affiliated with the school which, like the state hospitals, was operated in a custodial manner. As at Goldsboro, small iron cages were used to restrain "excited" students. To alleviate the crowded conditions at Caswell and to reduce the waiting list of 800 as much as possible, Greenhill noted that the State had appropriated $3,905,750 for an expansion program that was to provide 980 more spaces at the institution. The Greenhill report reads like an expanded copy of the Jimison articles and the report of the Spears investigation of 1942.

Beyond detailing the deplorable conditions that existed in the North Carolina hospital system two years after they were supposedly corrected, Dr. Greenhill's investigation corroborated the fact that the Morganton "problem" was considered by the Governor and the Legislature as an isolated disturbance in an otherwise orderly system. Sadly enough, but as might have been expected, the results of the investigation were relegated to the files of the Department of Charities and Public Welfare and the Hospitals Board of Control. If a copy of the report was submitted to Governor Broughton, it was not made a part of his hospital papers. In any case, the lack of coordination between departments and agencies in the state is demonstrated by the fact that a document as significant as the Greenhill report was not forwarded to Governor-elect R. Gregg Cherry who assumed office less than a month later. In reply to an inquiry from the Chairman of the Hospitals Board of Control almost two years later, Governor Cherry noted that he "had not had an opportunity to examine a copy of Dr. Greenhill's report on the Mental Institutions in North Carolina." The Governor assured Dr. Lineberger,

Chairman of the Hospitals Board of Control, "that an effort will be made to obtain a copy."[35]

Dr. Greenhill must have anticipated the demise of his report because at the same time he submitted the document to Commissioner Bost, he was completing "The Present Status of Mental Health in North Carolina" which appeared in the North Carolina Medical Journal, January, 1945. At least the medical profession would be made aware of the plight of the mentally ill in North Carolina. The report and the Journal article furnished sufficient evidence that the "new day" promised by Governor Broughton and hailed by editor Dowd in July, 1943, had failed to materialize. What had happened to the promise?

In retrospect, it appears that Governor Broughton's selections to the new Board were unwise. His appointment of men to the new Board who had served as trustees under the old system weakened the new form. The influential political figures on the Board were content to assume that the Morganton exposé was little more than a surface disruption of the way they had traditionally operated. Their continuation on the Board served to entrench and perpetuate the very practices the new administrative system was supposed to eliminate. Yet, Broughton's political tactics had been so skillful at every step along the way up to this point that it is difficult to understand why he suddenly seemed to lose his touch. Was he unable to pursue another course? In securing passage of the all-important hospital reform bill, did he incur political debts that required him to make the appointments he did? Perhaps political considerations were not a part of Broughton's selections as he stated in his remarks prior to swearing in the new Board members. Were the appointments nothing more than a recognition of the years of service these men gave under the old system? If Governor Broughton's actions were motivated by this latter consideration, does it follow that he actually failed to recognize the underlying causes of the hospital's problems as revealed by the investigation?

For want of more specific documentary evidence, only speculation on these
matters is possible; but it appears that Broughton was governed by both considerations.
First, the mental hospital system, like any other state agency that relies on the
support of the Legislature and the whims of the voting public, is by its very
nature political. Broughton's appointments to the Hospitals Board of Control were,
in part, a tacit recognition of this political reality. Second, one must assume
that Broughton was sincere in his intentions when he wrote to Harry Riddle, Secretary
of the Morganton Hospital, that his appointment to the new Board was based solely
on Riddle's years of devotion to the Morganton Hospital. Clearly, the course of
events surrounding the investigation at Morganton and the creation of the consolidated board indicate that Broughton's concern was "to put out a fire." Since a
North Carolina Governor cannot succeed himself for a second term, Broughton's
only chance to set matters straight came at the 1943 session of the Legislature,
and his political future rested on a successful conclusion to the affair that
would allow for a quick return to normal. The actions taken by Broughton during
the last eighteen months of his administration and the actions of the Hospitals
Board of Control during this period tend to corroborate the conclusion that the
promise of a new day remained nothing more than a promise for several reasons:
the available evidence strongly suggests that Governor Broughton neither fully
understood the problem nor was he in a position to be able to secure adequate
reform legislation to mold a new agency guaranteeing that "no political consideration whatsoever would enter into the selection of the newly formed consolidated
board."[36] While he was successful in securing in the Hospitals Board of Control
a coordinating mechanism of great potential, neither Governor Broughton nor the
Board were effective in their attempts to correct the long-standing problems of
the hospitals. While Governor Broughton undoubtedly deserves great credit for
the political skill he demonstrated in laying the groundwork for a major reform

of the hospital system, the fact remains, his reforms did not carry through to
an enduring success.

Fortunately, other groups in the state recognized the difficulties facing
the Hospitals Board of Control and took action. The investigation at Morganton
aroused widespread interest in the care for the mentally retarded. Petitions were
circulated in six western counties of the state urging the establishment of a
school to serve the West as a counterbalance to Caswell in the East. These
petitions were forwarded to Governor-elect R. Gregg Cherry on December 20, 1944.
At the same time, influential residents from the western areas lent their personal
support to the petitions. Hospitals Board member J. H. Beall urged Cherry to
include care for the mentally retarded in his inaugural address.[37] Robert L.
Doughton, 9th District Congressman, sought Cherry's support for the petitions
and also asked him to make the care of the mentally retarded a part of his
administrative program.[38] Roger Winborne, President of the Bernhardt Furniture
Company, Lenoir, went a step further and urged Cherry to extend the scope of
the Spears Committee and investigate all the state hospitals.[39] If these
individual pleas had an impact on the incoming Governor, an institutional appeal
following soon afterward proved even more effective in goading him to action.

The Charlotte Mental Hygiene Society had publicly supported the reorganization of the state hospital system in 1943, and probably more than any other agency
or group it recognized the problems inherent in the laws of North Carolina relating
to hospitals for the mentally disordered. To improve the lot of the mentally ill
and to reduce the political pressures that existed in the Hospitals Board of Control,
the Legislative Committee of the Charlotte Society submitted a list of suggestions
for legislative action.[40] The Society urged the substitution of modern psychiatric
terminology in place of the verbiage currently used in the North Carolina statutes
relating to mental illness. The Society also advocated the revision of the laws

110

governing commitment "upon patient's own application," the adoption of a period

of observation before commitment, the revision of the laws which provided for

care of mentally ill patients in jails, the adoption of a law providing for

immediate admission of acute cases to state hospitals without court procedure,

the revision of the statute which dealt with interstate transfer of mentally

ill patients, the appointment of a commission to study the revision of all

statutes relating to psychiatric problems, and finally the extension of the

term of employment of the General Superintendent of Mental Health from two to

six years.

The recommendations of the Charlotte Society, as it turned out, were

about ten years ahead of their time. The final recommendation struck a vital

chord, however. The Charlotte memorandum argued conclusively that no capable

man would accept the position of Superintendent unless given a longer term

that would allow him some freedom of action in establishing new therapeutic

programs and necessary administrative changes in the state hospital system.

Thus, as a result of several significant streams of advice reaching

him in December, 1944, Governor Cherry was not totally in the dark when a

sequence of fortuitous events concerning the Hospitals Board of Control required

action on his part in the first month of his new administration.

Chapter VI

THE END OF MAKE BELIEVE:

THE BEGINNING OF A COMPREHENSIVE HOSPITAL SYSTEM

The legislation of 1943 creating the Hospitals Board of Control had been
aimed at putting the Morganton scandal to rest once and for all by providing a
system that would upgrade the state hospitals and restore the peoples' confidence
in the institutions charged with the care and treatment of the state's insane.
One of the prime purposes of the newly created Board was to present a united front
to the Legislature in order to prevent duplication of effort and to insure the
development of a unified program that would benefit equally all the mentally ill
in North Carolina.   Ironically, the new quasi-political-administrative structure
that provided separate executive committees for each hospital served to perpetuate
the old system.[1] Hospital Board of Control officials serving as members of the
local executive committees remained more interested in the operation and control
of their own hospitals than in the system as a whole. While the Board members
presented a picture of unity in most matters, critical issues often tended to
divide members and block decisions when a Board member felt that the unit for which
he was responsible was not faring as well as the others.[2] One such critical point
was reached when the hospital budget request for the 1945-46 biennium was presented to the Advisory Budget Commission for consideration.

Senator William T. Clark of Tarboro was keenly aware of the attention
that had been given to the State Hospital at Morganton as a result of the investigation, and he was determined to secure similar aid for Dix, the hospital of

112

his primary concern. Clark was a powerful political leader from the eastern section of the state having served in the Legislature for seven terms and on the Board of Trustees at Dix Hospital for more than fifteen years. At the budget hearing he was granted the opportunity to emphasize the dire conditions that existed at Dix as a means of supporting the budget request. When Budget Commission Chairman Thomas Pearsall, of Rocky Mount, expressed concern that Senator Clark's requests for Dix would require more funds than the total appropriations asked for by the Hospitals Board, Clark responded with the statement that the Commission did not know the truth of the matters at Dix. Clark demanded that the Commission investigate conditions at the hospital. In the heated discussion that followed, Clark told Pearsall that an investigation would be of little value, anyway, since the all-powerful report issued by the Advisory Budget Commission that did most to decide the size of the appropriation would probably be a whitewash. "Cousin Willie" Clark had maneuvered the Commission into a corner.[3]

Chairman Pearsall rose to the challenge. Representative John W. Umstead, Jr., of Chapel Hill, was in the room as an observer. Spotting Umstead, and knowing that he was a life-long friend of Clark's, Pearsall pointed to the Representative from Orange County and asked if he thought John Umstead would whitewash the report of any committee he headed. "No," Clark shouted, and Pearsall immediately asked Umstead to make an investigation of Dix Hospital.[4] Senator Clark won his point. He would have his investigation, and by a personal friend. But why rock the boat with another investigation? The answer lay in Clark's conviction that an investigation had paid off for the Morganton Hospital and another might do the same for Dix. But Clark could not foresee the ramifications of his maneuver.

An investigation at Dix alone might well have led to the demand for similar action at Goldsboro and Caswell and increased the internal struggle for favors and attention among the Board members. Divisive action of this nature, if permitted to develop, would have brought about the eventual destruction of the Board as had happened in 1921. Such an eventuality was prevented, however, by the quick action of Governor Cherry. With nothing more than his personal knowledge of the Morganton investigation and the memorandum sent directly to him in December, 1944, before he assumed office, and entirely without the benefit of the Greenhill report, Governor Cherry called Umstead to his office and requested a full-scale investigation of the entire hospital system. Umstead agreed to the Governor's request and selected three members of the Hospitals Board along with a past board member of the Caswell Training School to serve with him. The four members respectively were N. E. Edgerton, of Raleigh; Harry Riddle, of Morganton; W. G. Clark, of Tarboro; and Thomas O'Berry, of Goldsboro. The six day tour of the State Hospitals at Morganton, Raleigh, and Goldsboro and the Caswell Training School at Kinston made Umstead so physically ill that on several occasions during the tour he had to excuse himself from the group. The shock of recognizing conditions within the hospitals, heretofore brought home to the public through exposé, swung John Umstead to the support of the hospital system. For the first time in its history there was now someone in a position of power at the state level who was interested in the needs and problems of North Carolina's state hospitals.

On his return to Raleigh, John Umstead had made up his mind on two points. First, he would dedicate his time and effort to the cause of the mentally ill in memory of his son, John Wesley Umstead, III, who was killed in action on the island of Saipan, June 14, 1944; and second, he would see where Governor Cherry actually stood on the issue before submitting a report of the investigation. When Cherry assured him that he wanted a report of what actually had been found, Umstead set about detailing his criticisms of the management of the hospitals. The report struck out at the paternalism and political influence that controlled the hospital

114

system.[5] Umstead was critical of the superintendents at Caswell and Goldsboro for operating on a "make-do" philosophy. Not one of the superintendents of the hospitals as they existed before unification nor the new Hospitals Board had pressed properly for adequate appropriations. While there was certainly political influence in the hospital system, it was not the kind to provide the hospitals with their needs.

Under the existing organizational structure of the Hospitals Board, there was almost a total lack of coordination between the hospitals and political districts in the state. Umstead argued that there had to be a local political tie that could be used to bring proper pressure to bear on the Legislature. According to Umstead, the sum and substance of the report was so damaging that the three members of his committee from the Hospitals Board of Control refused to sign it.[6] Umstead knew that improper handling of the report could easily alienate Clark, Spruill, and Riddle who had the power to block any proposed revision in the structure of the Hospitals Board. The political situation was so critical that the report could have blown the top off the hospital system in much the same manner as the Jimison expose had exploded three years earlier. Umstead's recommended solution to the problems raised in his report was an even greater political time bomb.

The only way to divest the hospitals of political intrusion, Umstead concluded, was to rid the Hospitals Board of Control of as many persons as possible who had politically vested interests. Such a move required a reorganization of the Board, but no simple reorganization would accomplish this task. A mere name change would achieve nothing nor would a reshuffling of the organizational structure retaining the same individuals in office. Similar reorganization had been tried before and failed. Umstead and Cherry agreed on the idea of reorganizing the Hospitals Board of Control along congressional district lines in order to assure a more equitable representation on the Board and to provide the political coordination they

115

felt was necessary for the development of a sound, progressive hospital system.[7]
Under this plan there would be one person from each of the twelve Congressional
Districts and three members-at-large. Governor Cherry drew up a list of potential
Board members that included Umstead. The list contained so many persons that
John Umstead thought were not qualified that he countered Governor Cherry's list
with one of his own. The Governor accepted ten of Umstead's nominees.

What brought Cherry to such quick agreement with John Umstead--possibly
the fact that John Umstead was a powerful leader in the Legislature? The Governor
could not forget that John Umstead's brother William B. Umstead had managed
Cherry's campaign for Governor. Undoubtedly, these two factors were important
in the Governor's thinking but probably the more decisive consideration was Cherry's
recognition that time was past due for a thorough overhaul in the hospital system.
Gregg Cherry was not one to be overly sensitive to the social problems of the state.
There was little in his previous record to indicate any compelling interest in
mental health. He came at this problem because the state had obviously reached a
point where the issue was critical. Moreover, it was politic to move constructively
in this area, and Cherry was an astute politician.[8] Quick to recognize the needs
of the state and the wishes of the political leaders, Cherry believed that the
mark of a good and successful Governor was the ability to implement state programs
the people wanted. Cherry's handling of the state's mental hospital problems is
an indication of his position on social issues and his concept of good governorship.
The new governor could not afford another "Morganton."

While Governor Cherry was not responsible for Umstead's appointment to
the investigating committee, he recognized the advantages accruing to an investigation and reform of the system sponsored by his administration. In any case,
with the list of possible new board members in hand, Governor Cherry and John
Umstead set out to reorganize the Hospitals Board of Control. Both men were

concerned with keeping the matter as quiet as possible in order to prevent a public airing of the known opposition to their plan. It was at this point that Umstead and Cherry showed their political mettle.

John Umstead was a shrewd and experienced political operator. He had served in five Legislatures prior to 1945 and had earned a reputation for being somewhat of a maverick and a liberal, particularly in regard to spending money on state obligations.[9] As a graduate of the University of North Carolina and a resident of Chapel Hill, he had been educated to the social needs of the state. For years the Umstead family had provided room for as many needy students at the University of North Carolina as their home would hold. Convinced that Dr. Frank Graham was the right man for the University in the 1940's, Umstead had organized the Alumni Association in support of Graham's presidency. He had carefully culti- vated legislative leaders in the early years of his political career and was fond of asking his colleagues when they were going to do what was needed in the state wihout regard to political ambitions. Umstead fought the "gag" rule in every legislative session, and in 1943 he introduced the bill providing for a nine month school term.

Of particular interest to the prospects of the proposed reorganization of the Board of Control was the veteran legislator's capacity for playing one issue off against another. During the 1943 session, the "wet forces" in the state had attempted to get approval for a referendum authorizing state Alcoholic Beverage Control stores through the Legislature. Josephus Daniels, publisher and editor of the Raleigh News and Observer and a stalwart "dry," was generally reputed to control fourteen Senate and forty-five House votes against the A.B.C. bill. Umstead, being a political realist, recognized the only chance his school bill had was through a political "horse trade" with the Daniels' forces. He persuaded Daniels to "lay off" the A.B.C. referendum until the school bill passed. When

117

the Raleigh paper suddenly fell silent on the liquor issue, Umstead gained enough support to secure passage of his bill. The day after the nine months school term was approved, Daniels struck out at the liquor bill "two a day" in the press until the end of the session.[10] Why couldn't similar tactics be applied to secure passage of the hospitals reorganization plan? With what Burke Davis later described as a "typical directness,"[11] Governor Cherry ordered Secretary of State Thad Eure to draw up the reorganization bill; and John Umstead began to attack the forces marshalled against the plan.

Opposition developed from both political and professional groups in the state. Potential opposition within the Legislature was silenced when Umstead reminded Senator Clark that there were several votes in Clark's political career that would have failed without Umstead's support and there could be more in the future. Umstead told Clark he would not hesitate to break openly with him if Clark chose to fight the reorganization. Senator Clark's life-long personal friendship was not to stand in the way of what John Umstead believed to be absolutely necessary legislative action. Clark fell in line and was rewarded by being selected as one of four members of the original Hospitals Board of Control to be retained on the new Board. In Umstead's estimation, Senator Clark was an honest and dedicated man and "too damn good a business head" to be lost to the state hospital system.[12]

Professional opposition was led by Dr. Maurice Greenhill because of the scheme of dual control for administering the hospitals. Greenhill's objection was that the non-professional business managers who controlled the purse strings would also control the professional programs in the hospitals. Greenhill could see no possible way of separating the business affairs of a hospital from the professional care of patients. Umstead countered this objection by pointing to a history of mismanagement and lack of fiscal coordination in the state hospitals. No General Superintendent, Umstead argued, should be burdened with the day-to-day problems of property management. The conditions in the hospitals, he pointed out, were so bad that when a competent superintendent was located he would have his time completely occupied by demands for his professional medical services. It would be asking too much, he concluded, to expect a qualified psychiatrist to be an expert business administrator too, and the state hospital system sorely needed both.[13] Umstead combined political skill and a surprisingly thorough understanding of the problems facing the Hospitals Board of Control to win his case.

The uncommon ability and unquestioned political strength of Cherry and Umstead is indicated by the speed by which these two men initiated an investigation of the hospitals, drew a plan for reorganization, defended the plan, and secured legislative approval of the reorganization bill--all in less than three months.[14] Furthermore, the farsighted views of these two men and their understanding of the contributory role of politics in a state institution was demonstrated in the draft of the bill to reorganize the Hospitals Board of Control and in their defense of the new Board.

To insure as little political influence as possible, the new law abolished the separate executive committees and vested all policy making authority in the unified board. The new board was structured along the lines of the state's ten Congressional Districts to provide Umstead's "necessary local political tie that could be used to bring _proper_ political pressure to bear on the Legislature." To support the work of the new Board, Governor Cherry authorized and appointed a Medical Advisory Committee of prominent physicians, surgeons, and psychiatrists to advise on technical policy and procedures.[16] On political matters relating to the appointments, Governor Cherry set the record straight when he answered Sam Erwin's charge that the appointment of a Republican to the Hospitals Board from Burke County would ruin the Democratic Party in that area with the statement that

119

if such were the case then there was something wrong with the Party.[17] As a capstone to his legislative program for the hospitals, Governor Cherry secured a six million dollar appropriation for capital improvements.

Thus, it turned out that a maneuver launched by Senator Clark in an effort to gain particular favor for "his" hospital ended in a complete reshuffling of the Hospitals Board of Control and a new attack on the problems of the state mental hospitals quite beyond anything imagined by the State Senator from Tarboro.

The new Board began to function as a close-knit unit almost from the start. At the swearing-in ceremony in Governor Cherry's office, Dr. H. O. Lineberger, a Raleigh dentist and foster brother of the Governor, was elected Chairman of the Board.[18] Cherry was determined to keep a close tie with and an open ear to the Board. The first official action of the new Hospitals Board was a request to the Medical Advisory Committee to assist in locating a General Superintendent. Within two months, on June 5, 1945, Dr. David Young, Assistant Clinical Professor of Psychiatry, University of Utah, was appointed to the position.[19]

In his interview with members of the Hospitals Board, Dr. Young frankly expressed his views on the poor physical and administrative condition of the hospital system. It was his intent to reorganize the system, to secure competent professional assistance, and to establish training and treatment programs that were so desperately needed. To accomplish these goals, if he were elected Superintendent, Young told the Board he would have to have the administrative authority to carry out the policies of the Board. Dr. Young defined the difference between the policy function of the Board and the executive function of the Superintendent in the day-to-day operation of the hospitals. Young further recognized the potential conflict between the medical and business divisions under the dual control system. As long as the medical requirements of the hospitals were given priority over all other expenditures, he would be willing to work under such an organization. Medical requirements might include buildings, food service, grounds facilities; but in any case, they were to be determined by the professional medical staff. By establishing the ground rules before accepting the position, Dr. Young was able to structure the beginnings of a sound administrative organization on which his successors could build.[20] Selection of a General Superintedent was not the only problem or opportunity to face the new Board in the first year of its existence. The superintendency at Raleigh was vacated almost a year before the old Board was dismantled, and in April, Dr. Saunders resigned from Morganton to enter private practice. The new Board acted with dispatch. Dr. Louis Beall was named Superintendent at Morganton and Dr. Eugene Blackwelder was appointed Acting Head at Dix. The By-laws and regulations for government of the state hospital system which were written and approved by July[21] are an indication of the administrative ability of Dr. Young.

The By-laws spelled out in specific terms the duties of the General Superintendent, the Superintendents of the several institutions, and the General Business Manager. They also provided a procedure for settling of controversies and the appointment and removal of personnel. The General Superintendent was responsible for all professional care, treatment, and welfare of patients. This charge included the development of recognized therapy and treatment for patients. All professional services were placed under his control, and he was authorized to promulgate contracts with medical schools for the purpose of gaining their assistance in treatment and research. Schools of nursing and training schools for attendants were to be established at all hospitals under the General Superintendent's direction. The By-laws further charged the Superintendent to institute research and preventive measures for public education on mental illness and deficiency that might further the understanding and treatment of mental disorder.

The comprehensive rules governing the authority and responsibility of the General Superintendent stipulated that he should cooperate with the General Business Manager in financial affairs and in planning for the future needs of plant and equipment necessary to the "treatment, care, and welfare of patients." As a further charge, the Superintendent was made responsible for establishing cooperative liaison with the State Department of Health, State Board of Public Welfare, State Department of Public Instruction, Juvenile Courts, and correctional institutions on problems of mental health and for the development and direction of psychiatric social service in the institutions and out-patient clinics. Finally, the General Superintendent was to be the legal officer of the state responsible for the execution of laws pertaining to custody, care, and treatment of insane, mental defectives, epileptics, and inebriates who were charges of the state.[22]

The broad scope of authority and responsibility granted by the By-laws was far beyond the immediate capacity of the General Superintendent since he first would have to face the realities of a poorly trained, inadequate staff as well as overcrowded and run-down physical facilities. Under the circumstances it might initially appear that the Hospitals Board of Control was not realistic in its job description, but the latitude afforded the General Superintendent in the By-laws assured him the greatest possible opportunity for developing his own programs as rapidly as he could. The duties of the Superintendents of the separate hospitals paralleled those of the General Superintendent in that the policies and procedures established by the Hospitals Board of Control were to be carried out on the local level by the hospital Superintendents.

Similarly, the By-laws delineated the authority and responsibilities of the General Business Manager who was to be responsible for supervision of fiscal control and management of all physical properties and equipment. The By-laws required the cooperation of the General Business Manager with the medical staff in all matters relating to the medical care and treatment of patients. The Hospitals Board members obviously recognized the possibility of friction between the professional and business divisions and included in the By-laws a statement on how controversies were to be settled. The executive committee of the Board was given the power to adjudicate disputes, their decision being final and binding unless either party sought appeal to the full Board of Control.[23] In a charge to all employees, the By-laws concluded with the statement that:

> All officers and employees of the several Institutions, whether engaged in the custody, care and treatment of patients, or in the business affairs, are admonished ever to bear in mind that those Institutions were established and are maintained for the sole purpose of rendering service to the unfortunate members of our society entrusted to them, and that it is the primary obligation of all persons serving or in any way connected with these Institutions to work in harmony and with a conscious effort to promote and sustain the efficiency of the Institutions in the protection and care, and, in so far as possible, the relief and cure of the patients, and that all other activities and programs are secondary to this one overall purpose and are justified only as they make a contribution to the attainment of this goal.[24]

The high purpose to which the Hospitals Board of Control set itself was given content when several opportunities to improve the hospital system were provided to the State from outside sources. Three such opportunities arose during the 1945-46 fiscal year.

Following the lead of John Umstead, the Board displayed its untiring interest and political sagacity by taking advantage of the first opportunity that came to the hospital. In 1945 World War II was drawing to a close and the Army was beginning to deactivate some of its temporary training camps. In April, word was received that Camp Sutton, near Charlotte, was going to be abandoned by July 15. By filing a letter of intent with the War Assets Administration, the Hospitals Board secured the camp for the purpose of housing five hundred senile patients from

Morganton and Raleigh. Governor Cherry supported the request for funds necessary to sign a three-year lease on the camp site. Between the initial inquiry made by the Board and the signing of the lease, John Umstead and State Senator Thomas O'Berry had convinced the federal fiscal officer that the appraisal value of Camp Sutton was too high. As a result of their negotiations, the rental price was reduced from $350,000.00 per year to $10,421.00.[25] The camp was opened on August 1, 1945, and senile patients were immediately transferred to the Sutton Unit in order to relieve severe overcrowding at the other hospitals. This action provided some relief, but it was recognized as being only temporary. The State was still in desperate need of expanded permanent facilities.

The second opportunity came for the reconstituted Board when Congressman Carl Durham, Chairman of the House Military Affairs Committee, met Umstead on the street in Chapel Hill and told him Camp Butner, located just outside of Durham, was to be closed. Umstead recognized the worth of this "advance information" and took immediate action. A state mental hospital facility at this camp could draw on the services of the University of North Carolina at Chapel Hill and the staff of the Duke University Medical School besides providing a ready-made answer to the problem of physical space for patients. While the Army was still making use of Camp Butner and before the Camp Commander was even aware that the unit was to be deactivated, John Umstead made an exploratory visit of the facility. At the December meeting of the Board of Control, Umstead presented the possibility of securing the Camp for the state.[26] The Board agreed to investigate the matter and set up a special committee of the Hospitals Board of Control and the Medical Advisory Committee which toured Butner in January[27] to determine the availability of the camp and the suitability of the hospital cantonment for the care of mental patients. The Hospitals Board received a favorable report at the regular meeting in February that prompted the Board to pass a resolution calling for acquisition of the Camp Butner area. The Board then created a Camp Butner Committee naming John Umstead Chairman and State Senators O'Berry, McBryde, and Clark, and board representatives Richardson and Whiteside as members.

The actions of the Butner Committee, spearheaded by Mr. Umstead, were a model of precision timing and political maneuvering. Umstead acted first to secure the equipment in the hospital so that the unit would be available for immediate operation if a transfer was made to the State. With assistance from Governor Cherry and the cooperation of Kenneth C. Royall, a native North Caro-linian and Undersecretary of the Army, a freeze order was secured on the hospital.[28] The Army justified the order on the grounds that Butner might be reopened or that the Veterans Administration might accept it for use. Following the holding action on equipment, Governor Cherry and Umstead took their next step toward securing the camp. Along with Dr. Young, General Superintendent of Mental Hygiene, the two flew to Washington, D.C., and met with the full North Carolina delegation to explain the purpose of their visit and to secure unanimous backing for their request. At the same time, Governor Cherry filed a notice of intention with the War Assets Administration to exercise the State's priority for the property.[29]

During the summer of 1946, and in fact for the remainder of the year, it appeared that it might not be possible to purchase the hospital area after all or to secure it on a federal grant because the Veterans Administration would not disclaim interest in the property. As an insurance measure, therefore, Umstead and O'Berry made efforts to secure release of the property on a lease basis similar to the arrangement that secured Camp Sutton. A second appraisal was made of the facilities by the Butner Committee to keep the issue alive. The appraisal showed that the water supply was adequate and that the laundry, bake shops, and cold storage facilities were in good condition. There was considerable space for

125

storage and sufficient land available in the reservation for all farming needs.[30]
Although no commitment had been made to the State by the War Assets Administration, Umstead felt prospects were good enough to push for supporting funds.
Senators Clark and O'Berry assured Umstead they could "do what was necessary"
from their side to see that funds were made available.[31] The commitment to
Umstead by Clark and O'Berry to secure funds for the hospitals was based on two
important points. Both men were convinced of the necessity of securing legislative approval for the hospitals program, and they controlled a significant block
of votes in both houses of the Legislature. Equally important, however, was the
fact that during and after World War II North Carolina tax revenues were mounting
rapidly thus making it easier to raise funds after 1946 than it had been before
1940. Receipts to the General Fund in 1945-46 amounted to $90,453,171.[32] This
amount represented a 57.4% increase over the annual average for the five year
period 1935-1940, and a 21.5% increase over the 1940-41 receipts to the general
fund. As the chart indicates, even in a period of rising inflation the state
managed to secure a percentage increase in revenues that produced a substantial
annual surplus.[33] Knowing that funds were available, Umstead, working in concert
with the Governor, was able to secure a commitment from the Advisory Budget
Commission to set aside additional funds for the operation of Camp Sutton or Camp
Butner on an expanded scale.[34] During the early part of 1947, plans for the
operation of Butner were made, submitted, and approved by the Board. True to
their word, Clark and O'Berry managed the legislative work to secure approval of
a $1,372,786.00 budget. The appropriation was won over the protest of Assistant
Budget Director, Robert Dayton, who looked upon the Butner facility as a "white
elephant."[35]

   While Senators Clark and O'Berry were managing the appropriations battle,
Umstead struck on an idea to further influence the Legislature and to cut weeks of

North Carolina Department of Revenue Reports 1960

General Fund Revenues   Revenue Comparison 1942-43 - 1959-60

YEAR	RECEIPTS	PERCENTAGE INCREASE OVER PREVIOUS YEAR	SURPLUS
1942-43	$ 70,445,137		$39,370,000
1943-44	76,622,101	8.76%	57,648,000
1944-45	80,697,290	5.31%	25,405,000
1945-46	90,453,171	12.08%	47,975,000
1946-47	119,996,404	32.66%	42,087,000
1947-48	129,568,152	7.97%	80,093,000
1948-49	140,843,645	8.7 %	13,937,000
1949-50	132,837,931	5.68%	13,260,000
1950-51	162,072,863	22. %	25,838,000
1951-52	178,887,834	10.37%	38,621,000
1952-53	180,978,102	1.16%	32,490,000
1953-54	184,709,897	2.06%	27,704,000
1954-55	189,111,046	2.38%	14,990,000
1955-56	224,613,939	18.77%	38,485,000
1956-57	237,768,203	5.85%	65,066,000
1957-58	242,111,765	1.82%	29,347,000
1958-59	253,670,563	4.77%	18,744,000
1959-60	310,207,655	22.28%	44,654,000

red tape from the negotiations. While the Legislature was still in session, plans for the transfer of equipment and the operation of the hospital were drawn and filed with Representative Carl Durham and the War Assets Administration. The state received a license in March, 1947, to occupy and use the hospital subject to final determination of arrangement for transfer.[36]

The Board lost no time taking control of the property. Mr. T. B. Huneycutt was appointed Acting Business Manager and Dr. James W. Murdock, Acting Superintendent of the new facility. Within two months the hospital at Butner was ready to receive the patients from Camp Sutton. There were no direct admissions to Butner in 1947, but by December, Sutton was closed and a total of 275 patients were transferred from Raleigh and Morganton, bringing the Butner census to 750. The spaces opened at Morganton and Raleigh allowed for new admissions to those institutions.

The War Assets Administration set the final fair value of the hospital area, the water and sewer plants, and 1,700 acres of land at $5,330,849.15; and a grant was offered to the Hospitals Board of Control at 100% discount plus one dollar to be paid as a legal binder. Umstead paid the dollar at the same time a check for $1,350,000.00 for the cantonment area was given the federal representative bringing the land area of the hospital unit to 2,950 acres.[37] The signing of transfer papers giving the Hospitals Board of Control complete control of Camp Butner consummated eighteen months of negotiations that required no little political skill and a vast amount of personal dedication in pursuing the issue with single-mindedness. The question yet to be answered was whether John Umstead would be able to continue to display this skill in attempting to secure funds and programs for the state's mental hospitals.

The hospital program which was materially upgraded through the physical expansion provided by the Butner acquisition was further augmented in the first year of the new Board's existence by the third opportunity which came in the form of two federal acts aimed at upgrading the hospitals of the nation as a whole. Public Law 486, "The National Mental Health Act," and Public Law 725, "Hospital Survey and Construction Act," better known as the Hill-Burton Act, were passed by the 79th Congress.[38] The Hill-Burton Act provides funds to states, local communities, and private non-profit hospital corporations on a matching-funds basis for the construction, modification or expansion of hospital facilities. The National Mental Health Act provides funds to the states for the development of mental health clinics, the training of personnel to work in mental hospitals, and sponsoring research and training programs in mental health. The Act also created the National Institute of Mental Health to aid in the public and private development of research in mental health. When these Acts were promulgated, Governor Cherry designated the Hospitals Board of Control as the fiscal agency for federal funds received for state hospital construction and for all funds in the area of mental health. Governor Cherry stipulated that the Hospitals Board work in complete cooperation with the Department of Public Welfare and the State Board of Health "insofar as such related agencies may be useful in the accomplishment of the purpose set out in the Federal Act."[39] The first funds became available to the State in 1947. Prior to assistance from the mental health program, only three communities in the state had mental health clinics which provided an equivalent of twenty-seven days a week of professional services.[40] According to Dr. Young, Superintendent of the hospital system, the participation policy opened the way for further community clinics and stimulated a new public interest in the problems of mental illness. By the end of the second year, the number of communities with clinics had doubled from three to six. The professional service provided by state clinics had increased from an equivalent of 27 to 80 days a week.[41]

No less significant than the opportunities for physical expansion and program development was the change in attitude on the part of the hospital administrators and the approach to administrative problems by the Governor. Dr. David Young was set on establishing a professional standard for the hospitals that would raise their stature in the public eye. This was not to be accomplished by hiding behind long-standing inadequacies. Dr. Young admitted freely the shortcomings of the hospitals. When relatives complained of the mistreatment of patients and investigation justified the complaint, Young frankly accepted responsibility for the occurrence and took firm action to prevent a repetition. He was equally quick to point out, however, that in some instances not much else could be expected with so few ward attendants, most of whom were still inadequately trained.[42]

Coupled with Dr. Young's willingness to admit error was a significant procedural change in the relationship of the Governor's office to the hospitals. Governor Cherry established the practice of referring all complaints and requests for admission directly to the General Superintendent for action. The Governor merely acknowledged receipt of such letters. With the Cherry administration, the Governor and the members of the Hospitals Board of Control ceased to be de facto admitting officers for the state hospitals. From Governor Cherry's administration through that of Governor Terry Sanford, there was no indication of direct executive interference in the operation of the hospitals although pressure from constituents continued to be exerted on the Governor for special favors such as the admission of "emergency cases." Unfortunately, many of the emergency cases, properly classified as such, could not be admitted for lack of space at all the hospitals.[43]

In spite of the physical expansion and change in official attitude, there continued to be severe shortage of facilities. As a result, mental patients were being lodged in jails when they reached the point where they could not be maintained

130

without forcible restraint. The Mental Health Section of the North Carolina Board of Health reported that during the 1947-48 fiscal year some 1,174 patients were lodged in jails, at least temporarily, although some remained for periods of over 90 days.[44] Again Dr. Young recognized a continuing situation that was a source of embarrassment to the State and the Hospitals Board. Rather than ignore the problem, however, he developed a system of classification that would at least give priority to the genuinely critical or emergency cases seeking admission.

Governor Cherry also acted to help alleviate the problem in 1947 by securing an appropriation of $12,568,000.00 for capital improvements. These funds were taken from the 1945-46 surplus of the State. Both Governor Cherry and the Hospitals Board of Control attempted to face up to the reality of the problems before them. The first question was to decide what steps were to be taken. Should the State expand and improve facilities first or develop staff and therapeutic programs? Both, of course, were needed immediately, but which had priority? The Cherry administration attempted to carry both forward at the same time, but the obvious took precedence over the intangible, and emphasis was placed on physical improvements and expansion. Problems of professional staff shortages and inadequately trained, overworked attendants continued to plague the hospitals. At almost every meeting of the Hospitals Board during the Cherry Administration, and indeed to this very day, the matter of low salaries was a major topic of discussion. Salary raises that have been provided have never brought the scale of attendants or physicians to the competitive level of the surrounding community.

Despite the continuing shortage of space and the personnel problems within the state hospital system, Governor Cherry and John Umstead, through the reorganized Hospitals Board of Control, laid a foundation for progressive leadership in the area of mental health. Officially, at least, North Carolina had begun to accept

131

its moral and fiscal responsibility for the mentally ill in the State. Probably Governor Cherry's greatest contribution to the cause of mental health was that he brought to an end the make-believe notion that problems in the hospitals were isolated instances in an otherwise smoothly running system.

Cherry and Umstead put the hospital house in order by erecting a sound administrative organization, an agressive staff, and a shrewd political relationship to support them. To Governor Cherry's successors fell the task of using these assets to see that the North Caroling mental hospital system caught up with the standards elsewhere in the nation.

Chapter VII

CATCHING UP:

THE COMING OF PROFESSIONALISM

John Wesley Umstead, Jr. often quoted the remark Winston Churchill is
eputed to have made during the dark days of the London Blitz: "No need to say
e are doing our best. We have got to succeed in doing what is necessary." This
hilosophy became the guideline for the Hospitals Board of Control as it undertook
o develop, simultaneously, the many programs necessary to meet the total needs
f the hospital system. One of the things to be done first was to educate the
pcoming governor-elect W. Kerr Scott to the needs, problems, and programs of the
ospitals. Following the December, 1946, meeting of Cherry, Umstead and Scott,
mstead reported to the members of the Board that Governor Scott was very receptive
o their program and had promised his full cooperation in the Board's effort to
ove the hospital system forward.[1] Prompted by strong political support and an
merging system that was able to communicate its needs, the Governor was ready
nd able to take positive action when funds became available.

The first tangible indication of Kerr Scott's cooperation came during the
egislative session of 1949. North Carolina experienced another large surplus in
he 1947-48 Biennium, and Scott directed $11,387,000 to the Hospitals Board of
ontrol for capital improvements.[2] Receipts for the sale of surplus material and
uildings at Camp Butner amounted to $458,101 between July 1, 1947, and January 1,
949.[3] The Hill-Burton funds made available to the State were $543,978. These
unds, added to the $9,465,276 appropriated by the 1947 Legislature, gave the
ospitals Board of Control a total of $21,859,493 for plant improvements and

expansion.[4] The funds were allocated to each of the units in the system on the basis of "critical need." When Governor Scott assumed office, $7,014,733 had already been allocated. Of the remaining $14,844,000, the Board approved $6,579,000 for new construction directly related to patient care. The remaining $8,265,000 was used for renovation and construction of allied facilities. Construction of quarters for nurses and staff in all units amounted to $1,900,000. The patient area projects were aimed primarily to create additional space to relieve overcrowding and to reduce the waiting lists in the State.

Overcrowding was acute. On July 1, 1949, Dr. Young, General Superintendent, reported to Governor Scott that the census of the hospitals showed a resident enrollment of 8,763 patients. The rated capacity of all hospitals was 6,336. On a unit basis, the breakdown showed the following:

	Rated Capacity	Census-July 1949	%Excess Over Cap.	Net New Beds	Total
Raleigh	1898	2226	+14	470	2,368
Morganton	2254	2592	+13	385	2,639
Goldsboro	2284	2765	+17	689	2,973
Butner		1180	-59	2900	2,900
	6336	8763		4444	10,880

At the same time, Dr. Young noted that there were 66 alcoholics and 530 epileptic patients at Raleigh and 158 epileptics and 310 mental defectives at Goldsboro. These groups were not ordinarily housed in state hospitals. North Carolina, however, did not have special facilities for alcoholics or Negro feeble-minded, so the state mental hospitals had to receive these groups. The overcrowded conditions at Caswell were temporarily relieved by using a section of the Butner hospital. In 1949 the state was attempting to care for 1,050 mental defectives. Two hundred and thirty-eight of this group were at Butner where facilities were not adequate for care or training.[5] While the Building Committee of the Hospitals Board worked at solving the problems of overcrowding, Dr. Young began to develop two programs to upgrade the care and treatment of alcoholics and the mentally ill under his care.

Early in 1949 Dr. Young proposed establishing an alcoholic rehabilitation center at Butner. Such a center was necessary, he insisted, in order to get the alcoholic out of the mental hospital where his resentment toward doctors and hospitalization in general, already at a critical stage because of his forced commitment, was further aggravated by his presence in a mental institution. Furthermore, the spacious grounds and the type of buildings found at Butner offered maximum opportunity for recreation and rehabilitation not available at Raleigh. The transfer of alcoholics to Butner would help to relieve desperately needed space at Raleigh. Young's proposal was referred to the Medical Advisory Committee which Governor Scott reappointed in July for a second four-year term.[6] After consideration of the proposal, which received only minor opposition, the Advisory Committee recommended that the Alcoholic Rehabilitation Center be established. Plans were developed for the program, and the Hospitals Board of Control assigned a section of the hospital area entirely separate from the mental unit for the Center. In April, 1950, the Hospitals Board appointed Mr. S. K. Proctor director of the alcoholic unit and appropriated $35,000 from current funds to develop a training and rehabilitation program.[7]

The problems of care and treatment for the mentally ill were more complex and pressing at the moment than those in the area of alcoholic rehabilitation, and Dr. Young asked that a special study be made of the problems. The Hospitals Board approved the request and asked the American Psychiatric Association to conduct a general survey of the state's mental hospitals.[8] The A.P.A. survey completed in June, 1950, presented first a general history that traced the development of the state system and then dealt with specific problem areas.[9] Notable among the areas singled out for criticism was the practice of jail detention and the use of police to transport patients to the hospital. The investigators urged

135

the removal of every implication of a criminal process in the commitment of patients
admission to a state mental hospital should rely on medical examination and voluntary admission of patients. The A.P.A. investigators were also critical of the
farming operations conducted by the hospitals because of the possible diversion
of interest from the main purpose of the institutions. The report, of course, took
special note of the extensive overcrowding at the three older units. Rather than
expand existing units further to accommodate any future increases in demand, the
investigators recommended limiting existing hospitals to 2,000 beds and construction
of entirely new hospital units near large population centers.

On the matter of construction, the investigating committee recognized the
fact that where new capacity had been so badly needed,"...it is hard for authorities
not to emphasize new buildings and repairs."[10] Nevertheless, the report emphatical-
ly declared that the best constructed buildings would be of little or no good without proper personnel. In 1950 "proper personnel" meant compliance with the recommended standard of the American Psychiatric Association of one doctor for each 100
patients plus a quota of occupational therapists, nurses, and attendants who togethe
would make possible a genuine program of active treatment rather than mere custodial
care. In North Carolina the doctor-patient ratio for the mental hospital system
averaged 1 to 210, a substantial decrease from 1942 ratio of 1 to 425 but still
twice the recommended average. At the same time, however, the recommended doctor-
patient ratio of 1 to 150 in 1940 became 1 to 100 in 1950 so that as North Carolina
struggled to catch up, the national ideal rose to even higher standards. To increas
the number of professional and semi-professional staff members in the hospitals
and to reduce high rates of turnover at all levels, the A.P.A. investigators urged
development of policies to insure job security, better wages, more reasonable
working conditions, and more adequate supervision.

In matters of patient care, the investigators also urged more direct treatment through psychotherapy and the use of drugs. Restraint and seclusion, still in use at all the North Carolina hospitals except Butner, were condemned in the report as was the mixing of the mentally deficient, the alcoholic, and the epileptic with the mentally ill. Of considerable concern to the A.P.A., was the practice of admitting senile persons to psychiatric hospitals in the state. The investigators argued that the senile should be kept in their home communities where they could be better cared for in more normal surroundings. The trend toward passing the problems of the aged from family to city or county and then to the state was recognized in 1950 as potentially the greatest problem the hospitals would have to cope with in the future. Finally, the investigators noted the very limited amount of funds and effort being put into research on mental illness and retardation.

The real value of the American Psychiatric Association study and report was not only its disclosures of inadequacies and needs, which were already recognized by the Board, but also the impartial, professional base the report gave to the evaluation of care and treatment of patients. This "outside" study served to validate what the professional staff of the hospitals and the Hospitals Board of Control had been contending all along. Dr. Young and the Board now faced the task of closing the gap between the realities described in the A.P.A. report and the association's recommended goals. Each success in areas such as reduced waiting lists and improved patient care was met with a counter-productive action--especially in the areas of senile admissions, research and public education. Ideally, the new construction Young sought should have been placed near large population centers such as Charlotte, and facilities to accommodate geriatric patients should have been established in local communities. The present mode of community oriented psychiatric services is severely hampered by lack of in-patient facilities that might have been established twenty years ago. Young recognized the validity of the A.P.A. goals, but he also knew that he had to contend with political and social realities that existed within the state. It is to Dr. Young's credit that he was able to isolate critical problems and to determine which problems could be solved immediately and which ones would have to be contended with at a later time. Redirecting the institutional form was to be a slow and arduous task. Nevertheless, both Dr. Young and the members of the Board were quick to use the A.P.A. report as a basis for further expansion of facilities and development of programs.

In spite of the funds allocated for capital improvements in 1947 and 1949, there still existed a severe shortage of space for patients. As a result of continued demands for admission and an average 35% overcrowding, the Hospitals Board of Control requested an additional capital improvements grant from the 1951 Legislature. Because of the expected relief that was to come from current building and from space still available at Butner, the Legislature denied the request. Despite the set-back, Dr. Young renewed the battle for funds. In a special report to the Board of Control on August 28, 1951, Young pointed up the dilemma of the hospital system.[11] The time required to estimate needs, to make plans, secure funds, construct buildings, and then recruit able people in order to have staff available to operate the new facilities required a minimum of three years. Under these restrictions, Young told the Board, it was almost impossible to plan in a manner that would satisfy the hospitals' needs. Before one planning program was completed, new contingencies arose to make it inadequate. Renovations alone, he argued, could not be made without dislocating patients and causing further overcrowdi Under such conditions, proper treatment of patients was all but impossible. Coupled with these basic problems of space, Young pointed out, was the factor of an ever-increasing census of senile patients who had no hope of returning to their home

communities. Prior to September, 1950, Butner received only transfer patients
from Raleigh and Morganton,so the admission load continued to be extremely heavy
at those two hospitals. The relief gained when Butner began admitting its own
patients did not reduce the in-patient load on the staffs at Morganton and Raleigh.
Waiting lists still existed at Raleigh where 74 were on the emergency and 203 on
the deferred lists. Goldsboro had a waiting list of "all types" of 240. Morganton
had a list of 128. Patients not classed as "emergency" remained on the waiting
list in come cases as long as eighteen months.[12]

Dr. Young raised two other issues that were related to the total problem
of overcrowding, issues which had also been reviewed in the A.P.A. report of 1950.
First, although the newly opened Butner Hospital had a patient census below rated
capacity, for lack of personnel many wards were unused from time to time, and no
new wards could be opened although space was available. It was clear Young told
the Board, that this situation "will cause more frequent deferrals and longer
waiting lists."[13] Butner could not take care of counties currently under the
jurisdiction of Morganton or Raleigh without a staff to care for the patients.

Second, the admission of new patients implied the dismissal of others--
either as improved and able to adjust to home situations again or as persons un-
suitable for state hospital care. Young reported difficulty with counties in many
instances that pointed up the prediction of the A.P.A. report of a growing tendency
for cities and counties to depend upon the state for care of mentally ill and senile
patients. In this situation Young urged the use of Hill-Burton funds to construct
rooms for psycniatric patients in general hospitals so that they could be maintained
in their own counties for short hospital stays. By this means,those waiting to be
admitted to one of the state hospitals would not have to jailed. Failure to implement this specific proposal was a double blow to the hospital program. Initial
relief was denied patients requiring hospitalization for almost six more years--

the time it took to reduce the patient census at state hospitals to below capacity
levels through new treatment programs. The nucleus for community based psychiatric
and geriatric in-patient treatment was delayed indefinitely. Young pointed out
that the basic problem on the local level was probably the attitude of county
officials and the general public.

Since political pressure could no longer "get a patient in," the next recourse was to apply pressure on hospital authorities by placing the patient in jail.
In some cases Young admitted there was probably no recourse; but in most instances,
the method of jailing a patient was a cruel ruse. The practice was condoned by the
public whose feeling of indifference toward the mental patient was the same as a
hundred years earlier. In 1958 the North Carolina Health Council reported that
county officials freely admitted that "holding a patient in jail gets quicker action
from the hospital for admission."[14] The action was justified on the 18th century
concept that when a person is out of his mind it doesn't make any difference where
he is; so why not in jail? "How could the state move forward in the mental health
field," Young asked, "with this attitude prevalent in society?"[15] Dr. Young's
solution was to educate the people; and the education would have to begin, he
realized, within the system.

Dr. Young sought a formal cooperative psychiatric residency program
between the hospital system and the Duke University Medical School since 1948.
An agreement was reached in 1949 that established a two-year residency program,
but there were no funds to support the plan, and student interest in the program
did not develop. Now with the A.P.A. report in hand to support them, Dr. Young and
John Umstead pushed for several programs that would benefit the state hospitals
and the recently approved four-year medical school at Chapel Hill.[16] With the
opening of the Alcoholic Rehabilitation Center at Butner in 1950, the Hospitals
Board of Control allocated an annual appropriation of $35,000 to support a cooper-
ative training program with Duke University and the University of North Carolina

Medical Schools. As a further aid to the new medical education program at Chapel Hill, the Board transferred $100,000 from the Alcoholic Rehabilitation Fund to the University of North Carolina for construction of an alcoholic treatment and reseach unit at the Medical School.[17]

Through the efforts of Dean Berryhill and Dr. George Ham, Chairman of the Department of Psychiatry, and the Planning Committee of the Hospitals Board, chaired by Mr. Robert Richardson, an agreement was reached in 1951 to establish a psychiatric residency program in the state hospitals under the supervision of the U.N.C. Medical School. To support the program and to further the Medical School development, the Board transferred one million dollars from building funds to aid in the construction of a psychiatric unit at Chapel Hill.[18] Under this agreement, the state hospitals at Raleigh and Butner were to make use of the teaching facilities and personnel at the University of North Carolina Medical School as well as the Duke University Medical School under the terms of an earlier agreement concluded in 1949. A three-year residency program, which included one year of training in the state hospitals' facilities, provided training for twenty-four residents.

The worth of the program was demonstrated when eleven of the first twenty-six residents to complete the program stayed in the state system.[19] By 1965 there were thirty-one psychiatric residents in training at Raleigh and at Butner. Moreover, the residency program was augmented by a twelve-week psychiatric nursing program at Raleigh which trained student nurses from general hospitals throughout the state. But the residency program was only one of the many significant improvements that stemmed from the A.P.A. report. That survey also opened the door to a study of mental defectives in North Carolina.

Some members of the Hospitals Board, including Dr. Young, John Umstead, and H. W. Kendall, editor of the Greensboro Daily News and a 1949 Scott appointee to the Board,[20] contended that the comments in the A.P.A. report on the care of the mentally deficient called for an extensive study of the state training school. The Hospitals Board agreed and in August, 1951, a Caswell Training School Study Committee began to survey the program for the care of the mentally deficient in North Carolina. The survey was conducted by the Bureau of Educational Research and Service of the School of Education, the University of North Carolina. Dr. Allan S. Hurlburt, Director of the Bureau, was named to serve as Director of the survey and Chairman of the Survey Advisory Board. Mr. H. W. Kendall, Mrs. E. H. Lasater, and Senator O'Berry represented the Hospitals Board of Control on the Advisory Board. The report issued by the Advisory Board on April 15, 1952, listed fifteen recommendations for the Hospitals Board's consideration and future action.[21]

The Advisory Board recommended that Caswell Training School to be held to a resident capacity of 1,250 and be utilized only as a facility for long-time care of grossly retarded cases. The recommendation was based on the conviction that "it would be almost impossible to reorient the staff of the institution to a new philosophy of training children for community living."[22] To compensate for this proposed reduced size and specialized use of Caswell, the Advisory Board recommended the immediate construction of a new school for white boys and girls. The Board condemned the practice of housing the mentally deficient with, or in close proximity to, the mentally ill. The removal of all Negro mentally deficient from Goldsboro State Hospital was called for under a construction plan that would provide a Negro training school for the State. Also recommended was special consideration in the selection of personnel and the location of new schools along with an after-care program that included a strong home-care and clinic program. The Advisory Board further recommended changes in the commitment law to assure proper handling of cases.

By way of general organization, the Advisory Board suggested that for proper administration of the problems of mental deficiency by the General Superintendent of Mental Hygiene, a Division of Mental Deficiency should be established as a separate unit within the Hospitals Board of Control. The report asked that steps be taken by the University of North Carolina to set up a training center for preparing teachers in the methods and techniques of teaching mentally handicapped children. Finally, the report called for a definite allocation of funds for research.[23]

The surveys conducted by the A.P.A. and the Bureau of Educational Research between 1950 and 1952 provided the basis for immediate action in the development of cooperative programs in education and training. The surveys also served to strengthen the Hospitals Board's discussions with Governor Scott and the Advisory Budget Commission. Most significantly, they helped to secure a ten percent salary increase for all hospital employees in the fiscal years 1951-52 and 1952-53, the last two years of Governor Scott's administration. In their efforts to improve the physical facilities and to develop long-range plans for the care and treatment of patients, neither Governor Cherry nor Governor Scott lost sight of the fact that personnel needs were a concomitant factor of critical significance in the continual struggle to upgrade.

While salaries were still below a competitive level with the surrounding communities and doctor, nurse, and attendant ratios remained distressingly far above the desirable level recommended by the American Psychiatric Association, the advances accomplished in these areas between 1945 and 1952 were no less significant than the physical expansion that took place. When Governor Cherry assumed office in 1945, the doctor-patient ratio was 1 to 390. The nurse-patient ratio was 1 to 160, and the attendant-patient ratio was 1 to 17 - a slight improvement over the 1942 ratios reported by the Spears' Board of Inquiry. In 1952, the doctor-patient ratio was 1 to 169, exclusive of dentist, residents and interns. The nurse-patient ratio was 1 to 77, and the attendant-patient ratio was 1 to 8.6.[24] Between 1945 and 1952, the population at the mental hospitals and the training school had increased from 8,919 to 12,506, or by 40%. The budget increase for the same period was from $4,470,233 to $13,037,527, or 190%. The average number of employees increased 155%.[25] Per capita daily cost rose from $1.37 to $2.64, of which 48 cents was for purchased raw food. The farms produced an average 18 cents of food per day, bringing the daily food cost to 66 cents.

Significant strides were also made during the Scott administration in up-grading the hospital system, and the members of the Hospitals Board of Control worked as a man to secure their programs. In October of 1951, Broad Chairman Dr. H. O. Lineberger died. He was succeeded by Senator William T. Clark who resigned in May, 1953, because of ill health. During Senator Clark's Chairman-ship, John Umstead was Vice-Chairman of the Board; and he succeeded to the Chair upon Senator Clark's resignation. This sequence of events placed John Umstead in an even more strategic position than he had previously occupied to fight for the needs of the mentally ill and mentally deficient in North Carolina. Armed with factual evidence and the strong recommendations of the A.P.A. survey and Bureau of Research report, Umstead and News Editor Kendall prepared to attack the space problem once more in the 1953 Legislature. Here again the fortunes of politics played a significant role.

The winner of the Democratic Primary for Governor in North Carolina was for all practical purposes, Governor-elect, and in 1952 William B. Umstead, Durham attorney and brother of John Umstead, won the nomination. During the summer of 1952 John Umstead and Kendall developed a proposal for expansion and capital improve-ments of the hospital system that called for an expenditure of $25 million. On two successive Sunday afternoons following the General Elections, the Umstead

brothers sat on John's front porch in Chapel Hill while John argued the cause step

by step. William finally agreed on a $22 million program if the Legislature would

approve and the funds could be secured by a bond issue referendum.[26] John was

more than willing to accept this arrangement. But when some of William Umstead's

strongest supporters heard of the proposed bond issue, they suggested a program.

Give the mental hospitals $10 million from the surplus and forget the bond issue,

they urged. The party leaders who had maneuvered Umstead's nomination were,

according to political commentator Burke Davis, pledging Senators to hold the line

against any tax increases and to fight proposed bond issues.[27] During the second

week in February, the Governor was told that thirty members of the Senate had

joined the movement and that big bond issues chiefly for mental hospitals and

schools were doomed.[28] John immediately set out to prove to William's satisfaction

that $10 million would not do. A check by William's friends in the Legislature in-

dicated that the Senate would back his money program 32 to 18. Why was John Umstead

willing to risk all on a $22 million bond issue when a smaller request failed in the

Legislature in 1951 and when he faced strong opposition in 1953?

The Hospitals Board's thoroughly detailed description of the projects for

permanent improvements, undergirded by John Umstead's philosophy of fiscal respon-

sibility, convinced him that the issue would be approved. The major expenditures

in the funds requested were for two training schools at Goldsboro and Butner to meet

the needs of the State's mentally deficient population. Building costs for these

two units, estimated at $9 million, were justified by the studies conducted during

the Scott administration. All other expenditures could be readily justified by the

same reports or by a visit to the hospitals by the Legislature. John Umstead's

opponents knew that in addition to having a well-planned program he was known to drive hard for his demands while taking cognizance of other state needs. The Representative from Orange County had convinced the Appropriation Committee that he asked only for what he needed - not all that could be spent but all that could wisely be spent in two years. Umstead's basic philosophy was "never to get caught with more than you can wisely spend in one legislative period."[29] The philosophy had worked for him in the past, and he was convinced it would work for him again in 1953; furthermore, the fact that John's brother was the Governor would not hurt matters.

During the legislative debate on the bond issue, Governor Umstead suffered a heart attack and was confined to the Governor's Mansion. John was one of three persons allowed to see the Governor during this illness, and his opponents accused him of exercising undue influence on his stricken brother. John swept the criticism aside with a characteristic invitation for his accusers to step to a warmer climate.[3] John Umstead would not bow to political pressure. The Governor's supporters rallied and the issue, when carried to a vote, was passed by the Legislature on April 20, 1953.[31] The referendum was approved on October 6 of the same year.[32] The bond issue, a singular success in itself, was not the only gain secured by the Umstead forces in the 1953 Legislature. A ten percent salary increase was voted for all hospital employees for the 1953-54 and 1954-55 fiscal years.

Passage of the money bills eased certain personnel and space problems, but it accentuated others. The Hospitals Board of Control now seemed to be able to complete plans to make the hospital system adequate and functional. Within weeks after the bond issue was secured, however, the Board began to sense that the task of spending $22 million was a truly formidable one that would require the utmost care and measured deliberation in order to prevent waste and costly errors. Robert R. Richardson, current Chairman of the Building Committee, along with members H. W. Kendall, D. W. Royster, Wayland Spruill, Senator O'Berry, and Warren R. Williams

146

settled on a building schedule aimed at completion of all projects by January, 1956. In a report to Governor Umstead, Richardson outlined the building program, suggested the dates for the sale of the Hospital Bonds, and recounted the difficulties already experienced by the Board in selecting architects for the many projects in the total program.[33]

Governor Umstead was not pleased with the report. While he recognized the difficulties outlined by Richardson, the Governor thought it was "absolutely necessary to proceed faster than indicated in your letter."[34] Governor Umstead reminded Richardson that the Board had told the people of the State "that the facilities were pressingly needed....It would be a great mistake," he concluded, "to proceed too slowly with this program."[35] It seems apparent that Governor Umstead wanted the building projects completed during his tenure. Pressure to move the building projects as rapidly as possible stirred a debate among the members of the Board, and editor Kendall took the lead in opposing undue haste in the planning and execution of the program. In a lengthly letter to John Umstead, Kendall presented his views on the matter, especially as they related to the new training schools.

Kendall's letter dealt with the dangers of building too rapidly, the philosophy underlying the concept of therapeutic treatment as opposed to custodial care, and the responsibility the Board and the State had to the people entrusted to them. "I want to get relief for the State's mentally ill and deficient just as quickly as anybody else," he wrote, "but I want to do what we do right." In an admirable example of logic and persuasion, Kendall argued:

> I want to get the most we can for the money that the people have entrusted to our spending and to come up with a program which will assure the humane and effective results for those whom it directly affects. The field in which we are dealing is highly specialized and I believe we should get the best possible advice from persons who know it. Undue haste will make waste from any number of angles; planning represents the groundwork, the foundations upon which we shall build not only for the present but for the years ahead. It is much cheaper to do right now, to avoid mistakes such as have occured in the past, rather than to live to regret them and to have to spend money to correct them. A few weeks or even months difference in the completion

of our program will not actually mean much so far as time itself is concerned; but it may mean many, many a mistake avoided, headache averted, material saving to the state and incalculable saving to the persons for whom this program is being undertaken.

In this latter connection I cannot urge too strongly ... that we keep clearly in mind our objectives, our obligations and our commitments. The board ... has been working to institute therapy, to get away from the costly, frustrating program of custodial care .... Until we do begin treating, training and dismissing more of these people entrusted to us, we shall never stabibilize our building program but will come back to Legislature after Legislature asking for huge sums for custodial care and even huger for capital outlay for more buildings in which to keep human beings for the rest of their dark lives .... North Carolina is rich enough in resources to provide its mentally deficient children with whatever training they are capable of taking and thus assuring them and itself of their earning power and their greater happiness.

We know that Caswell has had no training program, in the accepted sense of the word. We know that the committee which conducted our Caswell survey stressed the need for a training program and made it a primary recommendation .... What is happening to these children, whom we are not now training? The state has the responsiblity to take the lead and provide for those children who are institutionalized under standards clearly defined in our Caswell study commission report.

... Even though we might turn out only a handful of children in North Carolina annually, that would be that much in its inspiration, and in its human and material saving. The saving, mind you, is double; the trained working boy or girl becomes a wage earner and economic asset and his or her dismissal from a training school lifts that much cost off the state and makes additional physical facilities for our feebleminded that much less pressing.

Let us not forget these considerations and sacrifice what we have envisioned to haste, to shortsighted costliness or to the economic and social gains which will come of a long-range program.[36]

Kendall's letter received the unanimous endorsement of the Board; and in John Umstead's opinion, it marked the real beginning point of long-range planning for therapeutic treatment in the State's hospital system.[37] The natural inclination of the Board, according to Umstead, was to "get things done." Until Kendall began to drive home the need for careful long-range planning that would insure the coordinated development of building programs with sound, progressive therapy and administrative practices, there was little consideration given to the relationship between the building program and the program of medical administration and therapy. Kendall reminded the Board that the primary function of the State hospital system was to care for, treat, and educate mentally ill and defective people with one goal in mind - their return to an active, productive role in society. Throughout his tenure on the Board, H. W. Kendall insisted that this principle be the major concern and the justifying cause for all the Board's actions. Acceptance of Kendall's position, according to Umstead, was the major cause for the dramatic increase of activity within the hospitals.[38]

Umstead's contention is born out by a study of the rate of patient admissions and discharges during the period 1955-60. Chart I which compares the average daily population with patient admissions at all North Carolina mental hospitals between 1946 and 1960 indicates a striking change in the pattern beginning with 1955. Admissions, which up to 1955 were gradually increasing, more than doubled between 1955 and 1960 while the average daily population (average census) of the hospitals leveled off. In effect, there was a halt in the rise of the resident population. This pattern change was accomplished only by a discharge rate that paralleled the admissions rate. Chart II represents the ratio of discharges to patients in residence as another means of demonstrating the significant, almost sudden, increase in hospital activity. In 1955, there were 33 discharges for each 100 patients in residence. In 1960, there were 75 discharges for each 100 patients in residence. The rate more than doubled in five years. There were several factors that led to these dramatic results, the more important ones being the introduction and increased use of psychotropic drugs, improved diagnostic practices which allowed hospital personnel to classify and treat patients more effectively, and a major personnel change.

Dr. David Young resigned as General Superintendent of Mental Hygiene in August, 1955, to enter private practice. He was succeeded by Dr. James A. Murdoch,

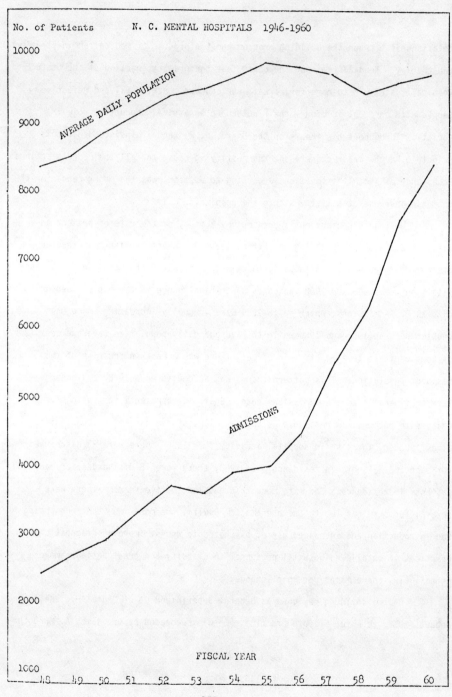

No. of Patients   N. C. MENTAL HOSPITALS   1946-1960

AVERAGE DAILY POPULATION

ADMISSIONS

FISCAL YEAR

10000

9000

8000

7000

6000

5000

4000

3000

2000

1000

48 49 50 51 52 53 54 55 56 57 58 59 60

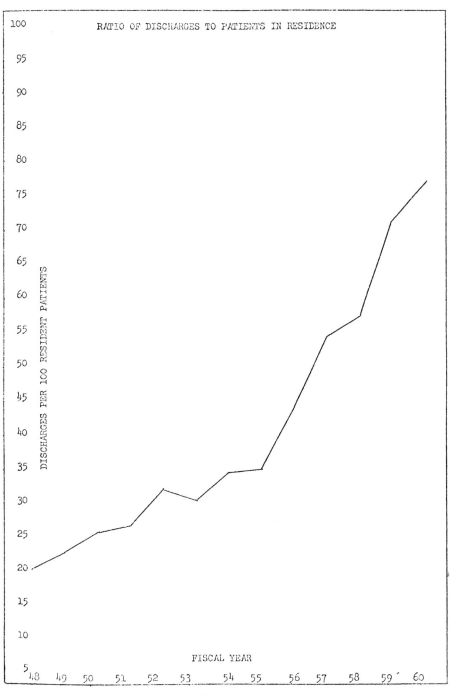

RATIO OF DISCHARGES TO PATIENTS IN RESIDENCE

FISCAL YEAR

former Superintendent at Butner State Hospital. Dr. Young's major concern had
been to lift the hospital system out of the deplorable condition in which he
found it and to establish a professional acceptance of the mental hospitals by
the people of the State.[39] The expansion and improvement of the physical plants,
the establishment of the cooperative training programs, and the significant salary
increases secured during his administration attest to the success of his efforts.
Whatever advances his successors managed to achieve must be seen as built upon
the improved institutional foundation he laid. Dr. Murdoch, on the other hand,
was more concerned with innovating administrative programs and treatment techniques that would improve patient care and therapy. Before being elected General
Superintendent, Murdoch ordered the removal of window bars from all but a few
doors; and a free movement system was established for the patients at Butner.

The free movement system opened patient areas and reduced the atmosphere
of jail confinement that prevailed in the heavily barred, tightly locked wards.
Under the new system patients were allowed to move more freely from ward to ward
and to the recreation and canteen areas within the hospital, thereby reducing the
need for routine regimentation. The plan also provided greater access to the
hospital grounds for those patients who did not require close supervision. An
advocate of voluntary admissions and intensive treatment, Dr. Murdoch insisted
that the latest admissions practices and therapeutic techniques be established in
all units of the hospital system. Patients committed to a state hospital by court
order were not allowed to leave the facility without permission. In 1955 there was
no voluntary admissions program to allow patients to enter the hospital on recommendation of their personal physician. The voluntary admissions proposed by
Murdoch and approved by the Legislature in 1959 provided that a patient freely
entering an institution is free to leave by filing an indication of intent. A
voluntary admission case could be retained by a hospital only if the medical staff

recommended such action, the patient's family approved, and a court order of commitment secured.[40] Under Murdoch, the emphasis was more away from bricks and mortar in favor of treatment. Just how extensive Dr. Murdoch's treatment methods were is indicated by the increased amount spent on drugs at Morganton State Hospital between 1955 and 1960. Total expenditures there for drugs was increased by 36.2%. The percentage of the total maintenance cost spent for drugs jumped from 1.42% to 4.40% during the same period.[41] Unfortunately, while Kendall's position was influential in undergirding the concept of long-range planning that allowed Murdoch and his staff to produce dramatic results in the area of patient administration and therapy, his stand in 1954 had little bearing on the immediate problems facing the Building Committee. Success in one area was again to be met with counter-productive action in another area.

The Hospitals Board was still under mounting pressure to produce immediate results. Governor Umstead's death on November 7, 1954, elevated Luther H. Hodges to the Executive Office. Hodges entered politics after retiring from a successful career as a textile executive. His first try for political office netted him the Lt. Governorship. Hodges owed no political debts, so he was free to insist upon a "hold the line" approach to the state's fiscal policies. The new Governor pressed for completion of the training schools within the limits set by the Legislature in 1953.[42] By 1956, however, building costs had increased by more than 15%, and the projects as originally planned could not be completed without an additional appropriation of three million dollars.[43] Governor Hodges insisted that the Board abide by its original commitment to the Legislature, and the building program was cut back to keep it in line with the original cost estimates.[44] The Goldsboro unit was completed and occupied in 1957, and the school at Butner opened the latter part of 1958. As a result of reducing the size of the two schools to meet the demands for economy, the Goldsboro unit was opened to accommodate 600 students, and Butner opened with a bed capacity of 825 in lieu of the planned 1,200 spaces for each unit.[45]

Governors Umstead and Hodges supported the building and personnel recommendations of the Hospitals Board, but their actions to force completion of
the training school building program "on schedule" was in direct contradiction
to the urgent pleas of H. W. Kendall that the program not be sacrificed to haste
or shortsighted costliness. The political necessity of demonstrating fiscal
responsibility to the people in every aspect of state government outweighed the
economic and social gains which were part of the board's long range program.
Neither Governor showed a willingness to explain to the people why there was a
need for additional funds or that the building program was being justifiably
delayed. John Umstead was willing to accept the Governor's demands to complete
the building within the established time span and fund allocation because he saw
at least a partial solution to the critical space problem in the abbreviated
building program. Besides, it did not pay to fight an issue that is clearly on
the side of the Governor and that would only serve to alienate forces that might
be needed for support at a later and more critical time. Umstead's political
philosophy was justified within two years when he was able to use his political
power and sense of timing to consummate advantage.

In 1958 the American Psychiatric Association conducted a survey of the
State Training Schools that included Caswell and Goldsboro. The report of the
Central Inspection Board noted that in December, 1958, Caswell Training School
had a resident student body of 2,220 while the rated capacity of the school was
1,807. The total unit was operating 22.9% beyond capacity. The new school at
Goldsboro, slightly more than a year old at the time of the A.P.A. inspection, had
an enrollment of 640 children against the rated capacity of 392. According to A.P.A.
standards, the Goldsboro Training School was 63.3% overcrowded.[46] The report
again called for a revision of the commitment laws, the establishment of a personnel department and an attendant training program at each school, a research

program, out-patient clinics, and a separate division of mental hygiene within the Hospitals Board of Control.[47] The fears expressed by Kendall were thus realized even before the new training schools were in complete operation.

There were, of course, some positive results from the general building program. More mentally defective children were being cared for, and by 1958 there was no longer an admissions waiting list at any of the State's mental hospitals.[48] The functional design of the new facilities was also a factor in the increased efficiency of patient care and treatment that permitted a greater turnover of patients. Again, buildings were not the sole concern during the years 1955-58. Governor Hodges aided the hospital program by supporting an Umstead request for another 10% salary increase for employees for the 1955-56 biennium.[49] Dr. Murdoch died in August, 1958, and Dr. Eugene A. Hargrove was named General Superintendent. Hargrove came to the State system from the Medical School at Chapel Hill where he had served for four years on the medical faculty in the division of psychiatry. Dr. Young had upgraded the physical facilities of the system while Dr. Murdoch had inaugurated new therapeutic techniques. Dr. Hargrove's training and ability would lead him to emphasize an improved administrative organization and an enlarged program of research aimed at improving the effectiveness of the therapy rendered to the mentally ill.

When he accepted the position offered by the Board, Hargrove told the members that the State must start a real research program, a step that would require men without too many time-consuming staff duties.[50] The new superintendent was convinced that research was the avenue to new ideas -- the real hope for a breakthrough in the care and treatment of the mentally ill. While research was being done elsewhere, Hargrove argued, "...it is no substitute for doing our own. When you do it at home your patients benefit and your staff and all others benefit too." Another major reason for Hargrove's emphasis on research was that it enabled the state system to attract able young doctors who otherwise would scorn service in a state institution. To insure the proper development of a research program, Hargrove urged the strengthening of the link between Chapel Hill's psychiatric unit and the State system. The expansion of the residence program initiated by Dr. Young not only provided better patient care; it was a source of "home grown" doctors who would be more willing to stay in the State after completing their formal education. Hargrove's goal of eventually having thirty residents annually in psychiatry was reached in 1965. Although Hargrove assumed the Superintendency late in 1958, he was able to propose several programs for legislative consideration in January, 1959.

The problem of interstate transfer of mental patients mentioned in the 1950 A.P.A. report was still unsolved. Hargrove recommended that North Carolina become a member of the Interstate Compact on Mental Health which was founded in 1955 by ten Northeastern states and drafted by the Council of State Governments.[52] The new superintendent also sought name changes for the State hospitals to relieve the stigma placed on them by their extant designations. In the general appropriations for the 1959-60 biennium, he requested funds to develop a research program within the State system.[53] Since the need for additional training facilities for the mentally retarded was still acute, Hargrove urged the Board to request funds for a new training school at Morganton to serve the western part of the state.[54] The Board concurred with the first three recommendations. After some discussion it was decided to postpone the school request until the 1961 legislative session.[55]

Backed by the Hospitals Board of Control and the full support of Governor Hodges, the Legislature adopted the Interstate Compact on Mental Health.[56] Under the terms of the act, North Carolina agreed to give treatment to any person found in the State who was in need of institutionalization by reason of mental illness or deficiency whether he was a citizen of North Carolina or not. The law permitted transfer of patients to an institution in another state when clinical determinations

156

indicated that such a transfer was in the best interest of the patient. Finally, interstate cooperative machinery was provided for after-care or supervision of patients on convalescent status of conditional release.

In response to Dr. Hargrove's proposals, the Legislature approved changes as follows: Morganton State Hospital became Broughton Hospital; The State Hospital at Raleigh was named the Dorothea Dix Hospital, thus giving offical sanction to a name that had been in use for years; Goldsboro State Hospital became Cherry Hospital; and Butner State Hospital was designated John Umstead Hospital. The Training School at Goldsboro was named in honor of Senator O'Berry, and the school at Butner was designated the Murdoch School.[57]

John Umstead was pleased with the legislative action, but he was not satisfied to let the chance go by to secure funds for the Morganton Training School. When the Appropriations Committee met to consider the Hospitals Board's budget request, he blew the session wide open by submitting a supplementary request of $11 million dollars for capital improvements at Kinston, Butner, and Goldsboro and a new school at Morganton. Umstead justified his action on the basis of having to get done what was necessary. "There are times," he declared, "when the people of the State need to be told what they must do, This is one such occasion."[58] The Appropriations Committee rejected the request out of hand, and Umstead upbraided its members for being shortsighted and "pinch penny." The Hospitals Board of Control was caught by surprise and was not prepared to fight the issue at the current session. Rejection of Umstead's request by the Appropriations Committee would have settled the issue but for the "slip of a tongue" and John Umstead's consummate political skill.

In the heated discussion that took place during debate of the Umstead proposal, news reporters sensed a major story. Umstead was a Hodges supporter, but would there be an open break between Umstead and the administration over this issue?

What was to be Umstead's next move? How did the Governor react to Umstead's demand? At a press conference, Governor Hodges attempted to smooth matters over with the comment that "Mr. Umstead is a great citizen who gets emotional on the problem." In answer to how he felt the matter would be settled, the Governor told reporters, "I imagine it will be considered with the rest of the laundry that goes to the wash."[59] Hodges meant to imply that the issue would be settled in conference, but John Umstead immediately seized upon the Governor's unfortunate choice of words. "How," he asked reporters, "could the Governor liken mentally deficient children to wash?"[60] Leading papers in the State carried the hospital issue on page one.[61] Pete McKnight, the reporter who covered the Morganton expose and was now editor of the Charlotte _Observer_, supported Umstead in a strongly worded editorial in which he demanded that the state delay "unnecessary administrative building" to provide the needed facilities for retarded children.[62] Henry Belk, political news commentator, termed the Governor's remark on emotionalism as "a great compliment" in a syndicated article carried by the state's major papers.[63] Umstead also noted that he was proud to be "emotional about human needs while not being emotional about "money, big business, or the big I."[64] Umstead had rocked the boat again, and this time it was the Governor who acted to bring it back to an even keel.

Legislative reaction to the news story and the exchange of words between Hodges and Umstead was just short of sensational. Mr. R. P. Richardson of the Hospitals Board was a personal friend of Hodges, and the Governor called him to see what he could do to quiet Umstead. Richardson came to Raleigh from his home in Reidsville to discuss the matter with the Governor's staff and Umstead. The latter was not to be budged. Throughout his years of service in the Legislature John Umstead had developed a strong network of friends, mutual obligations, and political favors that he knew he could count on at moments of critical need. Fearful that he might be in a position to hurt the administration's legislative program and to keep him quiet, Joe Eagles, legislative aid to Hodges, and members of the Appropriations Committee talked with Umstead and told him to list what he wanted.[65]   Umstead handed the Committee a copy of the original request of $11 million that included $4,500,000 for Morganton and all the requested improvements at the O'Berry, Caswell, and Murdoch Schools.

The Appropriations Committee approved the request the next day, and on the strength of Umstead's initial victory with the committee, the Legislature granted its approval when the 1959-60 Appropriations Bill was considered. At this same session the Legislature gave the Hospitals Board, and specifically Hargrove, the funds they sought for research purposes.[66] Thus, another of the major recommendations of the 1950 and 1953 A.P.A. studies was finally realized. Between 1959 and 1961 the Board supported Hargrove's recommendations for administrative reorganization and expansion as well as the research program he advocated. Plans were developed for construction of the Western Training School at Morganton. Riding the tide of success in the 1959 Legislative session, John Umstead moved to convince the Board that the time was right again for another major bond issue to effect needed improvements at the mental hospitals.[67]

Working with Governor-elect Terry Sanford, Hargrove and Umstead developed a proposal asking the 1961 Legislature for $16 million for capital improvements. Sanford was well aware of the needs of the state's mental hospitals. During the primary campaign he visited all of the state mental hospitals and training schools in an effort to familiarize himself with the problems of one of the state's major agencies. Sanford gave his full support to the proposal and agreed to include the request in an omnibus bond bill. With Umstead's urging the Legislature approved a bond issue referendum, and all parties involved were confident that the issue would receive public support in November when the referendum was to come to a vote.[68]

But the public rejected the entire referendum in what was considered a heavy voter turn out.[69] Shocked by the complete defeat of all sections of the money issue, the stunned supporters of the referendum raised a single question. Why did a bill that included such popular issues as education and mental health go down to defeat?

Umstead attributed the failure at the polls to overconfidence. There was no real effort, he felt, to organize a grass roots campaign to push the bill.[70] Others attributed defeat to the mistake of including in one money bill too many issues, some of which should not have been put to a vote of the people in the first place. Air-conditioning of the State College Library in Raleigh, for example, should have been provided for out of regular funds. Too many people apparently refused to countenance air-conditioned books when they did not enjoy such a luxury in their own homes. Still others may have viewed the wording of some issues as damaging. Improvements to the dairy barns at the State Hospitals were described as "cow lounges," and funds for swimming pools were requested with no mention of their need as therapy tools. These opinions, when combined, point to an ill-advised omnibus bill that was poorly written by the legislators and poorly managed on the local level. For all this criticism, it is doubtful that these reasons in themselves were cause for defeat. Voters rarely read the small print in a referendum issue, and many of the requests were normally popular with the voter. At least one significant answer to the question, "what happened?," is that given by some political observers who attributed failure to an "anti-Sanford" undercurrent in the State that grew out of the election campaign and the sales tax issue.

The Democratic Primary campaign between Terry Sanford and I. Beverly Lake had been waged over the race issue. While neither candidate openly accused his opponent of disloyalty to the white population of the state, the traditions of the party, or lack of personal integrity, the campaign did reach the level of the gutter through the mouthings of local fanatics on both sides. The conservative Lake forces went to defeat in a closely contested, hard-fought primary campaign. But they refused to give up or to support the Party Nominee in the General Election. Sanford won the gubernatorial race by one of the closest margins in the recent history of the State.[71] Following his nomination for Governor, Sanford led the delegation to the National Democratic Convention where he kicked over the traces by announcing his support of John F. Kennedy instead of Lyndon B. Johnson as it had been expected he would. The hostile undercurrent generated by Sanford's actions was further aggravated by the outspoken opposition of the State's housewives to the 3% State Sales Tax that Sanford successfully pushed through the Legislature.[72] The "Pennies for Sanford" signs posted on grocery store cash registers in some sections of the State served to keep the resentment alive through the summer months. When the referendum was approved by the Legislature, the generally conservative, grassroots politicians made little effort to organize the voters or to support the referendum. The money bill was defeated not as a result of vocal, organized opposition, but rather as a result of a deadly silence.[73] The failure of the bond issue was a bitter pill for John Umstead. He had suffered the first major defeat of his political career, and he was brutally reminded that the mental hospitals and training schools of the State are political in nature because their programs rest on the support of the Legislature and the whims of the voter. Furthermore, in this particular instance, "no one told the people what they needed to do."[74]

The experience of the Broughton, Cherry, Scott, Umstead, and Hodges administrations gradually revealed, after many painful steps of trial and error, that the necessary solution to the problem of state care of the mentally ill was a carefully structured partnership between the Executive and the Legislature, between the Hospitals Board and the representatives in the state-house, between the Hospitals Board and the state's medical schools, and between the hospital system and the people of the state. By virtue of imagination, dedication, and doubtless intuition, John Umstead sensed this and helped forge such a partnership. The underlying principle of the four-way relationship was fully recognized by Umstead, Commissioner Hargrove, and Governor Terry Sanford with the defeat of the 1961 Bond Referendum.[75]

Under John Umstead's leadership, there evolved in the state hospital system a subtle recognition of the necessity for a close working tie with the Legislature and the Executive Office in order to be assured of the support necessary for developing the other two areas that were vital to the maintenance of a progressive, treatment-oriented hospital system. These other areas were a sound, well-organized administrative structure to provide a sense of direction as well as continuity to the complex hospital system and a productive research and training program to serve as the foundation for development of new treatment programs and techniques. The general social attitude toward mental illness was most certainly an influential factor in the operation of the hospitals, and the Hospitals Board of Control under Umstead's and Hargrove's leadership accepted the responsibility of educating the people of the State in such a manner that they would not only recognize the problems of the mentally ill, but also accept the responsibility of supporting the State in its effort to alleviate them. In this venture, Governor Terry Sanford willingly joined with Umstead and Hargrove.

Two actions early in Sanford's administration indicate his genuine concern and appreciation for the remarkable intricate administrative problems confronting Hargrove and his staff. In his first year of office, Sanford was invited to be a participant in a panel discussion on the problems of mental health at the National Governors' Conference.[76] As Sanford told the Hospitals Board later, the invitation to participate in the panel discussion was an honor to the State because normally first-year Governors are not placed on panel groups.[77] More important, his participation gave the Governor a rare opportunity to become acquainted with the complex issues in mental health and to see how other states were handling these problems. Sanford thus came to his first meeting with the Board with an already awakened appreciation of the problems facing his own State agency. To reduce the amount of paper work in his own office and no doubt as a show of confidence in the Commissioner and his organization, Sanford notified Hargrove in February, 1961, that henceforth all letters of complaint or inquiry relating to the hospitals would be forwarded directly to the central office. While Sanford used the heavy load of paper work as the primary reason for his action, he made it clear that he would not be one to interfere in Hargrove's work when he noted that to handle such matters out of the Governor's Office

> might be an implication that the Governor is taking a direct hand in handling of the matter, which of course is a false impression. While the Governor's Office is available to every citizen, there should be no encouragement that this office is a shortcut, or a source of influence, for the orderly administration of your program.[78]

Sanford demonstrated his further interest in the area of mental health by his active support of Hargrove's recommendation for a reorganization of the administrative structure of the Hospitals Board of Control. The purpose of reorganizing the Hospitals Board was to put all phases of the care and treatment of mentally ill and defective people under one authority. At the request of the Governor, Hargrove and his staff worked with the Institute of Government at the University of North Carolina, Chapel Hill, in drawing up a plan for submission to the 1963 Legislature.

Sanford's actions demonstrated his understanding of the political relationship between his office, the Legislature, and the professional administration of the mental hospital system. His support of administrative reorganization and research development coordinated with the University of North Carolina Medical School reflected his appreciation of and support for,the fourth vital element in a successful state-wide mental health program.

With the recognition of the basic elements required to establish and maintain a progressive mental health program firmly established, the task now seems to be one of implementing the research developments in the treatment and cure of mental disease, and the continuing education of the general public on the problems of mental illness and retardation. Experience has shown that such a program will require a professional staff that is capable of developing sound administrative practices, that is willing to innovate, and that can maintain the subtle political and social orientation to guarantee continued statewide support of the system.

Chapter VIII

CONCLUSION

The institutionalization by the State of North Carolina of public concern, care, and treatment of the mentally ill of the State is a history shaped
by the medical, social, and administrative problems inherent in the mental hospital program itself. Overriding these problems, however, is perhaps the more
subtle and certainly the more powerful action upon the system of political
forces in the state. The action of social, administrative, and political
forces is evident in every stage of the historical development of the North
Carolina mental hospital movement. Within each period, and in the transition
between periods, the approach to mental illness by the public, the professional
administrator, or the elected officials of the state has determined the suc-
cesses and failures of the mental hospital program. The reaction of these
groups, be it indifference, undue meddling, intrigue, manipulation, genuine
concern, fiscal caution, protective defensiveness, or open frankness, directly
influenced the system of mental institutions. Within this context, this survey
set out to explore the changing response to the problems of North Carolina's
mental hospitals. Certain questions have been raised. How effective is the
technique of exposé in establishing social reform? What problems developed
within the institutions themselves and within the political structure of the
state that determined the programs of patient care and treatment? What is the
relationship between an effective and progressive mental hospital system and
the social, political, and administrative reaction to the problems of mental

illness? A comparison of current answers with those that evolved between 1848 and 1945 shows how far the state of North Carolina has progressed in little more than a hundred years.

The first hundred years of institutionalized care of the insane in North Carolina is best characterized as a period of public indifference and meager State appropriations which resulted in inadequate facilities, low salaries, insufficient and poorly trained staff, undermanned and overworked professional personnel, and the political structuring of the hospital system that fostered patronage and direct interference. The traditional attitude toward the mentally ill in North Carolina, "out of sight - out of mind," was apparent throughout virtually all of the period 1848-1945. The facts that Dorothea Dix Hospital could be authorized one day in 1848 by an eighty vote majority in the House of Commons and escape a recall motion by only two votes the next day, that the entire town of Morganton turned out in a circus atmosphere to see the insane marched double file from the train station to the new hospital in 1883, or that in 1948 county officials could justify holding patients in jail on the grounds that when a person is out of his mind 'it doesn't make any difference where he is, so why not in jail?' are indicative of the public attitude and political atmosphere that fostered and perpetuated the administrative practice of custodial care and an extemporizing policy of "least cost - least effort."

Appropriations for maintenance of patients from 1848 to 1945 clearly indicate that what appears to be substantial increases in allotments to the hospitals still afforded only bare subsistence. When pro-rated with the hospital population, apparent increases were, in many instances, marked decreases. The highest daily maintenance per patient prior to 1945 was sixty-five cents in 1920. The lowest was thirty-five cents in 1934. Per capita costs during this period were looked upon as a gauge of the economic efficiency of an institution. Superintendents were constantly urged to keep the per capita cost as low as possible and were often congratulated when the figure was lowered despite resultant decreases in staff and postponement of needed repairs. Dr. S. J. Thompson attacked this ludicrous practice in A Study of Mental Health in North Carolina in 1937. His comment that there is a point beyond which a smaller per capita cost is a discredit rather than an honor proved prophetic in 1942 when conditions at Morganton were elucidated by the James P. Jimison expose and the investigation of the Board of Inquiry appointed by Governor Broughton.

Coupled with chronically low maintenance support were the problems of overcrowding and of insufficient staff. Overcrowding was an accepted practice from the beginning because of efforts to hospitalize emergency cases that could no longer be cared for at home or in county jails. Furthermore, during the first fifty years of the hospital system, administrators were convinced that early hospitalization and treatment would afford a rapid cure for a majority of patients. Between 1850 and 1945, all hospitals experienced a patient census of six to twenty per cent beyond capacity as measured by actual bed space. From the opening of the hospitals through 1945, no hospital staff reached the level authorized by the Legislature. Turnover in medical staff, nurses, and attendants was extremely high. Of the twelve physicians employed at Morganton from 1916 to 1936, seven stayed for a period of less than four years. In 1942, the patient load per doctor at Morganton was 425 whereas the national average was 248 and the American Psychiatric Association recommended ratio, 150. The situation was comparable at Dix and Goldsboro. At times ratio studies can be misleading. Nevertheless, as the Board of Inquiry noted in 1942, at the level of staffing then prevailing in North Carolina it was humanly impossible for patients to obtain the proper care and treatment.

167

Despite overcrowding and inadequate personnel, pressure mounted in the State to secure admission for mental patients still in the local communities. In 1900, there were 400 patients in the area served by Dix and 500 in the area served by Morganton who could not be admitted. Approximately five per cent of these patients were lodged in jails. The situation remained relatively constant from 1900 to 1945 in spite of building and expansion programs completed during this period. The opening of facilities for epileptics in 1910 and the construction of housing for inebriates in 1922, and a building for the criminally insane in 1925, all at Dix, and the construction of special buildings for epileptics and tubercular patients in 1909 at Goldsboro, indicated a progressive approach to certain aspects of treatment. Even these accomplishments, however, were considered marginal. Overcrowding reached such proportions by 1903 that the progressive program of moral therapy developed by Dr. Patrick Murphy was abandoned for the practice of custodial care of inmates. The non-cure, custodial care philosophy of the North Carolina state mental hospitals between 1900 and 1945 was inefficient, medically worthless, and expensive. Even though the unit cost per patient was continually being reduced to the satisfaction of public officials, the low discharge rate and rising patient load forced the hospital officials to request more and more funds for buildings to house patients. In a system dependent directly on the Legislature for capital and operational funds, the superintendents found it expedient to acquiesce to the wishes of individual legislators, the Governor, and other state politicians who sought special admission of patients for friends. This practice led to unchecked and unavoidable political patronage. The pressure for admission and the need for more funds were but two of several elements that fostered unhealthy political and administrative practices in the hospitals.

Each hospital in the State was operated as a separate entity under the immediate control of a board of directors appointed by the Governor. These boards were accountable to the State Commissioner of Charities and Public Welfare. The individual boards, however, were responsible for the operation of the hospital: the hiring of the professional staff members including the superintendent, the recommendation of budgetary needs, the inspection of the hospital wards, records, and general plant. Periodic inspections were made by the Commissioner of Public Welfare, and annual reports from each hospital were filed with him. Complaints from patients, relatives, and doctors sent to the Governor or Commissioner were forwarded to the board of the particular hospital with a request for an investigation. An average of thirty to forty such letters were received and processed in this manner annually. Every investigation required special time of the superintendent and his staff. Almost without exception, the investigations were poorly conducted and drew the conclusion that allegations against the hospitals were incorrect or unfounded. In point of fact, to protect the integrity of the hospitals and the politically motivated trustees, the hospital staff developed a defensive attitude that obscured true conditions. The basis for such action was the belief that the hospitals were doing their best to justify requests for increased funds under existing circumstances and that a good front had to be presented to the Legislature.

The requirement that each institution argue its financial needs before the Advisory Budget Commission prior to the biennial meeting of the Legislature caused competition among the hospitals for funds. The legislator with the strongest political support secured the largest appropriation for his hospital. In actual practice, each hospital was run by a board that directed the everyday working routine of the institution in addition to controlling general policy and the purse strings. The chairman of the board wielded almost unlimited control over his domain. It was common knowledge that during the period from 1900 to 1945 the board chairman often acted as the admitting officer of the hospital, directing by letters to the superintendent persons to be admitted and, in many cases, those to be discharged. The administrative and political problems inherent in this system resulted in an untenable situation. Not until 1945, however, was such powerful political entrenchment effectively attacked.

The period 1848-1945 was marked by an alternating attitude in the Legislature toward the hospitals movement in North Carolina. This period was remarkable more for the durability of a few dedicated doctors and laymen who fought a valiant holding action against the erosions of politics and a neglectful society than for its progressive achievements. This was the period when the hospitals were partisan political institutions, though everyone, including the politicians, denied the fact. Not until the people of the State were aroused to the need for vigorous action and constant support, first through the 1941 exposé of Tom P. Jimison in the _Charlotte_ _News_ and later by the constructive political leadership of John Umstead and the professional administrative staff he recruited, did the movement become more than a mere custodial program for the mentally ill citizens of North Carolina.

The Jimison exposé in 1941 and the investigation of its charges prompted Governor Broughton to secure administrative reorganization of the state hospital system in favor of a unified Hospitals Board of Control in 1943. Although a structure for reform emerged, because the revised administrative structure incorporated so many of the practices of the past, the new system failed to solve the problems of legislative indifference, political intrusion, and administrative inefficiency. The routines of the past continued under the new form until 1945 when the threat of another investigation evoked the action of a politically astute, socially-minded legislator.

170

John Umstead recognized that the political nature of the state system needed to be organized on a non-partisan basis before imaginative leadership could develop a progressive therapeutic program to cure patients. Partly by design and political sagacity, partly by agonizing trial and error, the professional and political leaders in the hospital system have replaced their defensive protectionist attitude with an open, frank, and unified presentation of hospital affairs. An awareness of the past was encouraged by the new generation of administrators to avoid repeating old mistakes and forgotten methods. This is not to say that political considerations are ignored or downgraded. Indeed, the realization of the full meaning of political necessity provided a new direction to the efforts of the Hospitals Board of Control following its reorganization in 1945.

Between 1945 and 1960, under John Umstead's leadership, the Board attempted to face the reality of its problems. The two-fold needs to expand and improve facilities and to develop staff and therapeutic programs were equally pressing. Experience gradually revealed that the necessary solution to these problems was a carefully structured partnership between the Executive and the Legislature, between the Hospitals Board of Control and the state's medical schools, and between the hospital system and the people of the state. Only such a partnership could assure the support needed for a progressive, treatment-oriented hospital system. By dedication, imagination, and political sagacity, John Umstead helped to forge such a partnership.

During Umstead's tenure on the Hospitals Board, under the Cherry and Scott administrations, and during the short term of Governor William B. Umstead, emphasis was on physical improvements and expansion. This approach was not de-emphasized under Governors Hodges and Sanford, but greater effort was made to upgrade staff and to develop therapeutic programs. During this period, too,

expansion and renovation of old units, the acquisition of new facilities at
Camp Butner provided space to eliminate hospital waiting lists in the State.
A well-organized administrative structure to provide a sense of direction as
well as continuity to the complex hospital system and a productive research and
training program to serve as the foundation for development of new treatment
programs and techniques were developed. The use of psychotropic drugs, the
employment of specially trained doctors and nurses, and hospital-wide improvement in methods of treating patients has kept hospital population stable.
While the admissions rate increased three-fold during the period 1945-1960,
the discharge rate increased three and one-half times. A further sign of the
new approach to treatment is seen in the per capita cost index and the specific
expenditures for drugs. Between 1945 and 1960, per capita daily maintenance
costs rose 31%. The average expenditure for patient treatment rose from 1.46%
to 4.40% of total daily maintenance.

Despite the remarkable improvement in financial support granted by the
Legislature, the hospital system continued to suffer from chronic understaffing
in 1960. At the same time, there was a critical need to improve the facilities
of Cherry Hospital at Goldsboro. Nevertheless, in the face of these continuing
problems, the period 1945-1960 can be characterized as a period of general re-
newal of public concern, political and administrative reorientation, and innovation in which the State began to make a genuine effort to meet its responsibilities to its mentally ill citizens.

Future progress in the care and treatment of the mentally ill in North
Carolina will depend on the ability of professional and political leadership to
keep history alive in order to avoid repetition of mistakes. If those concerned
with mental health are to avoid the failures of the past, they must at the very
least remain aware of the relationship of the parts to the whole; which is to

172

say, they must comprehend the complex interplay in the roles of the Governor, the Commissioner, the Legislature, and the medical centers. And finally, if history is to have any meaning, future leaders must remain aware of the continual necessity to sell the concept of this relationship to the ever-changing political community. They must breed continuity of support and effective replacements on the political level and within the administrative structure of the hospital system itself. The North Carolina mental hospital system today, as in the years 1848-1945, is political. The difference now as opposed to the early period is that this fact is recognized and used with candor to control attempts at interference and to promote a positive approach to the many problems existing in the hospitals and in the State.

APPENDIXES

APPENDIX A

By-Laws, North Carolina State

Hospital for the Insane at

Raleigh, North Carolina

1898

Board of Directors

The Annual Meeting of the Directors shall be held on the First Wednes-
day in December; but all other meetings may be held at such stated times as
shall be agreed upon.

In the absence of the President, the senior Director shall preside at
the meetings; and when the Clerk is absent, a Clerk pro tempore shall be appointed.

All questions brought forward for the consideration of the Board shall
be submitted in writing, and decided by a majority of the members present.

The Executive Committee shall consist of three members, two of whom
shall reside in the city of Raleigh, and be fully competent to transact business.

They shall be, in the absence of the Board of Directors, the advising
body with whom the Superintendent of the Asylum shall confer in regard to the
business of the Institution; and they shall be clothed with full powers to do
all acts which may be necessary for the proper conduct and management of the
Institution, except in such cases as the law requires the action of a full
Board, or where prevented by a special order of the Board; and they shall meet
monthly at the Asylum, or such place in the city of Raleigh as may be agreed

upon, for the transaction of all business within the scope of their duties. On these occasions, it shall be their special duty to examine the books of the Treasurer, and to examine and audit the accounts of the Steward for the expenditures of the preceding month.

And shall report in writing at the regular Annual Meetings of the Board upon the general condition of the Asylum, and recommend such modifications of existing regulations as they may deem expedient, and that they also report the amount of the outstanding indebtedness of the Institution.

Duties of Superintendent

The Superintendent being required by law to reside in or near the Asylum buildings, and to devote his whole time to its welfare, becomes the chief executive officer under the Directors of the establishment, from whom all persons employed by him, with the approval of the Directors, will receive their instructions; while it shall be his duty to see that all the officers and employees of the Institution are energetic, industrious, punctual, exact, and in all respects faithful in the performance of their several duties as prescribed in these By-Laws.

He shall visit all the patients frequently and learn their condition, and shall visit those requiring it as often as necessary, and shall direct such medical, moral, and physical treatment as in his judgment will be conducive to their comfort and amelioration, or best adapted to their relief.

He shall keep a record of the name, age and residence of each patient, and the supposed cause of his insanity, and the length of time he has been afflicted; also of the time when received and removed, whether cured or relieved, whether eloped or dead, and, in case of death, of what he died, and shall conduct the correspondence of the Institution.

At each monthly meeting of the Executive Committee, he shall exhibit all the records of the Institution, its general state, the names of persons received or removed, with such remarks and suggestions as he may deem useful; and at the annual meeting, furnish a tabular view of the condition of the Institution for the year, deduced from the records.

It shall be his duty to give to all persons employed in the Asylum such instructions as are best adapted to carry into effect all the rules and regulations of this Institution; and he shall take care to see that these rules and regulations are strictly and faithfully observed and executed.

Subject to the instructions of the Board of Directors, and, in their absence, of the Executive Committee, he shall determine what attendants and other assistants are necessary, and with them arrange their rate of wages. When wishing to be absent from his duties for more than one day, he shall report the same to the Board of Directors or the Executive Committee.

No money shall be spent upon the premises, except for ordinary repairs and current expenses, nor for anything connected with the Asylum, unless so directed by the Board, or approved by the Executive Committee.

Assistant Physician

He shall assist the Superintendent in the medical, moral and physical treatment of the patients, keep a record of cases under treatment, and perform any other duty connected with the medical department, required by the Superintendent.

He shall have charge of the medical office, see that all medicines are properly prepared and put up, and shall report the same to the Superintendent.

He shall receive company and conduct them through the Asylum, in the absence or by the request of the Superintendent.

He is required to spend his time during the day, and in the night when necessary, in the Asylum, and in his intercourse with the inmates will exert what moral influence he can, and endeavor by every proper and lawful means to further the views and wishes of the Superintendent. He shall carefully study the character and pecularities of the patients, direct their exercises and amusements, and report to the Superintendent any neglect of duty or misconduct that may come under his notice. He shall discharge the duties of the Superintendent in his absence, and be clothed with his authority.

Steward, Matron, and Engineer

The Steward, Matron, and Engineer, shall, each under the direction of the Superintendent, make such purchases as may be necessary for their respective departments, and before making such purchases shall make out a requisition to be approved by the Superintendent, and they shall each be responsible for the due care and proper use of the property in their respective departments.

Steward--His Duties

He shall keep methodical and accurate accounts of all purchases, and of all moneys expended by him, as well on account of the patients as for the Institution.

He shall exhibit his vouchers, books and accounts to the Executive Committee at their monthly meetings, and shall furnish an abstract of the same to the Treasurer of the Asylum at the end of each month.

He shall constantly observe the condition of all persons employed in subordinate positions, see they do their duty, and report to the Superintendent any instance of neglect or misconduct that he may observe, or of which he may be informed.

Under the direction of the Superintendent, he shall attend to the business of the farm, stock, garden, grounds, fences and out-buildings, and see that they are always kept in order.

He shall assist in maintaining the police of the establishment; shall see to the opening and closing of the house, and that the attendants and servants rise and commence their business at the ringing of the bell, and retire in proper season at night; that the bell is rung at proper hours; that the warmth, cleanliness and ventilation of the house is attended to.

He shall, when directed by the Superintendent, receive visitors, give them all suitable information, and accompany them to such parts of the buildings as are open for examination.

It shall be the duty of the Steward to be in the presence of the male patients as much as possible, to see that they are kindly treated, that their clothes are taken care of, that their food is properly served and distributed, and that they take the same in a proper manner; that the rooms, passages and other apartments under his care are kept clean and in good order, and properly warmed and ventilated; and that the male attendants observe his orders and directions and in all respects do their duty.

It shall be his duty to devote his whole time to the Institution; to assist the Superintendent as Secretary, when desired so to do; to preserve order in the house and faithfulness amongst the assistants and to see that all the regulations here adopted shall be fully put in practice.

Matron

It shall be the duty of the Matron to look carefully to the female patients, to be with them as much as possible, to direct the nurses in their duty, to see that the patients are kindly treated, that their food is properly served and distributed, that their apartments are kept clean and in order, properly warmed and ventilated, and that the female attendants do their duty in all respects. She must also superintend the kitchen, the cooking, the washing and ironing, and take care of the clothes and bedding, and see that they are always clean and in order; keep a record of the clothing of patients when they enter and during their continuance in the Asylum, and watchfully superintend the bathing of the female patients.

Indeed, she must look into every department frequently and see to the good order of the whole house--direct the employment and amusement of the female patients, and spend as much time with them as her other duties will allow; and thus, by devoting her whole time to the Institution, spare no effort to promote the comfort and recovery of the patients, and the general welfare of the Asylum.

Supervisor

It shall be the duty of the Supervisor or chief attendant to see that the moral treatment of patients, and the conduct of the attendants conform in all respect to these by-laws and the instructions of the Superintendent and Assistant Physician.

He shall always be present when food or medicine is administered coercively; and he shall invariably be present when restraint is applied, and when patients take their baths. He shall keep a faithful list or record of the patients' clothes, and also frequently pass through the different wards, aiding and encouraging the attendants in their efforts to amuse or employ the patients; and in every way indeed endeavor to promote the good order and discipline of the Asylum, by seeing that the Superintendent's or Assistant Physician's instructions in reference to occupation and exercise are faithfully and cautiously fulfilled, and by guarding against disturbances, escapes, suicides, exposure, etc. He shall also wait upon visitors, when called on for that purpose, and perform any other service required of him.

Attendants

The Attendants shall treat the patients with uniform attention and respect--greet them with friendly salutations, and exhibit such other marks of kindness and good will, as evince interest and sympathy. They shall speak in a mild, persuasive tone of voice, and never address a patient coarsely, or by a nick-name.

On arising in the morning, every Attendant shall see that each patient confided to his or her care is washed, hair combed, and that he or she is decently dressed for the day. Attention shall be given to the person and dress of each patient during the day as often as required by disorder or any want of cleanliness.

One Attendant must always be with the patients, and must not leave them under any circumstances, but when relieved by another.

An Attendant must always be present at the meals--carve the food, and distribute it to such as are not competent to do it for themselves, and to see that each one has his or her proper supply, and that they take it in a proper manner.

Care shall be taken that no patient carries away a knife, fork, or other article from the table, and the knives and forks shall be counted after each meal, to prevent any being lost.

No Attendant shall ever apply any restraining apparatus to a patient except by order of the Superintendent, or of a resident officer under his direction.

The patients are to be soothed and calmed when irritated, encouraged and cheered when melancholy and depressed. They shall never be pushed, collared, nor rudely handled.

When Attendants receive insulting and abusive language, they must keep cool, and forbear to recriminate or threaten. Violent hands shall never be laid upon patients under any provocation; and a blow shall never be returned, unless in the clearest case of necessary self-defense. Sufficient force to prevent injury to themselves or others shall always be applied gently. Authority must be maintained by kindness of manner and dignity of deportment.

Attendants shall never place in the hands of patients, or leave where they can obtain, any razor, knife, rope, cord, medicine, or any dangerous weapon or article. Neither shall they deliver any letter or writing to or from a patient, without permission of the Superintendent--nor retain in their possession any writing of a patient.

Attendants must never leave the Institution without permission from an officer, and always return by nine o'clock at night, unless leave be expressly given to stay out longer. When abroad, the conduct and conversation of patients must not be reported. No company must be admitted into the apartments occupied by the patients, at any time, except by express permission of the Physician. But all other parts of the Asylum may be exhibited by the Steward or Matron, and it is expected that great respect will be shown to strangers who visit the Institution.

It shall be the duty of the Attendants to keep the patients' rooms and halls perfectly clean and well ventilated; to have the beds aired and sunned, and made in proper season; all the doors of rooms to be kept closed when the patients are in bed.

The Attendants must never give up the key of the passages, nor let any one into the halls without permission; and no male Attendant shall enter a female apartment without permission of an officer.

Every patient must be in the charge of some responsible individual at all times, unless permitted to be at large by the Physician.

No patient shall be permitted to go out of the ward in which his apartment is situated without the consent of an officer, and no new patient without the order of the Physician.

No Attendant shall discontinue service of the Asylum without giving to the Superintendent or Steward at least fifteen days' notice.

It is required that all persons who have the duty to perform in the Asylum will rise at the ringing of the morning bell.

Watchman

The duties of the Watchman are of a most responsible and important character. He should be careful, therefore, to keep up the strictest vigilance during the night, never allowing himself to sleep while on duty, or to fail in any particular to discharge his trust with fidelity.

He must commence his rounds at half-past nine o'clock at night, having first rung the Asylum bell to announce the hour for closing the Institution for the night; and after that time no employee must be out without the express permission of the Superintendent.

It shall be his duty to pass around the buildings at least every hour in the night, and have a particular care over the apartments occupied by the female patients, besides strictly observing such special directions for the night as shall be given him by the Superintendent or other superior officer.

He shall notice all unusual sounds in the patients' rooms, and give immediate information of the same to the proper attendant.

He shall report to the Superintendent all irregularities or violations of the rules of the Institution which may come under his notice, and enter in his watch-book any remarks he may have to make upon the occurrences of the night.

Should he discover fire in any part of the Asylum or out-buildings, he shall immediately give notice first to an officer, and then to the Attendants, but never raise a general alarm.

At daylight of each day he shall ring the Asylum bell again, when his duties will cease until the next night.

APPENDIX B

Resident Population

of

North Carolina Schools

for

the Mentally Retarded

1948 - 1962

Hospitals Board of Control

1943 - 1960

185

Fiscal Year 1948 - 1949

	*Murdoch	**O'Berry	Caswell	Total
Children In Institution	199		721	920
First Admissions	48		201	249
Readmissions	0		2	2
Total Admissions	48		203	251
Discharges	1		15	16
Deaths	1		17	18
Total Separations	2		32	34

* 12 Months estimated

** Not available

Caswell reported 140 transfers to Murdoch this year.

Fiscal Year 1949 - 1950

	**Murdoch	*O'Berry	Caswell	Total
Children In Institution	278		813	1091
First Admissions	70		170	240
Readmissions	0		7	7
Total Admissions	70		177	247
Discharges	1		26	27
Deaths	0		17	17
Total Separations	1		43	44

* Not available

** Caswell reported 71 transfers to Murdoch this year.

Fiscal Year 1950 - 1951

	*Murdoch	**O'Berry	Caswell	Total
Children In Institution	299		913	1212
First Admissions	0		138	138
Readmissions	0		5	5
Total Admissions	0		143	143
Discharges	3		24	27
Deaths	1		15	16
Total Separations	4		39	43

*   11 Months reported

** Not available

Fiscal Year 1951 - 1952

	**Murdoch	*O'Berry	Caswell	Total
Children In Institution	296		1038	1334
First Admissions	0		250	250
Readmissions	0		3	3
Total Admissions	0		253	253
Discharges	3		19	22
Deaths	2		17	19
Total Separations	5		36	41

* Not available

** Caswell reported 10 transfers to Murdoch this year.

Fiscal Year 1952 - 1953

	*Murdoch	**O'Berry	Caswell	Total
Children In Institution	293		1232	1525
First Admissions	2		298	300
Readmissions	0		3	3
Total Admissions	2		301	303
Discharges	2		45	47
Deaths	4		22	26
Total Separations	6		67	73

* Caswell reported 3 transfers to Murdoch this year.

** Not available

Fiscal Year 1953 - 1954

	Murdoch	*O'Berry	Caswell	Total
Children In Institution	292		1439	1731
First Admissions	0		256	256
Readmissions	0		7	7
Total Admissions	0		263	263
Discharges	1		78	79
Deaths	2		19	21
Total Separations	3		97	100

* Not available

Fiscal Year 1954 - 1955

	Murdoch	*O'Berry	Caswell	Total
Children In Institution	299		1593	1892
First Admissions	2		243	245
Readmissions	0		3	3
Total Admissions	2		246	248
Discharges	7		39	46
Deaths	2		2	4
Total Separations	9		41	50

* Not available

Fiscal Year 1955 - 1956

	*Murdoch	**O'Berry	Caswell	Total
Children In Institution	304		1738	2042
First Admissions	0		145	145
Readmissions	0		12	12
Total Admissions	0		157	157
Discharges	1		78	79
Deaths	1		8	9
Total Separations	2		86	88

* 12 months estimated

** Not available

Fiscal Year 1956 - 1957

	Murdoch	*O'Berry	Caswell	Total
Children In Institution	305		1785	2089
First Admissions	8		146	154
Readmissions	0		3	3
Total Admissions	8		149	157
Discharges	5		43	48
Deaths	2		14	16
Total Separations	7		57	64

* Not available

194

Fiscal Year 1957 - 1958

	*Murdoch	O'Berry	Caswell	Total
Children In Institution	312	195	1837	2344
First Admissions	75	114	96	285
Readmissions	0	1	7	8
Total Admissions	75	115	103	293
Discharges	5	14	48	67
Deaths	7	4	15	26
Total Separations	12	18	63	93

* 12 months estimated

Fiscal Year 1958 - 1959

	Murdoch	O'Berry	Caswell	Total
Children In Institution	472	460	1896	2728
First Admissions	192	354	101	647
Readmissions	0	0	9	9
Total Admissions	192	354	110	656
Discharges	17	8	33	58
Deaths	7	6	13	26
Total Separations	24	14	46	84

Fiscal Year 1959 - 1960

	Murdoch	O'Berry	Caswell	Total
Children In Instituion	715	588	1845	3148
First Admissions	470	49	127	646
Readmissions	0	1	2	3
Total Admissions	470	50	129	649
Discharges	50	34	36	120
Deaths	18	9	32	59
Total Separations	68	43	68	179

Fiscal Year 1960 - 1961

	Murdoch	O'Berry	Caswell	Total
Children In Institution	1053	641	1826	3520
First Admissions	151	134	133	418
Readmissions	0	2	2	4
Total Admissions	151	136	135	422
Discharges	29	5	35	69
Deaths	7	7	23	37
Total Separations	36	12	58	106

Fiscal Year 1961 - 1962

	Murdoch	O'Berry	Caswell	Total
Children In Institution	1267	709	1825	3801
First Admissions	417	65	161	643
Readmissions	0	10	2	12
Total Admissions	417	75	163	655
Discharges	96	28	52	176
Deaths	26	9	24	59
Total Separations	122	37	76	235

Hospitals Board of Control Membership 1943-1960

C. W. Spruill
Dr. Charles Poindexter
Harry L. Riddle
Dr. Yates Palmer
Mrs. Rivers Johnson
Dr. H. M. Baker
Dr. Roscoe McMillan
J. H. Beall
W. A. Dees
Dr. Lois Stanford
Dr. Wingate Johnson
L. L. Oettinger
J. Dwight Barbour
Mrs. Andrew Blair
W. G. Clark
N. E. Edgerton
Dr. R. H. Crawford
S. N. Clark
Dr. Carl V. Reynolds
B. G. Hardison
R. A. Whitaker
Dr. H. O. Lineberger
Thomas O'Berry
J. F. Strickland
W. P. Kemp
I. D. Thorp
Dr. Dewar W. Bridger
R. V. Liles

T. C. Byrum
R. P. Richardson
John M. Umstead
J. L. Dawkins
Ryan McBride
Dr. T. V. Goode
Francis A. Whiteside
Baxter L. Jones
Dr. J. W. R. Norton
Mrs. Reba Gavin
H. W. Kendall
Dr. W. H. Kibler
John S. Ruggles
Frank M. Kilpatrick
Kelly E. Bennett
Mrs. E. H. Lasater
Warren R. Williams
Bedford W. Black
John T. Rodgers
D. W. Royster
J. Melville Broughton, Jr.
N. C. Green
Mrs. E. F. McCollough
George R. Uzzell
W. Lumsford Crew
William A. McFarland
Mrs. W. Kerr Scott

APPENDIX C

Statistical Charts and Tables
North Carolina Mental Hospitals
1947 - 1961

JULY-DECEMBER 1960 ADMISSIONS BY DIAGNOSIS

```
1500 ─

1400 ─
                PSYCHOTIC
1300 ─          DISORDERS
                ─────────

1200 ─

1100 ─

1000 ─

 900 ─
                                                                    ALL OTHERS
 800 ─                                                              ─────────

 700 ─

 600 ─

 500 ─
                        ALCOHOLISM      SENIUM      PSYCHONEUROSIS
 400 ─                  ─────────    ─────────       ─────────

 300 ─

 200 ─

 100 ─

   0 ─   ─────────  ─────────  ─────────  ─────────  ─────────
```

FIRST ADMISSIONS DOROTHEA DIX HOSPITAL

(Average of Fiscal 1954 and 1955
Compared with 1959 and 1960)

600			
500			⌐‾‾‾⌐ INCREASE └___┘
400			
300			
200			
100			
50			
0			

54-55 59-60   54-55 59-60   54-55 59-60   54-55 59-60

Psychotic
Disorders   Alcoholism   Senium   Psychoneurosis

FIRST ADMISSIONS - BROUGHTON HOSPITAL

Comparing 1940 and 1960

(Percentages)

100	
90	Psychoneurosis ⟶
80	Senium
75	
70	
65	
60	
55	
50	
45	Psychotic Disorders
40	
35	
30	
25	
20	
15	All Others
10	
5	
0	

204

RESIDENT POPULATION OF

N. C. MENTAL HOSPITALS

July 1, 1960

(Total = 9753 patients)

No. of
Patients

No. of Patients	Schizophrenia (4599)	Category	Count
5000			
4800		All Other	650
4600			
4400			
4200		Alcoholic	93
4000		Psychoneurotic	160
3800		Involutional	199
3600		Syphilitic	382
3400			
3200		Manic-Depressive	622
3000			
2800			
2600		Convalsive Disorders	705
2400			
2200			
2000		Mental Deficiency	955
1800			
1600			
1400			
1200			
1000			
800		Senium	1188
600			
400			
200			
0			

1946 - 1947

	DIX	BROUGHTON	CHERRY	UMSTEAD	TOTAL
Mental 1st Admissions					
Male	213	146	307		666
Female	175	183	246		604
	388	329	553		1270
Alcoholic 1st Admissions					
Male	276				276
Female	46				46
	322				322
Readmissions (all)	179	129	33		341
Returns from Probation (all)	185	118	114		417
Transfers	-	9	-		9
Total Admissions					
Male	689	263	398		1350
Female	385	322	320		1027
	1074	585	718		2377
Total Admissions Minus Transfers					2350
Discharges (Direct)	124	0	0		124
Probations	584	449	343		1376
Transfers	20	20	-		40
Deaths	144	124	391		659
Total Separations	872	593	734		2199
Total Separations Minus Transfers					2159
Ave. Daily Population (for year)					
Male	1277	1270	1240		3787
Female	1086	1346	1350		3782
	2363	2616	2590		7569

1947 - 1948

	DIX	BROUGHTON	CHERRY	UMSTEAD	TOTAL
Mental 1st Admissions					
Male	194	184	279	6	663
Female	191	215	217	2	625
	385	399	496	8	1288
Alcoholic 1st Admissions					
Male	262				262
Female	65	-	-	-	65
	327				327
Readmissions (all)	179	149	63	-	391
Returns from Probation (all)	173	132	95	6	406
Transfers	-	2	-	1115	1117
Total Admissions					
Male	659	315	369		
Female	405	367	285		
	1064	682	654	1129	3529
Total Admissions Minus Transfers					2412
Discharges (Direct)	143	-	66	-	209
Probations	623	465	349	27	1464
Transfers	278	354	5	2	639
Deaths	108	111	285	49	553
Separations	1152	930	705	78	2865
Total Separations Minus Transfers					2226
Ave. Daily Population (for year)					
Male	1226	1199	1330	327	4082
Female	1115	1373	1458	374	4320
	2341	2572	2788	701	8402

	DIX	BROUGHTON	CHERRY	UMSTEAD	TOTAL
Mental 1st Admissions					
Male	255	216	244		715
Female	243	309	194	–	746
	498	525	438		1461
Alcoholic 1st Admissions					
Male	308		2		310
Female	56	–	0		56
	364		2		366
Readmissions (all)	199	168	63	3	433
Returns from Probation (all)	215	144	145	23	527
Transfers	3	2	–	294	299
Total Admissions					
Male	828	323	358	139	1648
Female	451	516	290	181	1438
	1279	839	648	320	3086
Total Admissions less Transfers					2787
Discharges (Direct)	155	–	67	–	222
Probations	819	427	399	73	1718
Transfers	201	103	–	5	309
Deaths	110	166	217	72	565
Total Separations	1285	696	683	150	2814
Total Separations less Transfers					2505
Ave. Daily Population (for year)					
Male	1186	1161	1321	492	4160
Female	1059	1354	1432	616	4461
	2245	2515	2753	1108	8621

1949 - 1950

	DIX	BROUGHTON	CHERRY	UMSTEAD	TOTAL
Mental 1st Admissions					
Male	306	383	240	1	930
Female	308	326	204	0	838
	614	709	444	1	1768
Alcoholic 1st Admissions					
Male	300				300
Female	60				60
	360				360
Readmissions (all)	187	174	59		420
Returns from Probation (all)	224	187	94	32	537
Transfers	8	6	-	384	398
Total Admissions					
Male	847	399	325	178	1749
Female	546	577	272	239	1634
	1393	976	597	417	3483
Total Admissions less Transfers					3085
Discharges (Direct)	198	-	82	-	271
Probations	928	545	350	131	1954
Transfers	134	256	-	14	404
Deaths	106	134	173	71	484
Total Separations	1357	935	605	216	3113
Total Separations less Transfers					2709
Ave. Daily Population (for year)					
Male	1166	1178	1315	566	4225
Female	1056	1422	1435	755	4668
	2222	2600	2750	1321	8893

1950 -1951

	DIX	BROUGHTON	CHERRY	UMSTEAD	TOTAL
Mental 1st Admissions					
Male	289	234	272	198	993
Female	254	296	194	232	976
	543	530	466	430	1969
Alcoholic 1st Admissions					
Male	310				310
Female	60	-	-	-	60
	370				370
Readmissions (all)	183	140	85	12	420
Returns from Probation (all)	236	203	107	74	620
Transfers	3	1	0	56	60
Total Admissions					
Male	852	346	362	261	1821
Female	483	528	296	311	1618
	1335	874	658	572	3439
Total Admissions Minus Transfers					3379
Discharges (Direct)	195	-	73	111	379
Probations	916	643	360	197	2116
Transfers	32	30	-	4	66
Deaths	119	123	158	114	514
Total Separations	1262	796	591	426	3075
Total Separations Less Transfers					3009
Ave. Daily Population (for year)					
Male	1170	1209	1352	620	4351
Female	1109	1418	1477	855	4859
	2279	2627	2829	1475	9210

1951 - 1952

	DIX	BROUGHTON	CHERRY	UMSTEAD	TOTAL
Mental 1st Admissions					
Male	279	249	268	301	1097
Female	239	302	215	400	1156
	518	551	483	701	2253
Alcoholic 1st Admissions					
Male	276		4		280
Female	69	-	0		69
	345	-	4	-	349
Readmissions (all)	163	112	80	56	411
Returns from Probation (all)	242	251	131	110	734
Transfers	4	5	-	39	48
Total Admissions					
Male	802	368	382	380	1932
Female	470	551	316	526	1863
	1272	919	698	906	3795
Total Admissions Minus Transfers					3747
Discharges (Direct)	166	-	65	313	544
Probations	921	734	437	387	2479
Transfers	21	24	3	10	58
Deaths	112	144	179	126	561
Total Separations	1220	902	684	836	3642
Total Separations less Transfers					3584
Ave. Daily Population (for year)					
Male	1198	1243	1407	653	4501
Female	1129	1439	1499	909	4976
	2327	2682	2906	1562	9477

1952 - 1953

	DIX	BROUGHTON	CHERRY	UMSTEAD	TOTAL
Mental 1st Admissions					
Male	230	214	264	308	1016
Female	240	259	186	377	1062
	470	473	450	685	2078
Alcoholic 1st Admissions					
Male	285		2		287
Female	83		1		84
	368		3		371
Readmissions (all)	165	135	83	98	481
Returns from Probation (all)	257	247	118	111	733
Transfers	3	6	-	79	88
Total Admissions					
Male	756	337	376	421	1890
Female	507	524	278	552	1861
	1263	861	654	973	3751
Total Admissions less Transfers					3663
Discharges (Direct)	177	1	47	418	643
Probations	883	659	360	368	2270
Transfers	39	52	5	6	102
Deaths	101	98	140	128	467
Total Separations	1200	810	552	920	3482
Total Separations less Transfers					3380
Ave. Daily Population (for year)					
Male	1221	1245	1445	675	4586
Female	1154	1453	1486	957	5050
	2375	2698	2931	1632	9626

212

	DIX	BROUGHTON	CHERRY	UMSTEAD	TOTAL
Mental 1st Admissions					
Male	264	241	249	292	1046
Female	232	317	222	373	1144
	496	558	471	665	2190
Alcoholic 1st Admissions					
Male	307				307
Female	67				67
	374				374
Readmissions (all)	220	144	85	131	580
Returns from Probation (all)	316	250	122	127	815
Transfers	6	4	-	84	94
Total Admissions					
Male	871	360	346	430	2007
Female	541	596	332	577	2046
	1412	956	678	1007	4053
Total Admissions less Transfers					3959
Discharges (Direct)	233	12	66	463	774
Probations	988	749	442	319	2498
Transfers	52	42	11	4	109
Deaths	100	121	120	126	467
Total Separations	1373	924	639	912	3848
Total Separations less Transfers					3739
Ave. Daily Population (for year)					
Male	1212	1242	1491	716	4661
Female	1136	1484	1498	983	5101
	2348	2726	2989	1699	9762

	DIX	BROUGHTON	CHERRY	UMSTEAD	TOTAL
Mental 1st Admissions					
Male	239	160	278	281	958
Female	212	215	206	330	963
	451	375	484	611	1921
Alcoholic 1st Admissions					
Male	336				336
Female	57				57
	393				393
Readmissions (all)	295	303	114	204	916
Returns from Probation (all)	318	263	152	111	844
Transfers	6	4	-	84	94
Total Admissions					
Male	944	346	411	436	2137
Female	519	599	339	574	2031
	1463	945	750	1010	4168
Total Admissions Less Transfers					4074
Discharges (Direct)	318	12	83	455	868
Probations	936	774	461	394	2565
Transfers	19	74	4	5	102
Deaths	63	135	114	133	445
Separations	1336	995	662	987	3980
Total Separations less Transfers					3878
Ave. Daily Population (for year)					
Male	1160	1233	1531	746	4670
Female	1251	1499	1491	1015	5256
	2411	2732	3022	1761	9926

214

1955 - 1956

	DIX	BROUGHTON	CHERRY	UMSTEAD	TOTAL
Mental 1st Admissions					
Male	215	204	306	269	994
Female	199	238	265	320	1022
	414	442	571	589	2016
Alcoholic 1st Admissions					
Male	266		3		269
Female	49		0		49
	315		3		318
Readmissions (all)	468	319	113	319	1219
Returns from Probation (all)	373	270	231	141	1015
Transfers	3	4	-	4	11
Total Admissions					
Male	972	399	476	432	2279
Female	601	636	442	621	2300
	1573	1035	918	1053	4579
Total Admissions less Transfers					4568
Discharges (Direct)	478	31	116	572	1197
Probations	1099	798	694	438	3029
Transfers	8	-	-	4	12
Deaths	114	165	110	137	526
Separations	1699	994	920	1151	4764
Total Separations less Transfers					4752
Ave. Daily Population (for year)					
Male	1246	1212	1605	750	4813
Female	1157	1494	1450	967	5068
	2403	2706	3055	1717	9881

1956 - 1957

	DIX	BROUGHTON	CHERRY	UMSTEAD	TOTAL
Mental 1st Admissions					
Male	312	243	346	312	1213
Female	334	307	308	342	1291
	646	550	654	654	2504
Alcoholic 1st Admissions					
Male	336		35		371
Female	71		10		81
	407		45		452
Readmissions (all)	443	312	173	386	1314
Returns from Probation (all)	638	297	227	165	1327
Transfers	5	-	-	4	9
Total Admissions					
Male	1268	450	576	518	1812
Female	871	709	523	691	2794
	2139	1159	1099	1209	5606
Total Admissions less Transfers					5597
Discharges (Direct)	507	74	294	680	1555
Probations	1523	1070	571	360	3524
Transfers	3	1	-	4	8
Deaths	134	174	149	173	630
Total Separations	2167	1319	1014	1217	5717
Total Separations less Transfers					5709
Ave. Daily Population (for year)					
Male	1210	1209	1653	707	4779
Female	1093	1472	1452	932	4949
	2303	2681	3105	1639	9728

216

1957 - 1958

	DIX	BROUGHTON	CHERRY	UMSTEAD	TOTAL
Mental 1st Admissions					
Male	377	285	390	353	1405
Female	387	346	329	444	1506
	764	631	719	797	2911
Alcoholic 1st Admissions					
Male	360	1	17		378
Female	61	0	8		69
	421	1	25		447
Readmissions (all)	700	361	188	430	1679
Returns from Probation	580	333	236	164	1313
Transfers	12	8	-	6	26
Total Admissions					
Male	1434	552	602	583	3171
Female	1043	782	566	814	3205
	2477	1334	1168	1397	6376
Total Admissions less Transfers					6350
Discharges (Direct)	704	111	341	802	1958
Probations	1454	986	717	375	3532
Transfers	9	4	116	5	134
Deaths	213	224	169	194	800
Separations	2380	1325	1343	1476	6424
Total Separations less Transfers					6290
Ave. Daily Population (for year)					
Male	1276	1222	1590	720	4808
Female	1124	1408	1396	905	4833
	2400	2630	2986	1625	9641

217

	DIX	BROUGHTON	CHERRY	UMSTEAD	TOTAL
Mental 1st Admissions					
Male	420	384	430	431	1665
Female	400	503	401	557	1861
	820	887	831	988	3526
Alcoholic 1st Admissions					
Male	487		33	53	573
Female	81		16	10	107
	568		49	63	680
Readmissions (all)	811	484	272	447	2014
Returns from Probation (all)	632	378	321	153	1484
Transfers	13	18	-	2	33
Total Admissions					
Male	1700	755	731	712	3878
Female	1144	1012	742	941	3839
	2844	1767	1473	1653	7737
Total Admissions less Transfers					7704
Discharges (Direct)	906	238	372	931	2447
Probations	1657	1223	916	314	4110
Transfers	37	5	-	3	45
Deaths	227	228	158	228	841
Total Separations	2827	1694	1446	1476	7443
Total Separations less Transfers					7398
Ave. Daily Population (for year)					
Male	1337	1177	1593	728	4835
Female	1108	1453	1355	939	4855
	2445	2630	2948	1667	9690

218

1959 - 1960

	DIX	BROUGHTON	CHERRY	UMSTEAD	TOTAL
Mental 1st Admissions					
Male	423	469	448	415	1755
Female	471	589	376	516	1952
	894	1058	824	931	3707
Alcoholic 1st Admissions					
Male	468	5	32	8	513
Female	105	1	10	2	118
	573	6	42	10	631
Readmissions (all)	724	639	295	705	2363
Returns from Probation (all)	730	463	409	162	1764
Transfers	10	29	-	24	63
Total Admissions					
Male	1700	884	782	813	4179
Female	1231	1311	788	1019	4349
	2931	2195	1570	1832	8528
Total Admissions less Transfers					8465
Discharges (Direct)	906	379	364	1138	2787
Probations	1776	1528	1035	368	4707
Transfers	27	7	-	13	47
Deaths	233	288	185	186	892
Separations	2942	2202	1584	1705	8433
Total Separations less Transfers					8386
Ave. Daily Population (for year)					
Male	1327	1204	1669	768	4968
Female	1104	1473	1283	951	4811
	2431	2677	2952	1719	9779

ALCOHOLIC REHABILITATION CENTER

	1951-52	1952-53	1953-54
Admissions	415	430	447
Discharges	180+	450	447

	1954-1955	1955-1956	1956-1957	1957-1958	1958-1959
Admissions					
Male	375	352	286	311	371
Female	66	56	67	83	68
Total	441	408	353	394	439
Discharges					
Male	376	345	281	310	363
Female	67	53	61	87	65
	443	398	342	397	428

	1959-1960
Admissions	
First - Male	339
Female	55
Total	394
Readmissions	
Male	71
Female	10
Total	81
Total Admissions	475
Discharges	
Male	410
Female	65
Total	475

BROUGHTON HOSPITAL

Business Manager's Office
Morganton, N. C.

(Figures below do not include Additions and Betterments)

TOTAL REQUIREMENTS AND PER CAPITA COSTS FOR PERIOD INDICATED

Year	Population	Per Capita Costs	Requirements
1940-41	2,487	185.91	462,361.68
1941-42	2,575	185.37	477,326.44
1942-43	2,601	261.87	681,132.31
1943-44	2,660	311.86	829,560.31
1944-45	2,705	332.10	898,385.97
1945-46	2,616	425.35	1,112,721.87
1946-47	2,601	568.08	1,477,581.06
1947-48	2,579	642.09	1,655,972.48
1948-49	2,530	707.47	1,798,897.09
1949-50	2,599	780.32	2,028,047.93
1950-51	2,622	849.75	2,228,047.62
1951-52	2,679	886.92	2,376,054.79
1952-53	2,702	980.92	2,650,432.74
1953-54	2,727	1,015.01	2,767,946.78
1954-55	2,725	1,016.01	2,768,625.07
1955-56	2,702	1,069.81	2,890,629.80
1956-57	2,680	1,163.68	3,118,659.51
1957-58	2,606	1,464.81	3,817,286.30
1958-59	2,626	1,503.68	3,948,658.29
1959-60	2,674	1,545.69	4,133,182.75
1960-61	2,615	1,656.35	4,331,362.73
1961-62	2,613	1,742.67	5,553,597.74

Per Diem Per Capita Cost 1961-62 $4.77

RAW FOOD COST IN FISCAL YEAR ENDING	6/30/57	6/30/58	6/30/59	6/30/60	6/30/61	6/30/62
Purchased from appropriation	473,765.83	398,372.43	367,012.46	401,867.62	413,484.85	362,309.97
Raised on Hospital Farm	254,889.91	328,650.47	309,191.70	281,003.38	319,397.36	355,445.00
Donated by Dept. of Agriculture	57,557.00	66,284.00	40,095.00	34,137.00	61,835.00	49,016.00
Total Raw Food Cost, All	786,212.74	793,306.90	716,299.16	717,008.00	794,717.21	766,770.97
Less Revenue Cafeteria		38,063.92	43,160.36	42,158.52	40,131.10	42,759.64
Total Raw Food Cost, Patients		755,242.98	673,138.80	674,849.48	754,586.11	724,011.33
Average Number of Patients	2,680	2,606	2,626	2,674	2,615	2,613
Average Number of Employees Fed (3 times daily)	430	(Deducted above)	(Deducted above)	(Deducted above)	(Deducted above)	(Deducted above)
Total Number Fed	3,110	2,606	2,626	2,674	2,615	2,613
Per Annum, Per Capita, Fed	252.80	289.81	256.34	252.38	288.56	277.08
Per Diem, Per Capita, Fed	.6926	.7940	.7023	.6896	.7906	.7591
Percentage of Food Purchased	60.26	50.22	51.24	56.05	52.03	47.25
Percentage of Food from Farm	32.42	41.43	43.16	39.19	40.19	46.36
Percentage Donated by Department of Agriculture	7.32	8.35	5.60	4.76	7.78	6.39
	100%	100%	100%	100%	100%	100%

Chapter I

1. Dorothea Dix, "Memorial to the General Assembly of the State of North Carolina," November, 1848, North Carolina Pamphlets, Peacock Collection, Vol. 17.

2. Dorothea Lynde Dix, Memorial Soliciting a State Hospital for the Insane, submitted to the Legislature of New Jersey, January 2, 1845.

3. Norman Dain, Concepts of Insanity in the United States, 1789-1865, Rutgers University Press, New Brunswick, New Jersey, 1964, p. 55.

4. Ibid., chapter 9 "The Public's Response."

5. Albert Deutach, The Mentally Ill in America, Doubleday, Doran and Company, Inc., Garden City, New York, 1938, p. 306.

6. Clifford W. Beers, A Mind that Found Itself, Doubleday, Doran and Company, Inc., 1937. and Dain, op. cit., chapter 9, for treatment of the role of journalism in bringing to light conditions in state mental institutions and the public attitude toward insanity.

7. The author is indebted to Professor George C. Cochran, Duke University Law School, for permission to cite unpublished research findings resulting from a study conducted by Duke University law students under the sponsorship of the North Carolina Department of Mental Health during the summer months of 1971.

8. Deutsch, op. cit., p. 307.

9. Joint Commission on Mental Illness, 1961, Action for Mental Health, Basic Books, Inc., New York, 1961, p. 5.

10. Mary Jane Ward, The Snake Pit, Random House, New York, 1946.

11. Frank L. Wright, Jr., Out of Sight Out of Mind, National Mental Health Foundation, Inc., Philadelphia, 1947, p. 133-34.

12. Ward, op. cit., p. 201.

13. Wright, op. cit.

14. Albert Deutsch, The Shame of the States, Harcourt, Brace and Company, New York, 1948.

15. Jimison's Articles were fashioned after the dramatic and gruesome revelations of the inner workings of both the Nazi and Communist parties in Germany in the nineteen thirties written by Jan Valtin and entitled Out of the Night.

16. Charlotte News, January 19, 1942, section 1, p. 6; Greensboro Daily News, January 19, 1942, section 1, p. 7.

17. The series also appeared in the Durham Evening Sun.

18. See Liston Pope, Millhands and Preachers, New Haven, 1942, for a description of the strike and the ensuing trials.

19. The author is indebted to several people for information relating to Mr. Jimison, among them Dr. Fletcher Nelson, in whose parsonage Jimison wrote the Morganton articles; Dr. John McKee, Superintendent at Broughton Hospital and a member of the Morganton staff during Jimison's hospitalization; and Messrs. J. Ed Dowd, Pete McKnight, and Brodie Griffith of the Charlotte News and Observer.

20. Journal of the Western North Carolina Conference of the Methodist Church, 1917, p. 29.

21. Conference Journal, op. cit., 1924, p. 67. "Permanent location" in the Methodist Church allows a man to assist in the priestly and prophetic rites of the church, but he is denied the privilege of directing these functions. Location is one step removed from defrocking.

22. Martindale-Hubbell, Law Directory, 1937-40. North Carolina Listings.

23. Interview with Mr. Brodie Griffith, op. cit.

24. The staff at Morganton proved the diagnosis of a "social disease" was incorrect.

25. Tom P. Jimison, "Out of the Night of Morganton," chapter 1. The sixteen original newspaper articles were later published in pamphlet form by the Charlotte News and Observer Publishing Company. All quotations from the series are taken from a copy of the pamphlet edition found in the papers of Governor Melville Broughton.

26. Ibid., chapter 1.

27. Ibid., chapter 1.

28. Ibid., chapter 11.

29. Ibid., chapter 4.

30. Ibid., chapter 12.

31. Ibid., chapter 3.

32. Ibid., chapter 2.

33. Ibid., chapter 7.

34. Ibid., chapter 7.

35. Ibid., chapter 5.

Chapter II

1. Samuel A. Ashe, Biographical History of North Carolina, Greensboro, North Carolina, 1907, Vol. VII, p. 207. When James C. Dobbin, one time United States Congressman, state legislator, and Secretary of the Navy, was asked why the Navy Department was so frequently given to North Carolinians, the questioner answered his own inquiry. "Because," he said, "North Carolina is the Rip Van Winkle of the states and the Navy Department is the Rip Van Winkle of our national defenses."

2. Lefler, North Carolina, Chapel Hill, North Carolina, 1954, p. 304.

3. Ibid., p. 298.

4. Lefler lists among those who migrated from North Carolina the families of three presidents of the United States - Andrew Jackson, James K. Polk, and Andrew Johnson: two vice presidents, Johnson and Willian King; three cabinet members; two speakers of the House of Representatives; more than a score of Congressmen; governors of seven states, including the first governor of Texas; the founders of Furman University, Mercer University, Cumberland University, Miami of Ohio and the University of the South; and among others the founder of Rochester, New York, and the first Negro to serve in the United States Congress. Ibid., p. 305.

5. Ibid., p. 321-22.

6. "Governor's Message," Legislative Documents, 1840, p. 7, 1842, p. 11.

7. "Governor's Message, "Journal of the Legislative Session, 1844 p. 12.

8. Margaret C. McCullock, "Founding the North Carolina Asylum for the Insane" The North Carolina Historical Review XIII (July, 1936), p. 187.

9. The Standard, XV, 733 (November 22, 1848) lists the party alignment as: House - 28 Whigs, 25 Democrats; Senate - 59 Whigs, 58 Democrats. However, J. G. Hamilton, Party Politics in North Carolina 1835-1860 states that the division was even, p. 124. The latter source seems more reliable since a compromise had to be reached over control of the two chambers. In the compromise the Whigs controlled the House, the Democrats, the Senate.

10. Albert Deutsch, The Mentally Ill in America, op. cit., p. 39.

11. Ibid., p. 47.

12. McCulloch, op. cit., p. 188; Legislative Documents, 1854-55, Raleigh, North Carolina, No. 5.

13. Marshall, Helen, Dorothea Dix, Chapel Hill, North Carolina, 1937, p. 117.

14. Journal of Legislative Session, 1848-49, p. 392.

15. Dorothea Dix, "Memorial Soliciting a State Hospital for the Protection and Care of the Insane," November, 1848, House of Commons, Document, No. 2.

16. Marshall, op. cit., p. 119.

17. Francis Tiffany, Life of Dorothea Lynde Dix, Boston, 1891, p. 136.

18. Raleigh Register, December 27, 1848.

19. North Carolina Standard, December 27, 1848.

20. Journal of Legislative Session, 1848-49, p. 155.

21. Marshall, op. cit., p. 193. Lefler, op. cit., p. 353.

22. Laws of North Carolina, 1852, pp. 137-39.

23. Laws of North Carolina, 1854-55, Chapter II.

24. Raleigh Register, March 5, April 9, 1856.

25. North Carolina State Hospital Reports, 1857-58, p. 9.

26. Ibid., p. 16.

27. Ibid., p. 4.

28. Ibid., p. 4.

29. Laws of North Carolina, 1856-57, Chapter III; 1858-59, Chapter II.

30. The author is indebted to Drs. Eugene Hargrove and Charles Vernon, North Carolina Department of Mental Health for their assistance in interpreting the problem of "pathologic dependence."

31. An Appeal, The Board of Public Charities of North Carolina 1900, pp. 10-11.

32. A Study of Mental Health in North Carolina, Report to the North Carolina Legislature of the Governor's Commission, appointed to study the care of the insane and mental defectives, Ann Arbor, Michigan, 1937, Chapter XI, Referred to hereafter as "Governor's Commission."

33. Dain, op. cit., p. 15.

34. Deutsch, op. cit., p. 187.

35. Ibid., p. 188.

36. North Carolina State Hospital Reports for the early years make repeated reference to this as a factor in cure failures.

37. Joint Commission on Mental Illness and Health, Action for Mental Health, 1961, pp. 28-31.

38. Dain, op. cit., pp. 123-130.

39. Ibid., p. 5.

40. Deutsch, op. cit., p. 250-51.

41. See Lefler, op. cit., pp. 460-473 for a discussion of Reconstruction politics.

42. Annual Report, North Carolina Board of Public Charities, 1868.

43. The report of William E. Anderson, Treasurer of the Asylum, for 1865, shows total expenditure for the year of $308.00. Supplies for the one hundred forty-seven patients were issued by the U. S. Army of Occupation. North Carolina State Hospital Reports, 1865-66, p. 12.

44. "Speech of Hon. Thomas J. Jarvis, Delivered in the Dr. Grissom Trial, for the Defense," 1889, p. 2.

45. Ibid., p. 5.

46. Legislative Journal, 1871-72, p. 176.

47. North Carolina Reports, Vol. 72 (Spring Term, 1873), Welker vs Bledsoe.

48. Annual Report, op. cit., 1868, p. 6.

49. North Carolina State Hospital Reports, 1868, p. 4.

50. Ibid., 1873, p. 3.

51. Legislative Documents, 1874, Document 26.

52. James K. Hall, "Psychiatry in Retrospect," Southern Medical and Surgery, Vol. 100 (November, 1938), p. 5.

53. Letter of Mr. Horace Payne, Morganton, North Carolina to Dr. James K. Hall, April 19, 1939, in the possession of Dr. Charles Vernon, State Department of Mental Health.

54. I am indebted to Dr. E. H. E. Taylor of Morganton for much of the information concerning Dr. Murphy and the early years of the Morganton Hospital.

55. Dr. Murphy's advocacy of colony therapy was expressed in two articles: "Colony Treatment of the Insane and Other Defectives," North Carolina Medical Journal, 1906; and "The Treatment and Care of the Insane in North Carolina," An address delivered before the Agricultural and Mechanical College, Raleigh, North Carolina, March, 1900.

56. Eugene Grissom, "Mechanical Protection for the Insane," American Journal of Insanity, July, 1877.

57. Report of the North Carolina State Hospital, Raleigh, North Carolina, 1912, p. 7.

58. Ibid., pp. 8-11.

59. Eugene Crissom, M. D., "A Statement to the Friends of the North Carolina Insane Asylum, 1889," published by the author.

60. Letter of Mr. Horace Payne, op. cit.

61. Wood vs Bellamy, 120, N.C., p. 89, (1897).

62. Ibid.

Chapter III

1. An Appeal, The Board of Public Charities of North Carolina, 1900.

2. Belknap, Human Problems of A State Mental Hospital, McGraw-Hill Book Company, Inc., New York, 1956, p. 17.

3. North Carolina State Hospital Reports, Raleigh, North Carolina, 1916, p. 7.

4. The law defines the term "mental defective" as "a person who is not mentally ill but whose mental development is so retarded that he has not acquired enough self-control to manage himself or his affairs, and for whose own welfare and that of others, supervision, guidance, care or control is necessary or advisable." The term is construed to include the feebleminded, idiots, and imbeciles. In "Report on the State Training Schools," by the American Psychiatric Association, December, 1958, p. 5.

5. Legislative Documents, 1911, Document 7.

6. "Governor's Commission," pp. 275-276.

7. Ibid., pp. 280-289.

8. Jimison's episode of the "Gospel Hens" in his expose is a graphic representation of this condition. See chapter I, p. 18.

9. "Governor's Commission," p. 335.

10. North Carolina Journal, 1921, p. 212.

11. Belknap, op. cit., p. 29.

12. Charlotte Observer, December 16, 1905, p. 1.

13. "Condition of Hospitals" a special publication by D. A. Tompkins, Charlotte, North Carolina, February, 1906. This publication is a re-print of Governor Glenn's report and an editorial printed in the Charlotte Observer, February 17, 1906, and written by J. P. Caldwell, Chairman of the Board of Directors of Morganton Hospital, Duke University Pamphlet Collection.

14. Ibid.

15. James K. Hall, "The War on Dr. Albert Anderson." A reprint of editorials in the Department of Human Behavior, Southern Medicine and Surgery, December, 1928 - July, 1929.

16. Ibid.

17. Ibid.

18. "Report of the Committee on Caswell Training School," Raleigh, 1926. This report to Governor A. W. McLean detailed the existing conditions at Caswell and listed the needs of the school in much the same fashion as earlier reports from the several superintendents. There is no record of any action being taken on the report.

19. "Governor's Commission," p. 296.

20. S. Kirkson Weinberg, Society and Personality Disorders, New York, Prentice-Hall, Inc., 1952, p. 375.

21. "Governor's Commission," p. xiii.

22. Minutes of the Meeting of the Governor's Commission, September 29, 1936. Files, State Department of Mental Health, Raleigh, North Carolina.

23. Ibid.

24. "Governor's Commission," p. 348.

25. Governor's Papers, State Department of History and Archives, Raleigh, North Carolina, Clyde R. Hoey, Dix Hill File, July 14, 1937. Hereafter cited as "Hoey Papers."

26. Ibid., March 3, 1937.

27. Ibid., Morganton file, August 12, 1937.

28. Ibid., Dix Hill file, June 7, 1937.

29. Personal papers of State Senator William T. ("Cousin Willie") Clark, Tarboro, North Carolina. Papers are in the possession of Senator Clark's son, W. T. Clark, Jr.

30. Hoey Papers, Box 60, Morganton file, July 1, 1937.

31. Ibid., Box 61, Dix Hill file, November 7, 1937.

32. Ibid., Dix Hill file, November 12, 1937.

33. "Governor's Commission," p. 223.

34. Hoey Papers, Box 61, Morganton file, May 30, 1938.

35. Ibid., Report of investigation of complaint, June 2, 1938.

36. Ibid., June 3, 1938.

37. Weinberg, op. cit., p. 418.

38. See Appendix A.

39. See Chapter I.

40. Dain, op. cit., p. 12.

41. Interview with Dr. Charles Vernon.

42. Wright, op. cit., report 279, p. 67.

43. See Chapter I.

44. James K. Hall, "Psychiatry in Retrospect," op. cit., pp. 9-10.

45. Ethel M. Speas. History of the Voluntary Health Movement in North Carolina. Raleigh, North Carolina, 1961, p. 3.

46. Ibid., p. 9.

47. The official papers of every Governor from 1900 through 1960 contain files of pathetic and outraged complaints from patients, lawyers, family members and friends of patients, and corresponding investigative reports from hospital staff members that universally deny charges of cruelty, malpractive, or mistreatment.

48. See above, page 56, note 31.

49. "Governor's Commission," p. 208.

50. Hoey Papers, Morganton file, Quarterly Report of Trustees, Morganton State Hospital, September 20, 1937.

51. "Governor's Commission," p. 179.

52. "Governor's Commission," p. 166.

53. Ibid., p. 173.

54. Ibid., p. 167.

55. Ibid., p. 174.

56. Ibid., p. 226.

57. Ibid., p. 368.

58. Ibid., p. 182.

59. Ibid., p. 361.

60. Ibid., p. 239.

61. Ibid., p. 226.

62. Ibid., See descriptive breakdown of facilities under discussion of separate hospitals.

63. Ibid., p. 176.

64. Ibid., p. 357.

65. Ibid., p. 357.

66. Ibid., p. 357.

67. Ibid., p. 357.

68. Ibid., p. 27.

69. Ibid., p. vi.

70. Governor's Papers. J. C. B. Ehringhaus, North Carolina Department of Archives and History, Raleigh, North Carolina, Box 158. Hereafter cited as Ehringhaus Papers.

71. Edward A. Oldham, "North Carolina in New York," Winston-Salem Journal, August 14, 1946.

72. Action for Mental Health, op. cit., p. xxxix.

Chapter IV

1. Governor J. Melville Broughton Papers, Agencies, Departments, and Institutions, 1941-44, State Department of Archives and History, Raleigh, North Carolina, box 48, file 3. Hereafter cited as Broughton Papers. These papers covering the investigation are in six archive boxes (47-52) and are not catalogued. The boxes contain files received from the Governor's office. The files are just as they were kept by the Governor's secretary. As a result, much of correspondence is not in chronological order. This investigator was given the privilege of numbering the files in each box in order to facilitate location of material.

2. Ibid., box 48, file 3, January 17, 1942.

3. Ibid., box 48, file 3, January 22, 1942.

4. Ibid., box 48, file 3, January 22, 1942.

5. Ibid., box 48, file 3, January 31, 1942.

6. Ibid., box 48, file 3, February 1, 1942.

7. Ibid., box 48, file 2, January 25, 1942.

8. Ibid., file 3, Letter from Broughton to Mr. Ira S.Griffen, Charlotte, February 3, 1942.

9. Ibid., box 52, file 2, February 3, 1942.

10. Charlotte News, editorials, January 22, 25, 27. 31, 1942, and interview with J. Ed. Dowd, op. cit.

11. Ibid., February 2, 1942.

12. Ibid., February 5, 1942, p. 14.

13. This was a series of eight articles written anonymously by a former patient at Morganton who told "The woman's side of the story." No other paper in the state carried this series, and it received little attention.

14. Broughton Papers, op. cit., box 48, file 2. Letter to Broughton from Dowd, February 6, 1942.

15. Gastonia Gazette, Gastonia, North Carolina, February 1, 1942, p. 5.

16. Fayetteville Observer, Fayetteville, North Carolina, January 29, 1942, p. 6. Asheville Citizen, Asheville, North Carolina, January 31, 1942, p. 9. The circulation of the Charlotte, Greensboro, Asheville, Fayetteville, Greensboro, Durham, and Raleigh papers combined, covered the state. Several smaller papers such as the Hickory Record supplied editorial coverage on the local level.

17. Greensboro News, Greensboro, North Carolina, February 3,1942, p. 4.

18. Ibid.

19. The Trustees' committee was established on February 5, 1942.

20. Broughton Papers, box 48, file 3, February 6, 1942.

21. Ibid., box 48, file 2, p. 4. Trustees' report to Governor Broughton, February 13, 1942.

22. Ibid., box 47, file 1, News release, February 13, 1942.

23. Broughton Papers, box 48, file 2, February 27, 1942.

24. Ibid., box 48, file 2, March 2, 1942.

25. Ibid., box 48, file 2, March 7, 1942.

26. Ibid., box 48, file 3, March 13, 1942.

27. Sessions were held in Morganton, March 18-20, Winston-Salem, March 25, and Charlotte, March 26-27, 1942.

28. Broughton Papers, box 48, file 3, May 22, 1942.

29. Ibid., box 48, file 2, May 23, 1942.

30. Ibid., box 48, file 2, May 27, 1942.

31. Charlotte News, June 5, 1942, p. 1.

32. Ibid., box 48, file 2, July 25, 1942.

33. Interview with McKnight and Dowd, August 26, 1963.

34. Broughton Papers, box 42, file 2, July 26, 1942.

35. Counsel Hines in a letter to Broughton, July 27, 1942. Broughton Papers, box 48, file 2.

36. Broughton Papers, box 48, file 2, July 30, 1942.

37. "Report of the Board of Inquiry appointed by his Excellency, J. Melville Broughton, Governor of North Carolina, to make an Investigation of the State Hospitals, Morganton, North Carolina," Broughton Papers, box 47, file 1. Hereafter cited as Report.

38. Ibid., pp. 6-7.

39. Ibid., pp. 7-10.

40. Ibid., pp. 10-11.

41. Ibid.

42. Ibid., pp. 12-15.

234

43. Ibid., pp. 16-17.

44. Broughton Papers, box 48, file 3, News Release, August 7, 1942.

45. Ibid.

46. Charlotte News, August 7, 1942, p. 8.

47. Letters from North Carolina residents thanking Broughton for correcting the situation at Morganton are filed in Broughton Papers, box 48, file 3.

48. Broughton Papers, box 48, file 2, News Release, August 19, 1942.

49. Ibid., box 48, file 2, Letter from Dowd to Broughton with editorial attached, August 21, 1942.

50. Ibid., box 48, file 2, Letter from Broughton to Dowd, August 27, 1942.

51. Ibid., box 48, file 2, Letter from Dowd to Broughton, September 2, 1942.

52. Ibid., box 48, file 2, Letter from Broughton to Dowd, September 3, 1942.

53. Ibid., box 48, file 2, Letter from Dowd to Broughton, September 10, 1942.

54. Ibid., box 48, file 3.

55. Ibid., box 48, file 2, Broughton to Dowd, September 14, 1942.

56. Charlotte News, p. 14.

57. Ibid., box 48, file 2, Morganton file, September 15, 1942.

58. Charlotte Observer, Charlotte, North Carolina, September 16, 1942, p. 7.

59. Ibid., p. 14.

60. Broughton Papers, box 48, file 2, September 19, 1942.

61. Ibid., box 48, file 2, September 21, 1942.

62. Ibid., box 48, file 2.

63. Ibid., box 48, file 2, September 21, 1942.

64. Ibid., box 48, file 2, October 15, 1942.

65. Charlotte News, Friday, October 16, 1942, p. 8.

66. Broughton Papers, box 48, file 2, October 18, 1942.

67. Ibid., box 48, file 2, October 19, 1942.

68. These reports are on file in the Broughton Papers, box 48, file 4.

69. *Ibid.*, box 48, file 3, December 9, 1942.

70. *Ibid.*, box 48, file 3, December 9, 1942.

71. *Ibid.*, box 48, file 3, News release.

72. Governor's Address to the Joint Session of the Legislature, January 7, 1943. *Journal of the Senate of the General Assembly of the State of North Carolina*, Session 1943, p. 20.

73. Action on the bills in the Senate and House are to be found as follows: For the Senate, *Ibid.*, pp. 94, 139, 162; For the House, *Journal of the House of Representatives of the General Assembly of the State of North Carolina*, Session 1943, pp. 140, 183, 205, 208, 224, 264.

74. Broughton Papers, box 48, file 2, Telegram, March 8, 1943.

75. *Hickory Record*, March 9, 1943, p. 6.

76. Broughton Papers, box 48, file 2, March 9, 1943.

77. *Ibid.*, box 48, file 2, "News release, Governor Broughton's appointments to Hospitals Board of Control."

78. *Ibid.*

79. *Ibid.*, box 48, file 2, Letter from Davis to Broughton, July 8, 1943.

80. *Ibid.*, box 48, file 2, July 9, 1943.

81. *Ibid.*, box 48, file 3, July 9, 1943.

82. *Ibid.*, box 52, file 2, July 12, 1943.

83. Minutes of the Hospitals' Board of Control, Raleigh, North Carolina, Files Department of Mental Health, Raleigh, North Carolina, July 16, 1943. Hereafter cited as Minutes of the Board.

84. *Ibid.*, p. 1.

85. *Ibid.*, p. 8.

Chapter V

1. Minutes of the Board, July 16, 1943.

2. Broughton Papers, box 48, file 2, Letter from Vernon to Broughton, June 9, 1942; from Johnson to Broughton, June 3, 1942.

3. Charlotte News, July 17, 1943, p. 7.

4. Broughton Papers, box 48, file 2, Letter from Broughton to Davis, July 19, 1943.

5. Minutes of the Board, op. cit.

6. Minutes of the Executive Committee of North Carolina State Hospital at Raleigh, August 3, 1943.

7. Minutes of the Board, October 4, 1943.

8. Broughton Papers, box 48, file 3. These reports dealt, for the most part, with the physical improvements being carried forward at Morganton.

9. "First Annual Report of the Hospitals Board of Control," July, 1944. Files, Department of Mental Health, Raleigh, North Carolina.

10. Maurice H. Greenhill, "The Present Status of Mental Health in North Carolina," North Carolina Medical Journal, Vol. VI (January - December, 1945) p. 8.

11. Ranked nationally in 1934, the North Carolina State Hospital system was 47th in per capita cost, 44th in patients per physician, 43rd in patients per nurse and attendant, 42nd in patients per total employees, 34th in first admissions per 100,000 population, and 41st in hospital population per 100,000 population.

12. Laws of North Carolina Relating to Hospitals for the Mentally Disordered, Reprinted from the General Statutes of North Carolina, Issued by the North Carolina Hospitals Board of Control. Chapter 122, Article 2.

13. Memo to Mrs. W. T. Bost, Commissioner of the State Board of Charities and Public Welfare, from Dr. James Watson, Director, the Division of Public Hygiene, August 19, 1943. Files of the Department of Mental Health, Raleigh, North Carolina.

14. Broughton Papers, box 48, file 3, "Constitutional Authority of the Board of Charities and Public Welfare over Hospitals Board of Control," February 9, 1944.

15. Greenhill, op. cit., p. 12.

16. Ibid., p. 11.

17. The author is indebted to a number of persons for insights into the political organization of the North Carolina Legislature during the 1940's and 1950's. Some were members of the Legislature during this period; others are newspaper editors and state employees whose positions place them close to the political operations in the State. My interpretation of the positions and relative strength of Clark, Spruill and others is derived from these conversations.

18. "First Annual Report," op. cit.

19. Report of R. M. Rothgeb, General Business Manager of the Hospitals Board of Control, August 9, 1944. Files of the Department of Mental Health, Raleigh, North Carolina.

20. "Annual Inspection of State Institutions for the Mentally Ill and Feebleminded by the North Carolina State Board of Charities and Public Welfare," 1944. Inspection made by Maurice H. Greenhill, M.C., Psychiatric Consultant for the State Board of Charities and Public Welfare, Hereafter cited as "Greenhill Report." Governor R. Gregg Cherry Papers, Agencies, Departments and Institutions, Box 27, 1945. Hereafter cited as "Cherry Papers."

21. "Greenhill Report," p. 1.

22. Ibid., p. 2.

23. Ibid., p. 4.

24. Ibid., p. 5.

25. Ibid., p. 6.

26. Ibid., p. 8.

27. Ibid., p. 10.

28. Ibid., p. 13.

29. As noted earlier in Chapter III, the A. P. A. recommended ratios were 1 to 8 for nurses, 1 to 12-14 for attendants and 1 to 150 for doctors.

30. "Greenhill Report," p. 15.

31. Ibid., p. 17.

32. Ibid., pp. 24-26.

33. Ibid., p. 27.

34. Ibid., p. 28.

35. Cherry Papers, box 84, Hospitals Board of Control File. Letter to Dr. H. O. Lineberger, October 10, 1946.

36. Minutes of the Board, July 16, 1943.

37. Cherry Papers, Box 16, Insane Asylum File, Letter from Beall to Cherry, December 20, 1944.

38. Ibid., Letter from Doughton to Cherry, December 21, 1944.

39. Ibid., Letter from Winborne to Cherry, December 18, 1944.

40. Ibid., Memorandum from the Charlotte Mental Hygiene Society, December 18, 1944.

Chapter VI

1. The Minutes of the Hospitals Board from July, 1943, through June, 1944, contain reports of the separate executive committees on such matters as ward repairs, painting, general maintenance, personnel hiring and patient discharge regulations indicating that the executive committees were still involved in daily operational decisions that rightfully fell in the province of the hospital staff.

2. Control and allocation of funds presented the most serious point of possible conflict.

3. The author is indebted to Mr. John W. Umstead for granting me a series of interviews which form the basis for information concerning the Hospitals Board of Control from 1945 to 1960 that is not available in the official minutes. These interviews, ten in number, were conducted between October 10, 1962, and April 7, 1963. Hereafter referred to as Umstead Interviews. Mr. Umstead's recollections are verified by supporting interviews from Mr. Robert Richardson, Reidsville, North Carolina, who came on the Board in 1945 and who is still a member and Representative Wayland "Cousin Bob" Spruill of Windsor who was on the original Board in 1943 and returned again in 1953 after an absence of eight years from the Board.

4. Ibid., October 10, 1962.

5. Ibid., October 20, 1962. The report which Mr. Umstead refers to is not in the public or private papers of Governor Cherry, but the events that followed the Umstead investigation tend to corroborate the contention that one was submitted to the Governor.

6. Ibid., November 7, 1962.

7. Ibid.

8. The author is indebted to several persons for insights into the political and social attitudes of Governor Cherry, among them Professor W. T. Laprade, Duke University, who knew Cherry from his student days. While the information provided by the people was helpful to me, the interpretation of Governor Cherry's social concern and political motivation is mine.

9. Political obervers in the state such as Burke Davis, Greensboro Daily News and Henry Belk, Goldsboro News Argos considered Umstead to be one of the state's few liberal politicians on fiscal policy and social action in mental health and public school education.

10. Ibid., November 9, 1962. See the Raleigh News and Observer for the month of April, 1943.

11. Burke Davis, Greensboro Daily News, February 22, 1953, p. 1.

12. Umstead Interviews, January 12, 1963.

13. Ibid., January 12, 1963.

14. The Advisory Budget Commission met on the hospital requests January 11, 1945, and the Mental Hospital Act, Senate Bill 170, 1945, was passed by the Senate on March 20, 1945.

15. The Congressional Districts were represented by Thomas C. Byrum, First District; Senator William G. Clark, Second; Senator Thomas O'Berry, Third; Dr. Henry O. Lineberger, Fourth; Robert Richardson, Fifth; John Umstead, Sixth; John Dawkins, Seventh; Ryan McBryde, Eighth; Dr. T. V. Goode, Ninth; D.. Yeates Palmer, Tenth; Francis Whiteside, Eleventh; Baxter Jones, Twelfth; and Leonard Oettinger, Mrs. Andrew Blair, and Mrs. Rivers Johnson, At Large. W. G. Clark, L. L. Oettinger, Mrs. Blair and Mrs. Johnson were retained from the original Hospitals Board of Control. For a complete list of members of the Hospitals Board of Control, 1945-1963, see Appendix.

16. The Medical Advisory Committee was appointed April 10, 1945. The fifteen members were: Drs. Hubert Haywood, Raleigh, Chairman; C. C. Carpenter, Winston-Salem; W. C. Davison, Duke University; W. R. Berryhill, University of North Carolina; Maurice Greenhill, Duke University; George T. Harrell, Bowman Gray School of Medicine; Lois Stanford, Durham; Charles Roindexter, Greensboro; James Vernon, Morganton; Charles Strosnider, Goldsboro; Paul Whitaker, Kinston; Carl V. Reynolds, Raleigh; Oscar Miller, Charlotte; C. C. Orr, Asheville; and J. B. Robinson, Wilmington.

17. Umstead Interviews, January 17, 1963.

18. Minutes Hospitals Board of Control, April 10, 1945.

19. Ibid., June 5, 1945.

20. Ibid., May 17, 1945.

21. "By-Laws and Regulations" Accepted by North Carolina Hospitals Board of Control for government of the State Hospital at Morganton, the State Hospital at Raleigh, the State Hospital at Goldsboro, Caswell Training School at Kinston, State Hospitals Extension - Camp Butner Unit, 1945, The Files North Carolina Department of Mental Health, Raleigh, North Carolina.

22. Ibid., pp. 2-4.

23. Ibid., p. 10

24. Ibid., pp. 11-12.

25. Minutes, Hospitals Board, July 1, 1945.

26. Ibid., January 11, 1946.

27. The Special Committee consisted of Board Chairman Lineberger, Umstead, Superintendent Young and Drs. Haywood, Greenhill and Berryhill of the Medical Advisory Committee.

28. Minutes, Hospitals Board, March 13, 1946.

29. Ibid., April 11, 1946.

30. Special report of Butner Committee to Hospitals Board, June 12, 1946.

31. Umstead Interviews, January 17, 1963.

32. North Carolina Revenue Report, 1959-60.

33. Ibid. The following chart details the gross revenue receipts to the General Fund from 1942-43 to 1959-60 showing the percentage increase over the previous year and the annual surplus.

34. Umstead Interviews, January 17, 1963.

35. Ibid.

36. Minutes of the Board, March 17, 1947.

37. Ibid., July 7, 1947.

38. United States Statutes at Large, 79th Congress, Second Session, 1946, Vol. 60, Part I, United States Government Printing Office, Washington.

39. Cherry Papers, Box 35, File Hospitals Board of Control, September 25, 1946.

40. Governor W. Kerr Scott Papers, Agencies, Departments, and Institutions, 1949-52, State Department of Archives and History, Raleigh, North Carolina, Box 19. Hereafter cited as Scott Papers.

41. Scott Papers, Box 19, "Progress Report, Twenty Months of National Mental Health Act in North Carolina." May 17, 1949.

42. Minutes of the Board, March 1, 1947.

43. "Do They Belong in Jail?" North Carolina Health Council and Mental Health Section of the North Carolina Department of Mental Health, Graphic Press, Inc., Raleigh, North Carolina, 1957.

44. Ibid.

Chapter VII

1. Minutes of the Board, December 11, 1948.

2. Ibid., July 6, 1949.

3. Ibid.

4. Ibid.

5. Ibid.

6. Ibid.

7. Census figures showing admission and discharge rates between 1950 and 1960 are available in Appendix C. A woman's division for alcoholics was opened in 1954.

8. Minutes of the Board, July 6, 1949.

9. The original report of findings and recommendations by the American Psychiatric Association was filed with the Hospitals Board of Control in July, 1950. This report is missing from the files. However, a summary of the report was submitted to Governor Scott. This summary is the basis for the findings described above. Scott Papers, Box 62, 1950.

10. Scott Papers, Box 62, 1950.

11. "Special Report to the Board" August 28, 1951, Files Department of Mental Health, Raleigh, North Carolina. Hereafter cited as "Special Report."

12. Ibid., August 28, 1951.

13. Ibid.

14. "Do They Belong In Jail," op. cit., p. 6.

15. "Special Report."

16. The 1949 Legislature approved a four-year school program at the University of North Carolina at Chapel Hill. The first four-year class entered in the fall of 1950 while a major portion of Memorial Hospital, the teaching unit of the Medical School, was still under construction.

17. Minutes of the Board, July 6, 1950.

18. Ibid., May 11, 1951.

19. Umstead Interviews, December 11, 1962.

20. Scott Papers, Box 19, Appointments, August 5, 1949.

21. "A Survey of the Program for the Mentally Deficient in North Carolina," Chapel Hill, North Carolina, April 15, 1952.

22. Ibid., p. 5.

23. Ibid., pp. 6-13.

24. The author is indebted to the Division of Statistics, the Department of Mental Health, for all statistical data used in this study for the years 1945-1963 and especially to Mr. Charles W. Pettus and Mr. Lacoe B. Alltop.

25. This figure includes all employees and not just those directly responsible for patient care.

26. Umstead Interviews, November 18, 1962.

27. Burke Davis, Greensboro Daily News, February 22, 1953.

28. Ibid., November 18, 1962.

29. Umstead Interviews, November 18, 1962.

30. Ibid.

31. Senate Journal, Session 1953, Senate Bill 10.

32. North Carolina Manual, 1954, Issued by Thad Eure, Secretary of State, p. 124.

33. Governor William B. Umstead Papers, Agencies, Departments and Institutions, 1953-54, State Department of Archives and History, Raleigh, North Carolina, box 16, October 23, 1953. Hereafter cited as Umstead Papers.

34. Ibid., Letter from Governor Umstead to R. P. Richardson, October 27, 1953.

35. Ibid.

36. Minutes, Hospital Board, February 12, 1954. Kendall's letter of February 10, 1954, was entered in the minutes of the Hospital Board of Control by John Umstead.

37. Umstead Interviews, November 19, 1962.

38. Umstead Interviews, November 19, 1962.

39. Interview with Dr. David Young, Chapel Hill, North Carolina, April 19, 1966.

40. Laws of North Carolina, 1959, Article 3, Sections 122-46.1 and 122-62 "Commitment on patient's application."

41. From an Analysis of Expenditures for Maintenance June 30, 1939 through June 30, 1962, Morganton State Hospital. The office of the Business Manager.

42. Letter from Governor Hodges to John Umstead, February 8, 1956. Governor Luther H. Hodges Papers, Agencies, Departments and Institutions, 1954-60. State Department of Archives and History, Raleigh, North Carolina, Box 18. Hereafter cited as Hodges Papers.

43. Special Meeting of the Hospitals Board of Control, February 22, 1956. This meeting was called at the request of Governor Hodges and the Advisory Budget Commission to consider alternate plans for completing current construction programs within the $22,000,000 authorization of the 1953 Legislature. Minutes, Hospitals Board of Control.

44. Ibid.

45. Minutes, Hospitals Board of Control, July 1958.

46. "Report on the Training Schools of North Carolina" made by the Central Inspection Board of the American Psychiatric Association, December, 1958, pp. 100 and 174 respectively.

47. Ibid., December 1958, pp. 7-11.

48. Minutes, Hospitals Board, July 12, 1958.

49. Session Laws, 1955, "Appropriations, North Carolina Mental Hospitals," Chapter 1038.

50. Minutes, Hospitals Board, October 1, 1958.

51. Ibid.

52. Ibid.

53. North Carolina Hospitals Board of Control. Appropriations Request to the Advisory Budget Commission for the Biennium 1959-60. Hospitals Board of Control, Raleigh, North Carolina, October, 1958.

54. Minutes, Hospitals Board, October 1, 1958.

55. Ibid.

56. Session Laws, 1959. "Interstate Compact on Mental Health in North Carolina," Chapter 1003.

57. Ibid., "Hospitals for the Mentally Disordered" Amendments to Article 1 paragraph 122-1 "Incorporation and Names," Chapter 1002.

58. Umstead Interviews, November 22, 1962. Quotation as recalled by Umstead.

59. Raleigh, North Carolina, News and Observer, March 10, 1959, p. 1.

60. Ibid.

61. Among the papers carrying the story were the Charlotte Observer, the Greensboro Daily News, the Raleigh News and Observer, and the Durham Morning Herald.

62. Charlotte, North Carolina, _Observer_, March 11, 1959, p. 1.

63. Raleigh, North Carolina, _News and Observer_, "A Great Compliment," by Henry Belk, March 18, 1959, p. 3.

64. Umstead Interviews, and Durham _Morning Herald_, March 11, 1959, p. 1.

65. Umstead and Richardson Interviews.

66. _Session Laws_, 1959. "Appropriations, Hospitals Board of Control." Chapter 1008.

67. Minutes of the Board, October 6, 1960.

68. _Senate Journal_, Session, 1961, Senate Bill 211.

69. Umstead Interviews, November 22, 1962, and Charlotte _News and Observer_, November 8, 1961, p. 1. A comparision of voter turnout with the 1959 bond election supports this position. The 1959 issue was carried by a 12% margin with a total vote of 110,473. The 1961 issue failed by a 10% margin in a total vote of 363,836. _North Carolina Manual_, 1963. Issued by Thad Eure, Secretary of State, p. 262.

70. In addition to election analysis and editorial comments in the Charlotte, Raleigh, and Durham papers, I am indebted to a number of people both in and out of state government service for their opinions concerning the 1961 State Bond Referendum, all of which tend to support Mr. Umstead's position.

71. Sanford won the General Election in November, 1960 with 54 per cent of the popular vote as against a "normal" margin of 64% in traditionally Democratic North Carolina. Luther Hodges, for example, was elected Governor in 1956 with 66.9% of the popular vote.

72. Editorial comment attributed the bond rejection as a reaction to the sales tax. Raleigh _News and Observer_, November 8, 1961, p. 3., Charlotte _Observer_, November 8, 1961, p. 1.

73. Governor Sanford accepted responsibility for the bond failure and attributed the voter's rejection of the issue to possible overconfidence and a lack of organized support for the omnibus bill. Raleigh _News and Observer_, _Ibid._, p. 1.

74. Umstead Interview, January 12, 1963.

75. Commissioner Hargrove's interviews consistently centered around this concept and the belief that the defeat of the bond issue produced at least one positive result by bringing into clear focus the interplay of political, administrative and research forces in the hospital system.

76. National Governor's Conference, Honolulu, Hawaii, January, 1961.

77. Minutes, Hospitals Board, July 1, 1961.

78. "Memorandum," Hugh Cannon, Assistant to the Governor, to the Commissioner of Mental Health, February 22, 1961, Files of the Department of Mental Health, Raleigh, North Carolina.

SELECTED BIBLIOGRAPHY

SELECTED BIBLIOGRAPHY

Primary Sources:

Government Documents

"By-Laws and Regulations," North Carolina Hospitals Board of Control, 1945. Files, Department of Mental Health, Raleigh, North Carolina.

"First Annual Report of the Hospitals Board of Control." 1944, Files, Department of Mental Health, Raleigh, North Carolina.

Greenhill, Maurice, M.D. "Annual Inspection of State Institutions for the Mentally Ill and Feeble-Minded," 1944. "Unpublished material," State Department of Archives and History, Raleigh, North Carolina.

Journal of the House of Representatives of the General Assembly of the State of North Carolina, 1943.

Journal of the Senate of the General Assembly of the State of North Carolina, 1943, 1945, 1951, 1961, 1963, 1965.

Journals of the Senate and House of Commons. State of North Carolina, Raleigh, 1841, 1844, 1849.

Laws of North Carolina. Raleigh, North Carolina, 1852, 1854-55, 1956-57.

Laws of North Carolina Relating to Hospitals for the Mentally Disordered. Charlottsville, Virginia: The Michie Company, 1959, 1961, 1963, 1965.

Legislative Documents. Also known as Legislative Journal. State of North Carolina, Raleigh, 1840, 1844, 1854, 1855, 1871-72, 1874, 1921, 1935.

Minutes of the Executive Committee of the North Carolina State Hospital at Raleigh. "Umpublished material," Files, Department of Mental Health, Raleigh, North Carolina, 1943.

North Carolina Board of Public Charities. "An Appeal," Raleigh, North Carolina, 1900.

North Carolina Board of Public Charities. Annual Report, Raleigh, North Carolina, 1868.

North Carolina Commission for the Study of the Care of the Insane and Mental Defective. A Study of Mental Health in North Carolina, Ann Arbor, Michigan, Edwards Brothers, Inc., 1937.

North Carolina Department of Mental Health. "Minutes of the Meeting of the Governor's Commission," "Unpublished material," September 29, 1936, Files, Department of Mental Health, Raleigh, North Carolina.

North Carolina General Assembly. "Report on Penitentiary and Lunatic Asylum," 1828.

North Carolina Hospitals Board of Control. "Minutes," 1943-1962, "Unpublished material," Files, Department of Mental Health, Raleigh, North Carolina.

North Carolina Hospitals Board of Control. "Statistical Reports," "Unpublished material," Files, Department of Mental Health, Raleigh, North Carolina.

North Carolina Reports. Supreme Court. Vol. LXXII, Spring Term, 1873.

North Carolina State Hospital Reports. 1858, 1865, 1868, 1873, 1912.

"Report of the Board of Inquiry appointed by His Excellency, J. Melville Broughton, Governor of North Carolina, to make an Investigation of the State Hospitals, Morganton, North Carolina," "Unpublished material," August 7, 1942.

"Report of the Committee on Caswell Training School." "Unpublished material," 1926. Files, Department of Mental Health, Raleigh, North Carolina.

Smith, Harvey L., Director. A Comprehensive Mental Health Plan for North Carolina. Chapel Hill: North Carolina Mental Health Planning Staff, Vols. I-V, 1965.

United States Statutes at Large. 79th Congress, Second Session, 1946. Vol. 60, part I, Washington: United States Government Printing Office.

Watson, James. "Memorandum to Mrs. W. T. Bost, Commissioner of the State Board of Public Welfare." "Unpublished material," Files, Department of Mental Health, Raleigh, North Carolina.

Manuscripts

Clark, William T. Private Papers, In possession of William T. Clark, Jr., Tarboro, North Carolina.

Governor's Papers. North Carolina Department of Archives and History, Raleigh, North Carolina, Governors Ehringhaus (1933-36), Hoey (1937-40), Broughton (1941-44), Cherry (1945-48), Scott (1949-52), Umstead (1953-54), Hodges (1954-60), Sanford (1961-64).

Jimison, Tom P. "Out of the Night of Morganton," Charlotte, North Carolina: News and Observer Publishing Company, 1942.

Payne, Horace. "Written Communication," Morganton, North Carolina, to Dr. James K. Hall, April 19, 1936. Files of Dr. Charles Vernon, North Carolina Department of Mental Health.

Books and Pamphlets

American Psychiatric Association. "Report on the State Training Schools of
    North Carolina." "Unpublished material," December, 1958, Files, Department
    of Mental Health, Raleigh, North Carolina.

Beers, Clifford. A Mind That Found Itself. New York: Doubleday, Doran and
    Company, 1937.

Bureau of Educational Research. A Survey of the Program for the Mentally
    Deficient in North Carolina. Chapel Hill: 1952.

Charlotte Mental Hygiene Society. "Memorandum to Governor Cherry," 1944.
    "Unpublished material." State Department of Archives and History, Raleigh,
    North Carolina.

Dix, Dorothea. Memorial Soliciting a State Hospital for the Insane. Submitted
    to the Legislature of New Jersey, January 2, 1845.

Dix, Dorothea. "Memorial to the General Assembly of the State of North Carolina,"
    November, 1848, North Carolina Pamphlets, Vol. 17.

Dix, Dorothea. "Memorial to the Massachusetts Legislature," Old South Leaflets.
    VI (January, 1843).

Grissom, Eugene, M.D. "A Statement to the Friends of the North Carolina Insane
    Asylum, 1889." "n.p."

Jarvis, Thomas J. "A Speech Delivered in the Dr. Grissom Trial, for the
    Defense," "n.p." 1889.

Joint Commission on Mental Illness. Action for Mental Health. New York:
    Basic Books, Inc., 1961.

Journal of the Western North Carolina Conference of the Methodist Church,
    "n.p." 1917, 1924.

Martindale-Hubbell. Law Directory, North Carolina Listings. New York:
    Martindale-Hubbell, 1933-40.

Packard, Mrs. E. P. W. The Prisoners Hidden Life or Insane Asylums Unveiled.
    Chicago, Published by the author, 1868.

Ward, Mary Jane. The Snake Pit. New York: Random House, 1946.

Secondary Sources:

Books and Articles

Ashe, Samuel. Biographical History of North Carolina. Greensboro, North
    Carolina: "n.p." 1907.

Belknap, Ivan. The Community and Its Hospitals, Syracuse University Press, Syracuse, New York, 1963.

Belknap, Ivan. Human Problems of a State Mental Hospital. New York: McGraw-Hill Book Company, Inc., 1956.

Bellak, Leopold. Handbook of Community Psychiatry and Community Health. New York: Grune and Stratton, 1963.

Dain, Norman. Concepts of Insanity in the United States, 1789-1865. New Brunswick, New Jersey: Rutgers University Press, 1964.

Deutsch, Albert, The Mentally Ill in America. New York: Harcourt-Brace and Company, 1938.

Deutsch, Albert, The Shame of the States. New York: Harcourt-Brace and Company, 1948.

Greenhill, Maurice, M.D. "The Present Status of Mental Health in North Carolina," North Carolina Medical Journal. Vol. VI (January, 1945).

Grissom, Eugene. "Mechanical Protection for the Insane," American Journal of Insanity (July, 1877), pp. 12-18.

Hall, James K. "Psychiatry in Retrospect," Southern Medicine and Surgery, (November, 1938), 1-8.

Hall, James K. "The War on Dr. Anderson," A reprint of editorials in the Department of Human Behavior, Southern Medicine and Surgery, (December 1928-July, 1929).

Hamilton, J. G. deRoulhac. Party Politics in North Carolina, 1835-1860. Durham, North Carolina: Seeman Printery, 1916.

Lefler, Hugh Talmage and Albert Ray Newsome. North Carolina. Chapel Hill: University of North Carolina Press, 1954.

Marshall, Helen E. Dorothea Dix. Chapel Hill: The University of North Carolina Press, 1937.

McCulloch, Margaret C. "Founding the North Carolina Asylum for the Insane," The North Carolina Historical Review., XIII (July, 1936), 185-201.

Murphy, Patrick. "Colony Treatment of the Insane and Other Defectives," Reprint from North Carolina Medical Journal, "n.p." 1906.

Murphy, Patrick. "Treatment and Care of the Insane in North Carolina," a speech delivered by the Agricultural and Mechanical College, Raleigh, North Carolina, March 16, 1900.

North Carolina Health Council. "Do They Belong in Jail?" pamphlet. Raleigh: Graphic Press, 1957.

Pope, Liston. Millhands and Preachers. New Haven: Yale University Press, 1942.

Speas, Ethel M. History of the Voluntary Mental Health Movement in North Carolina. Raleigh: North Carolina Mental Health Association, 1961.

Tiffany, Francis. Life of Dorothea Lynde Dix. Boston: Houghton, Mifflin and Company, 1891.

Tomplins, D. A. "Condition of Hospitals," Charlotte, North Carolina: Published by the author, 1906.

Valtin, Jan. Out of the Night. New York: Alliance Book Corporation, 1941.

Weinberg, S. Kirkson. Society and Personality Disorders. New York: Prentice-Hall, Inc., 1952.

Wright, Frank L. Out of Sight Out of Mind. Philadelphia: National Mental Health Foundation, Inc., 1942.

Newspapers

Asheville Citizen. Asheville, North Carolina.

Charlotte News. Charlotte, North Carolina.

Charlotte Observer. Charlotte, North Carolina.

Durham Sun. Durham, North Carolina.

Fayetteville Observer. Fayetteville, North Carolina.

Greensboro Daily News. Greensboro, North Carolina.

Hickory Record. Hickory, North Carolina.

Journal Sentinel. Winston-Salem, North Carolina.

Morning Herald. Durham, North Carolina.

North Carolina Standard. Raleigh, North Carolina.

Raleigh News and Observer. Raleigh, North Carolina.

Raleigh Register. Raleigh, North Carolina.

Interviews

Dowd, J. Ed. At Charlotte, North Carolina, August 26, 1963.

Ewing, Oscar. At Chapel Hill, North Carolina, January 21, 1967.

Griffith, Brodie. At Charlotte, North Carolina, August 26, 1963.

Hargrove, Dr. Eugene. At Department of Mental Health, Raleigh, North Carolina, extensive series from 1963-1966.

Laprade, Professor W. T. At Durham, North Carolina, November 15, 1966.

McKee, John. At Morganton, August 26, 1963.

McKnight, Pete. At Charlotte, North Carolina, August 26, 1963.

Nelson, Fletcher. At Durham, North Carolina, April 16, 1965.

Richardson, Robert. At Reidsville, North Carolina, June 1, 1966.

Spruill, Wayland. At Windsor, North Carolina, June 9, 1966.

Taylor, Dr. E. H. E. At Morganton, North Carolina, August 26, 1963, May 17, 1964.

Umstead, John W., Jr. At Chapel Hill, North Carolina, Extensive series from November 10, 1962 - April 17, 1963.

Vernon, Dr. Charles. At Department of Mental Health, Raleigh, North Carolina, extensive series from 1963-1966.

HISTORICAL ISSUES IN MENTAL HEALTH

An Arno Press Collection

American Psychopathological Association. **Trends Of Mental Disease.** 1945

Belknap, Ivan. **Human Problems Of A State Mental Hospital.** 1956

Berkley, Henry J. **A Treatise On Mental Diseases.** 1900

Bond, Earl D. Thomas W. **Salmon: Psychiatrist.** 1950

Briggs, L. Vernon. **Two Years' Service On The Reorganized State Board Of Insanity In Massachusetts, August, 1914 to August, 1916.** 1930

Briggs, L. Vernon. **A Victory For Progress In Mental Medicine.** 1924

Burrow, Trigant. **A Search For Man's Sanity.** 1958

Cahow, Clark R. **People, Patients and Politics.** (Doctoral Dissertation, Duke University, 1967). 1979

The Committee of the American Neurological Association for the Investigation of Eugenical Sterilization. **Eugenical Sterilization.** 1936

Cotton, Henry A. **The Defective Delinquent And Insane.** 1921

Dayton, Neil A. **New Facts On Mental Disorders.** 1940

Fein, Rashi. **Economics of Mental Illness.** 1958

Goldhamer, Herbert and Andrew W. Marshall. **Psychosis And Civilization.** 1953

Gosney, E.S., and Paul Popenoe. **Sterilization For Human Betterment.** 1929

Greenblat, Milton, et al. **From Custodial To Therapeutic Patient Care In Mental Hospitals.** 1955

Grob, Gerald N., editor. **Immigrants And Insanity.** 1979

Grob, Gerald N., editor. **Mental Hygiene In Twentieth Century America.** 1979

Grob, Gerald N., editor. **The Mentally Ill In Urban America.** 1979

Grob, Gerald N., editor. **The National Association For The Protection of the Insane And The Prevention Of Insanity.** 1979

Grob, Gerald N., editor. **Psychiatric Research In America.** 1979

Grob, Gerald N., editor. **Psychiatry and Medical Education.** 1979

Grob, Gerald N., editor. **Public Policy And Mental Illness.** 1979

Grimes, John Maurice. **Institutional Care Of Mental Patients In The United States.** 1934

Gurin, Gerald, et al. **Americans View Their Mental Health.** 1960

Hinsie, Leland. **The Treatment Of Schizophrenia.** 1930

Jahoda, Marie. **Current Concepts Of Positive Mental Health.** 1958

Joint Commission On Mental Illness And Health. **Action For Mental Health.** 1961

Koren, John. **Summaries Of State Laws Relating To The Insane.** 1917

Landis, Carney, and James D. Page. **Modern Society and Mental Disease.** 1938

Lewis, Nolan D.C. **Research In Dementia Praecox.** 1936

Malzberg, Benjamin. **Social And Biological Aspects Of Mental Disease.** 1940

May, James V. **Mental Diseases.** 1922

Myerson, Abraham. **Speaking Of Man.** 1950

The National Committee for Mental Hygiene. **State Hospitals In The Depression.** 1934

National Research Council, The Committee on Psychiatric Investigations. **The Problem Of Mental Disorder.** 1934

Plunkett, Richard J. and John E. Gordon,. **Epidemiology And Mental Illness.** 1960

Rapoport, Robert N., et al. **Community As Doctor.** 1960

Robison, Dale W. **Wisconsin And The Mentally Ill.** (Doctoral Dissertation, Marquette University, 1967). 1979

Sicherman, Barbara. **The Quest For Mental Health In America, 1880-1917.** (Doctoral Dissertation, Columbia University, 1967). 1979

Smith, Stephen. **Who Is Insane?** 1916

Stearns, Henry Putnam. **Insanity.** 1883

United States Surgeon General's Office. **The Medical Department Of The United States Army In The World War.** 1929

Wertheimer, F.I., and Florence E. Hesketh. **The Significance Of The Physical Constitution In Mental Disease.** 1926

White, William A. **The Mental Hygiene Of Childhood.** 1919

White, William A. **William Alanson White.** 1938